I0823318

THE DAY STARTS LIKE ANY OTHER.

A HOUSE OF DYNAMITE

A HOUSE OF DYNAMITE

A FILM BY KATHRYN BIGELOW

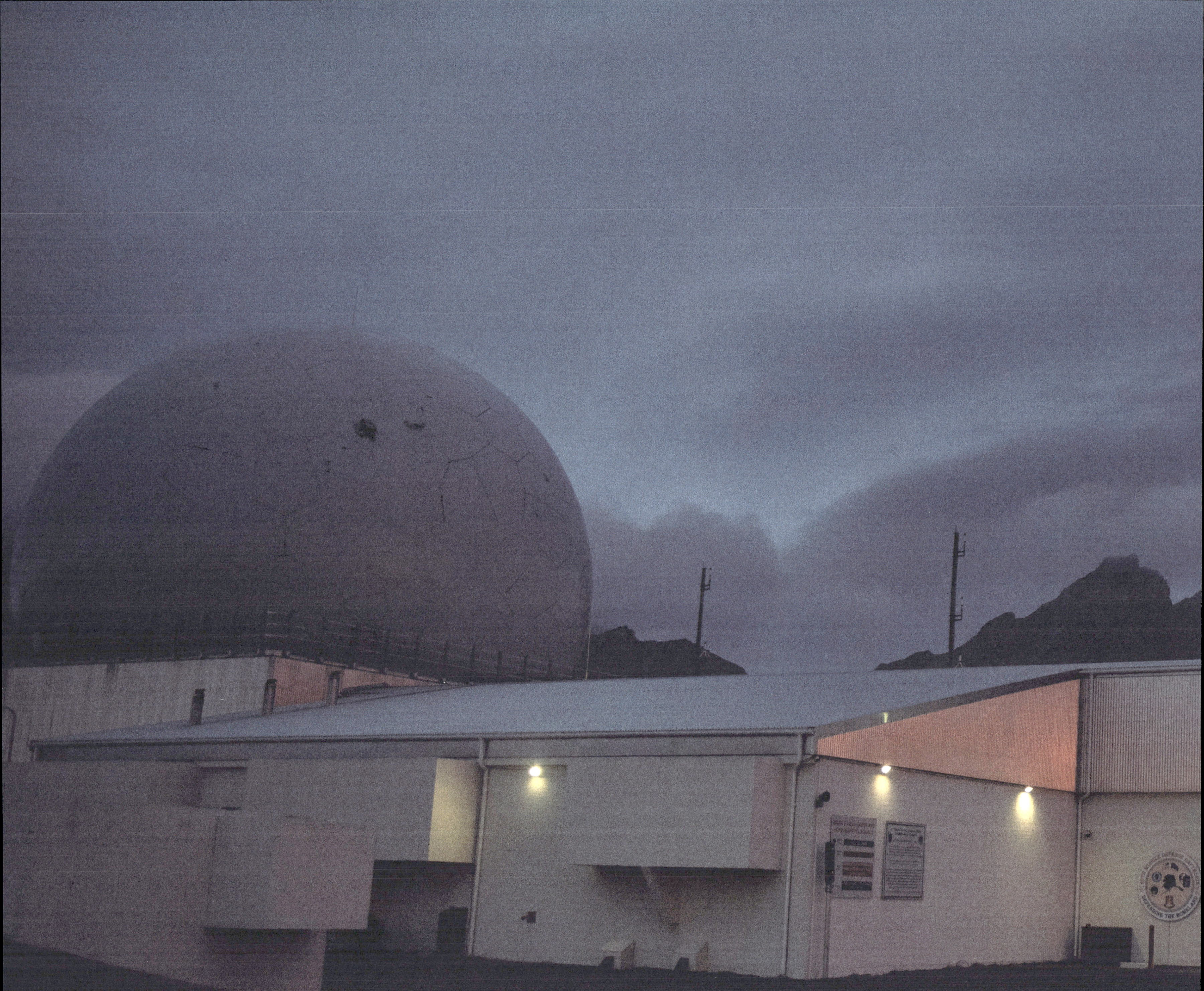
DEFENDING THE HOMELAND

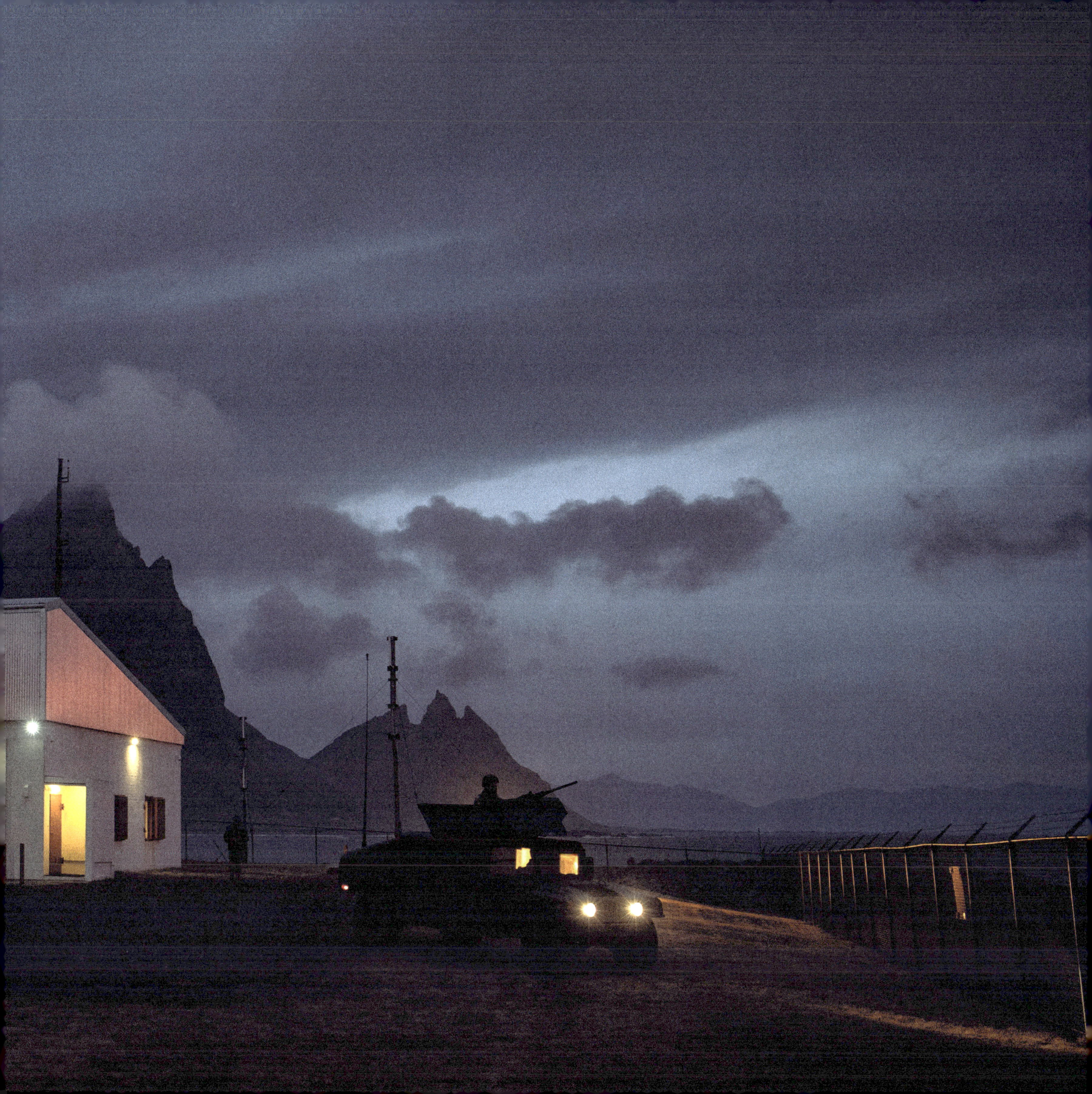

THE DANGER
HAS ONLY
ESCALATED.

I grew up in an era when hiding under your school desk was considered the go-to protocol for surviving an atomic bomb. It seems absurd now—and it was—but at the time, the threat felt so immediate that such measures were taken seriously.

Today, the danger has only escalated. Multiple nations possess enough nuclear weapons to end civilization within minutes. And yet, there's a kind of collective numbness, a quiet normalization of the unthinkable.

How can we call this <u>defense</u> when the inevitable outcome is total destruction?

I wanted to make a film that confronts this paradox—to explore the madness of a world that lives under the constant shadow of annihilation, yet rarely speaks of it.

—KATHRYN BIGELOW

MOVIES ABOUT NUCLEAR WAR MUST RELY PURELY ON THE IMAGINATION.

For filmmakers depicting the horrors of war, there is a long record of bloodshed and brutality to draw upon. We know exactly what modern trench warfare looks like because World War I veterans lived to recall it and journalists recorded it. There were military photographers on the beaches of Normandy, on the frozen battlefields of Korea, and in the jungles of Vietnam. The Nazis made movies of Auschwitz. War films feel real, and therefore pack an emotional punch, because storytellers can draw on these collective memories.

With one exception.

Movies about nuclear war must rely purely on the imagination. The worst kind of war has never been fought, and once it is, there will be no more war or movies. But how do we imagine the unimaginable?

Some films, as exemplified by On the Beach (1959), seek to depict the grim aftermath of an apocalypse. They find their pathos in the intimacy of small, human dramas—for instance, Threads (1984)—and sometimes by painting on a grand, fantastical canvas—see Planet of the Apes (1968) and the Terminator (1984) franchise. Either way, by portraying the collapse of civilization and the depravities faced by its few survivors, these movies seek to remind us of all we stand to lose if the world's nuclear arsenals are ever unleashed.

Others tell stories about the race to avert that moment. In Fail Safe (1964), a bomber receives mistaken orders to attack the Soviets, then loses radio contact and can't be recalled. In WarGames (1983), a primitive AI takes over the North American Aerospace Defense Command (NORAD) and tricks its human overlords into believing an attack is incoming. And, in my favorite example of the genre, Dr. Strangelove (1964), a deranged Air Force general orders a strike, sending the world on a tragicomic road to doomsday. (It's my favorite because its pitch-black comedy so perfectly captures the absurdity of nuclear weapons, which can never win a war, but only ensure everyone loses.)

In A House of Dynamite, we hope to contribute a unique note to this ongoing cry for civilization's attention to its own peril. We've done so by referencing the imagination not of fellow storytellers but of our own United States government's nuclear policymakers. For 80 years, they have envisioned, in granular detail, how a nuclear conflict might unfold, planning for almost every contingency. These plans, collectively, bring into sharp focus the terrifying fact that, if and when a nuclear crisis does arrive, just one person, the President of the United States, will have the sole authority to determine the fate of humanity. And, with almost no time for briefing, that one person will have mere minutes to make a decision.

The destructive potential of nuclear weapons may be underappreciated and difficult to dramatize. But just as terrifying are the flawed procedures that do so much to guarantee that if even a single nuclear missile is launched—by anyone, anywhere—we will quickly embark on a path toward mankind's collective suicide.

War films mine history so that we don't repeat it. A House of Dynamite—ike every nuclear war film—imagines the future we wish to avert. Unlike in our film, the power to do so rests not with one man, but with all of us. As in our film, the clock is ticking.

—NOAH OPPENHEIM

WE ONCE UNDERSTOOD
WHY WE SHOULD
FEAR NUCLEAR WAR.

We once understood why we should fear nuclear war. Not so long ago, the atomic destruction of Hiroshima and Nagasaki was within living memory. For almost five decades, the Cold War—and the risk it carried of an instant cataclysm—was part of daily life for everyone on the planet. We were afraid, and we knew why we were afraid. The leaders of the nuclear-armed nations felt the same way, which is one reason—along with a bit of luck—that we're all still alive.

When the Cold War finally sputtered out, however, so did the sense of doom that hovered over much of humanity. We gratefully let go of our anxieties about shelters and sirens, shedding them like ragged clothes we'd outgrown and made room for new worries: climate, terrorism, plagues. As the great struggle between East and West receded into a dimly remembered past, we packed up our fears about nuclear war and stowed them away in the attic of our collective consciousness.

The terror may have abated, but the weapons remain. Missiles still sit in their underground silos and traverse the seas aboard their submarines, silent sentinels who have never been relieved of their posts. Bombs still rest under the wings of their aircraft. At this moment, thousands of nuclear warheads and the crews who control them are still doing their duty and standing their watch. Thermonuclear payloads capable of destroying entire cities in moments and ending most of human civilization in a matter of hours are still aimed at billions of human beings around the world.

No one can be blamed for wanting to forget. Existential dread is exhausting, and years in its shadow can induce a sense of helplessness. But forgetting is dangerous: When we accept with resignation that large nuclear arsenals must always exist, that more countries will develop them, that leaders can speak casually about their use as if they are just another weapon of war, then we risk unspeakable disasters.

Memory is the path to survival. We must remember that these weapons are still with us, and that controlling their spread and averting their use is within our power. Preventing nuclear war is the most important job of our leaders. But choosing those leaders and ensuring that they are decent and humane people remains the most important responsibility of every citizen.

We can honor this responsibility by remembering.

—TOM NICHOLS

“THIS IS A
DIFFERENT KIND
OF WAR STORY.”

I've always chased conflict with my camera. As a photojournalist, I covered the wars in Iraq, Afghanistan, and Colombia. I photographed cartel violence in Mexico, a coup d'état in Haiti, and organized crime across Central America. Humanity's enduring appetite for war has long fascinated me, so my collaboration with Kathryn Bigelow was a natural fit from the start.

Photojournalism prepared me well for documenting films rooted in real-world gravity. Trust, discretion, and the ability to work unnoticed are essential in both professions. Each requires the careful construction of a cohesive narrative arc and an honest, nuanced portrayal of the subject. The artistic challenge of photographing this project—and its allure—was to create a body of work that exists not simply as a still facsimile of the motion picture but as a parallel interpretation of the filmmaker's vision.

Ground combat operations, counterinsurgency, and bomb disposal are all subjects deeply familiar to both Kathryn and me. But this tale, in many ways, is far more frightening.

"This is a different kind of war story," Kathryn told me on the first day of principal photography. Indeed. Despite my long relationship with armed conflict, I hadn't seriously considered the threat of nuclear destruction since my childhood in the 1980s. Perhaps, coming of age at the end of the Cold War, my generation was the last to do so. Soon, it seems, that may no longer be the case.

PHOTOGRAPHS BY

EROS HOAGLAND

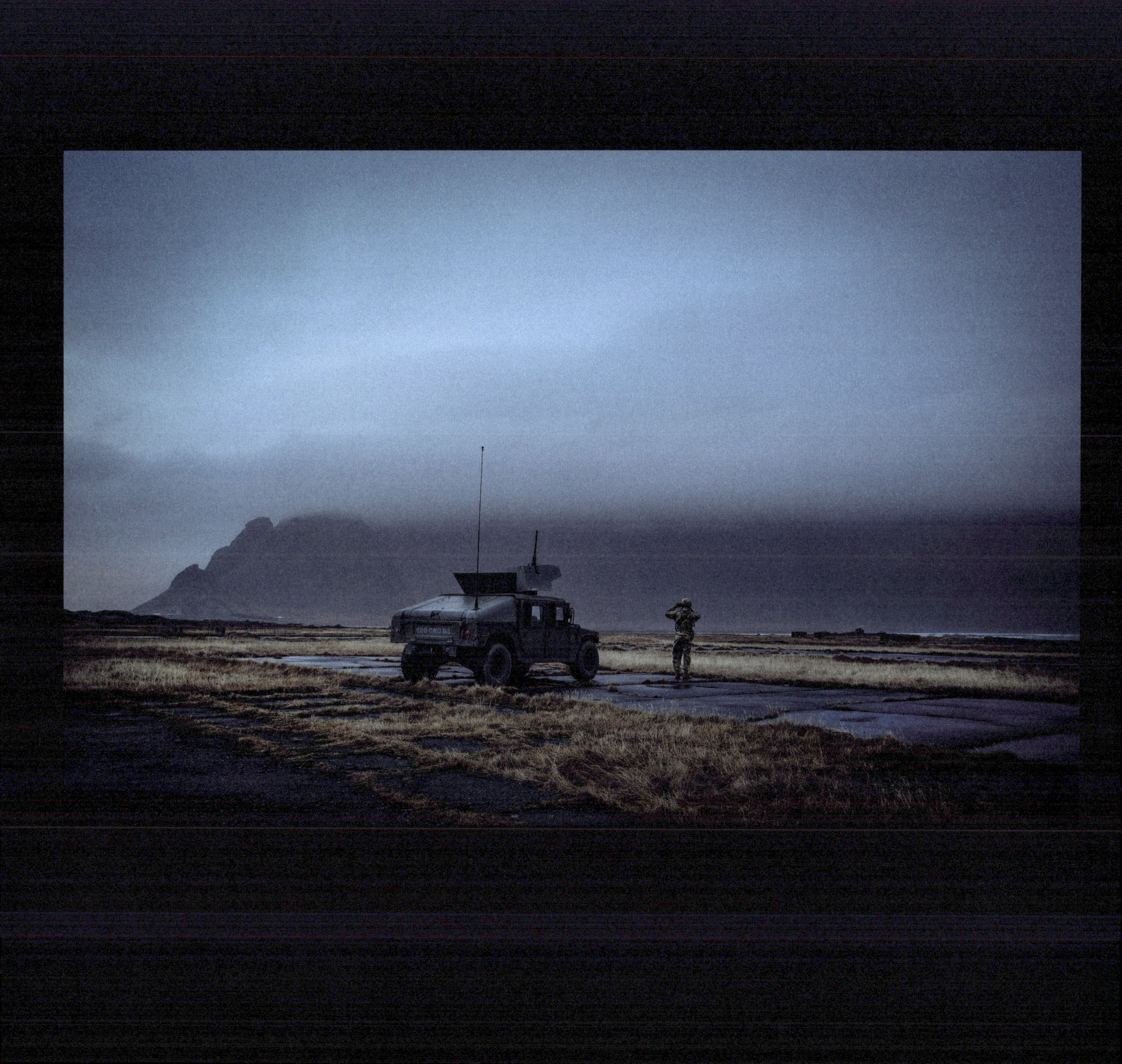

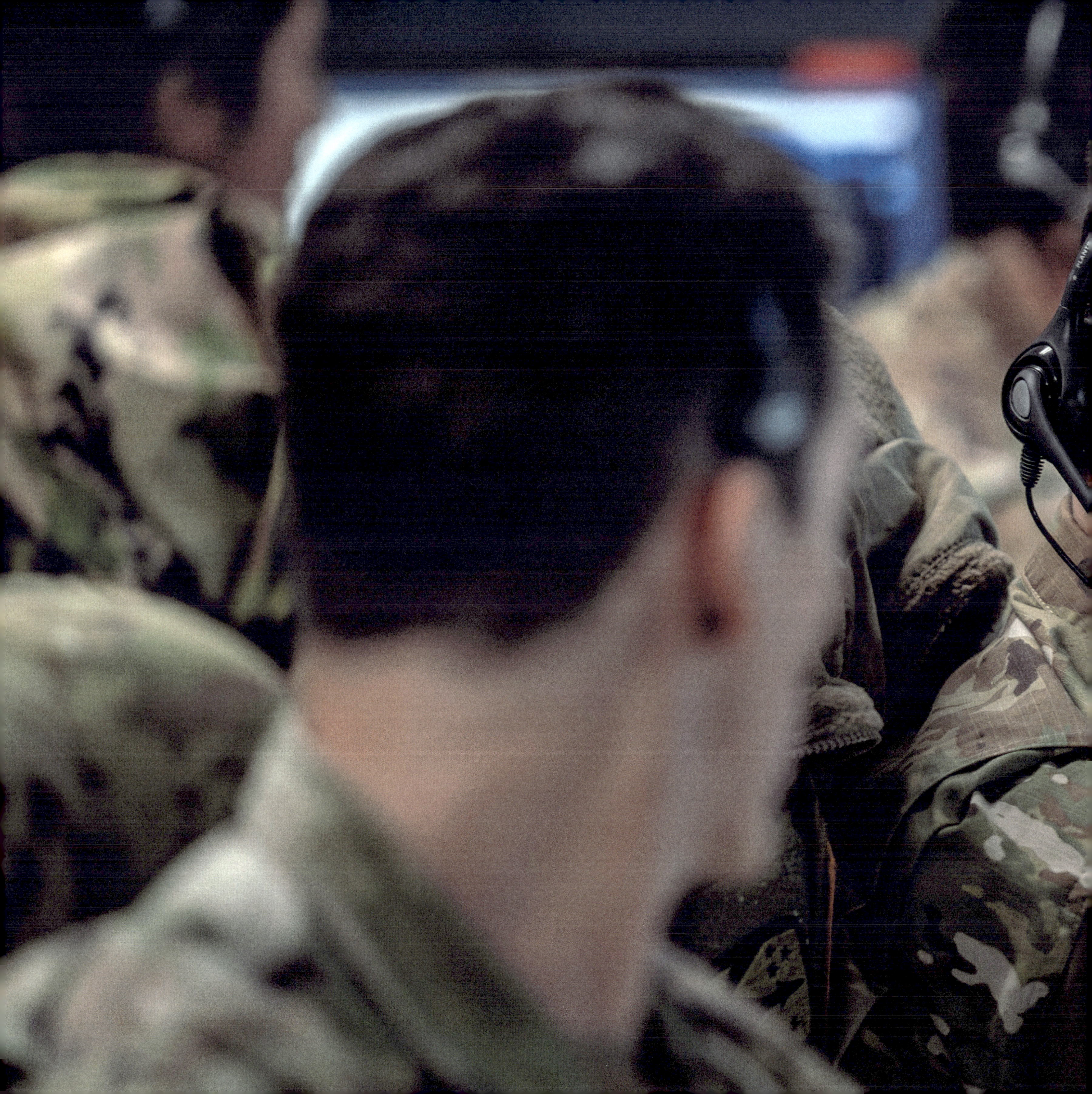

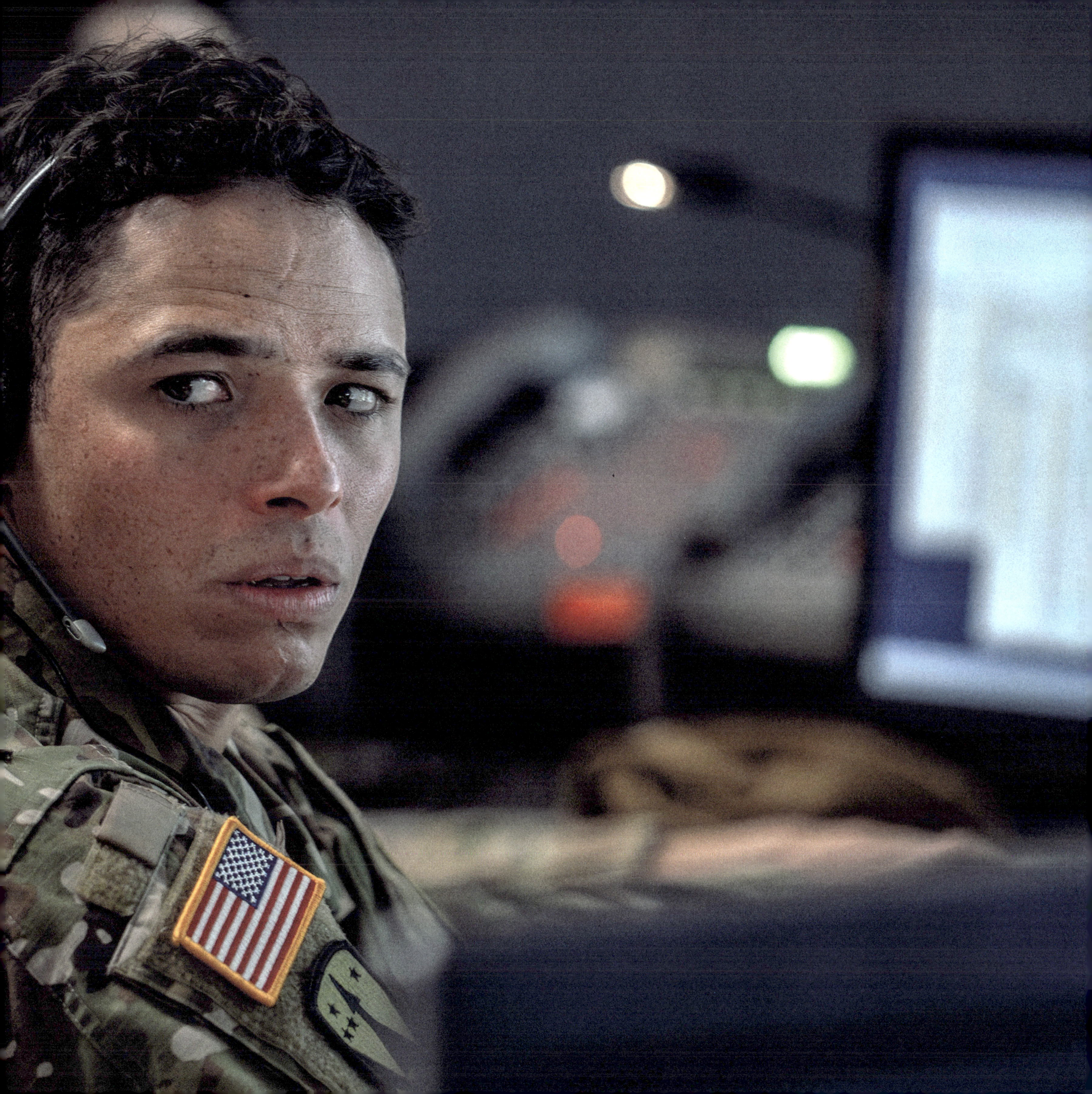

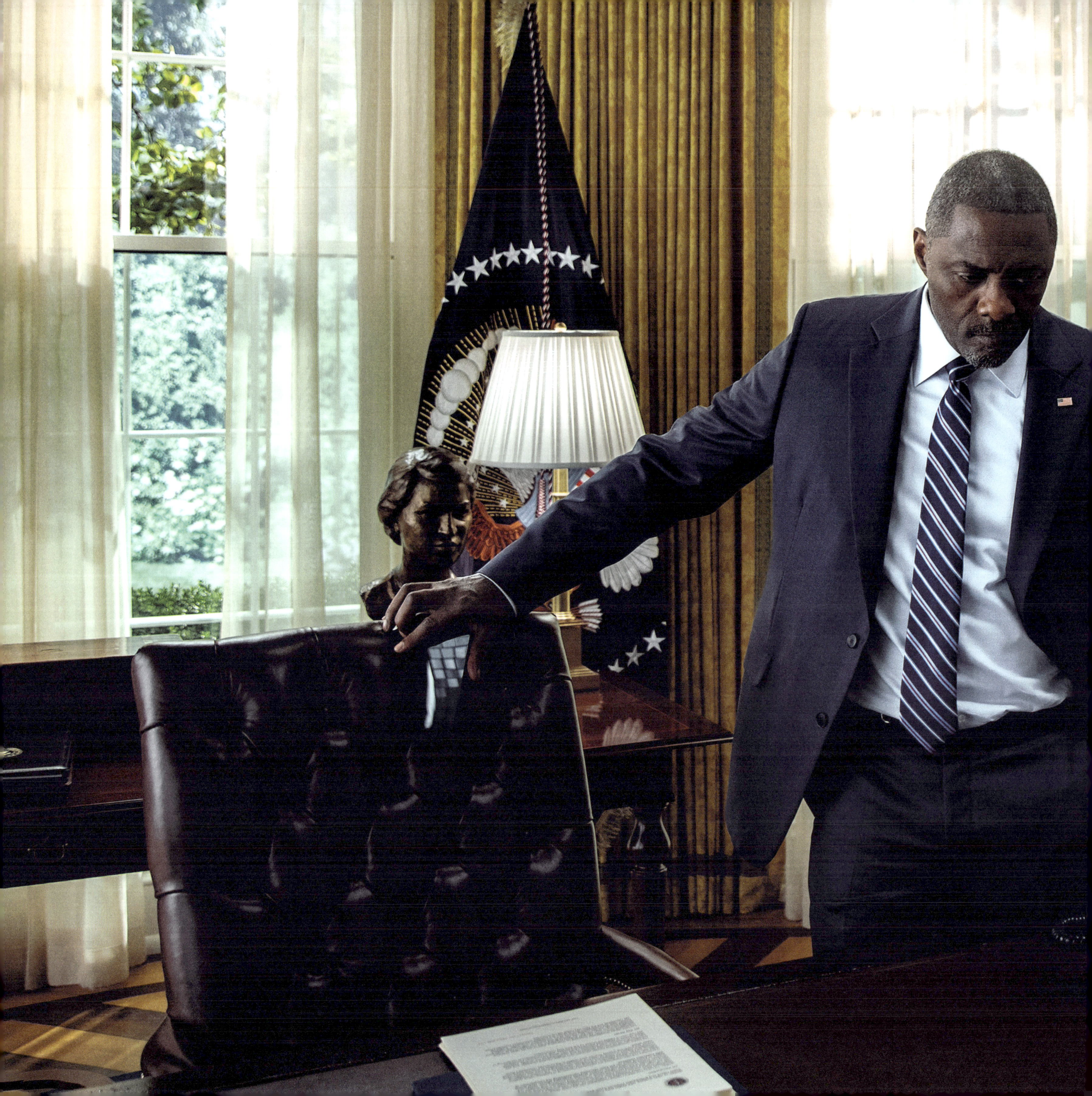

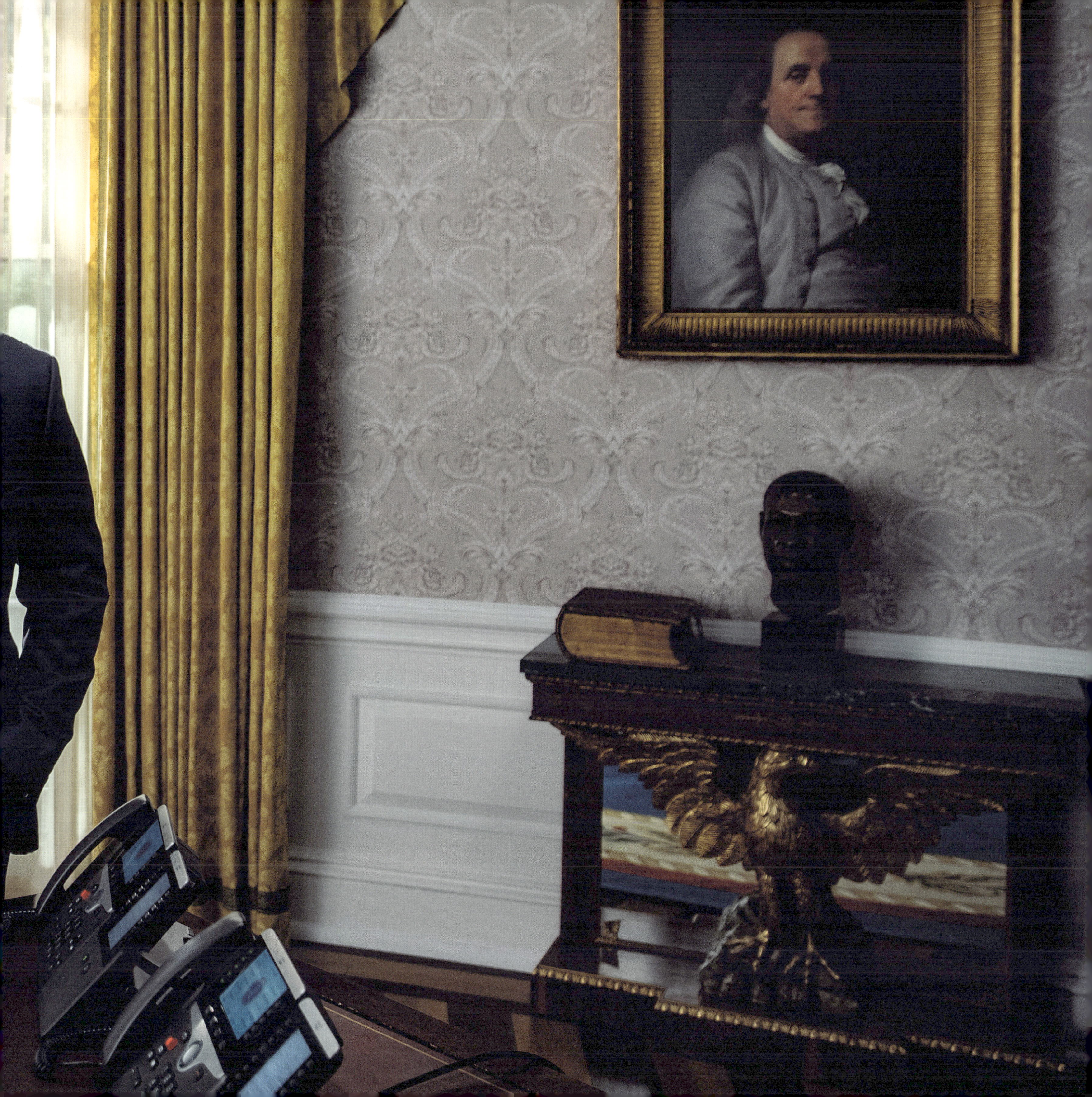

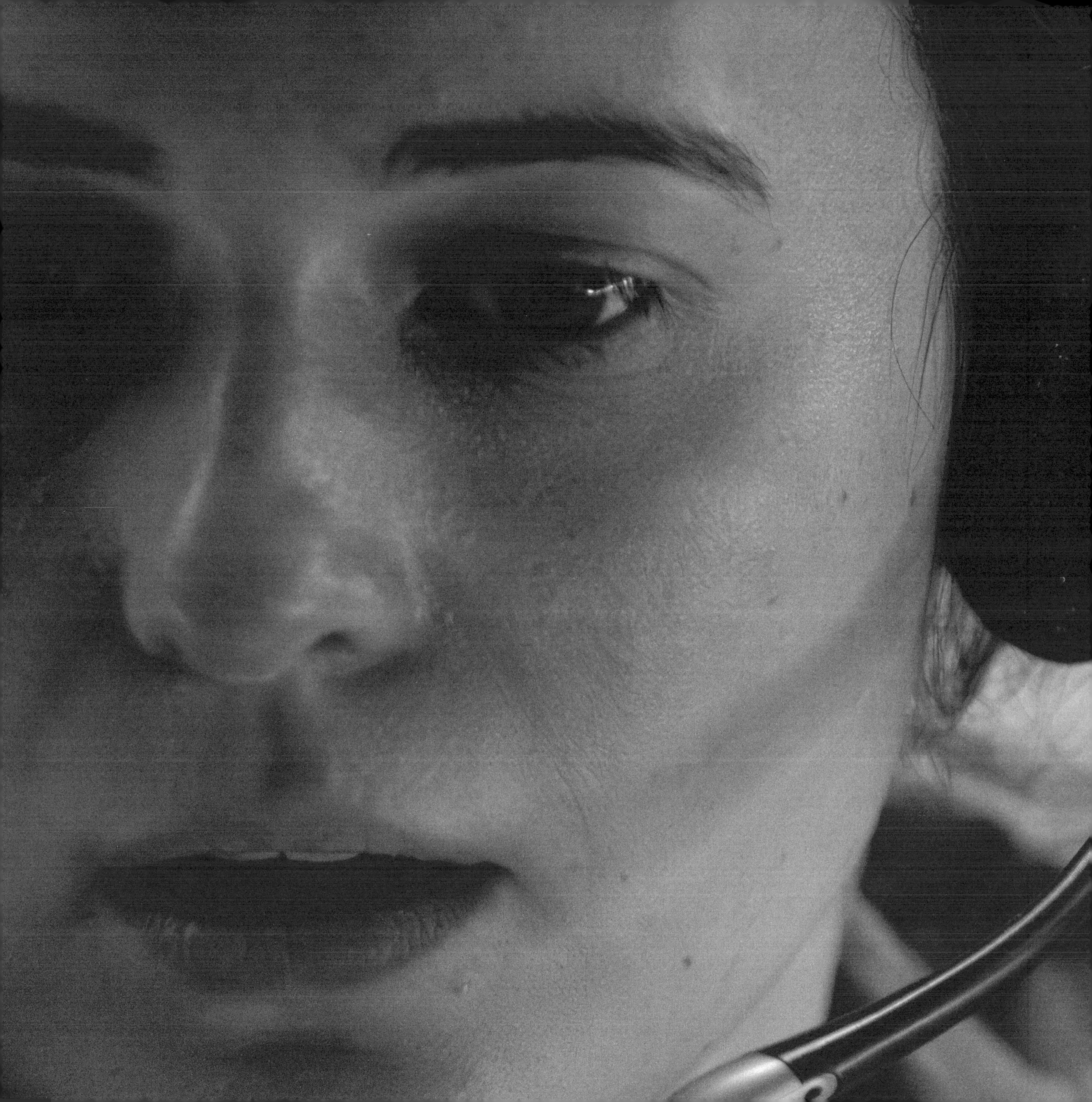

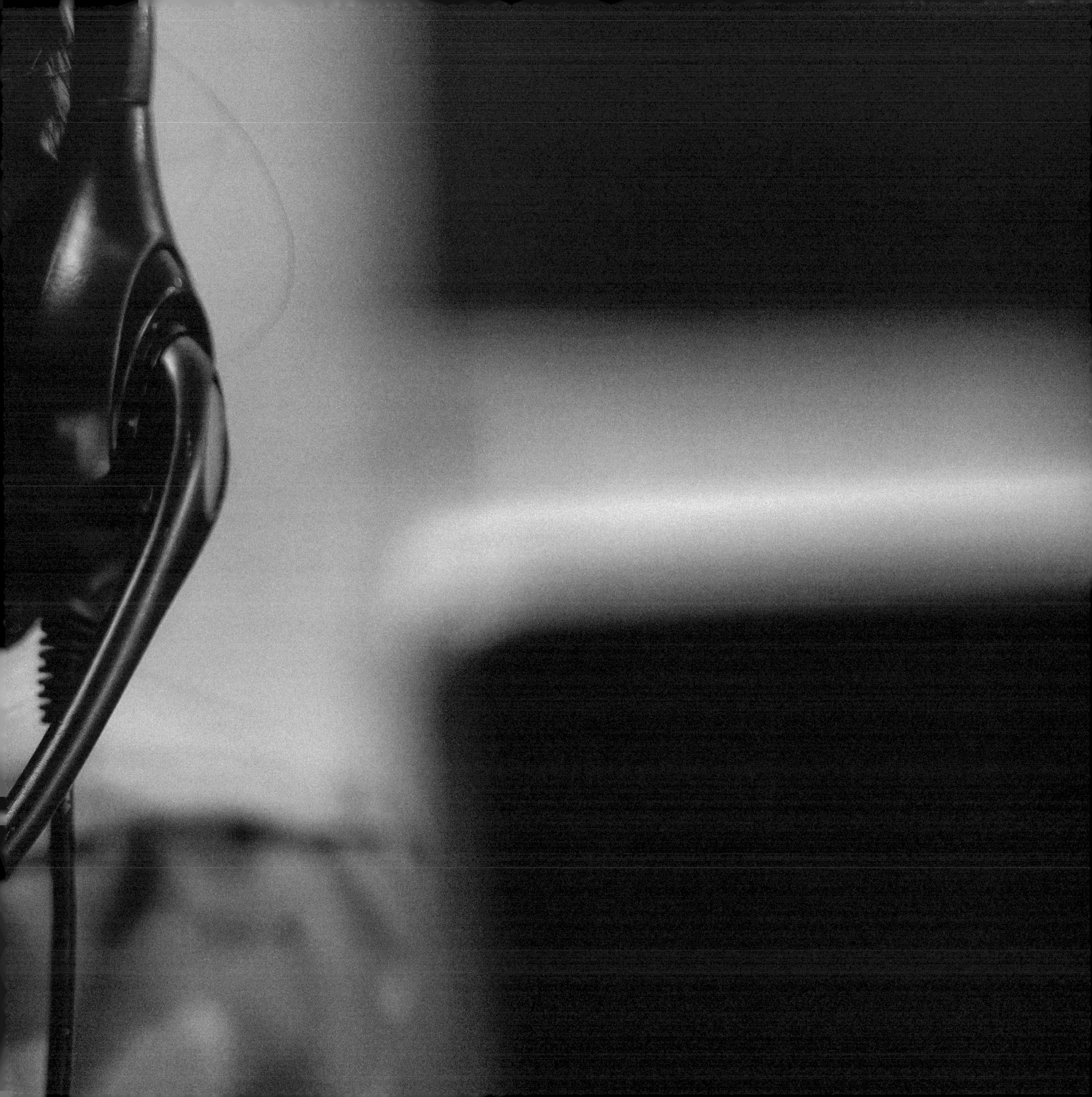

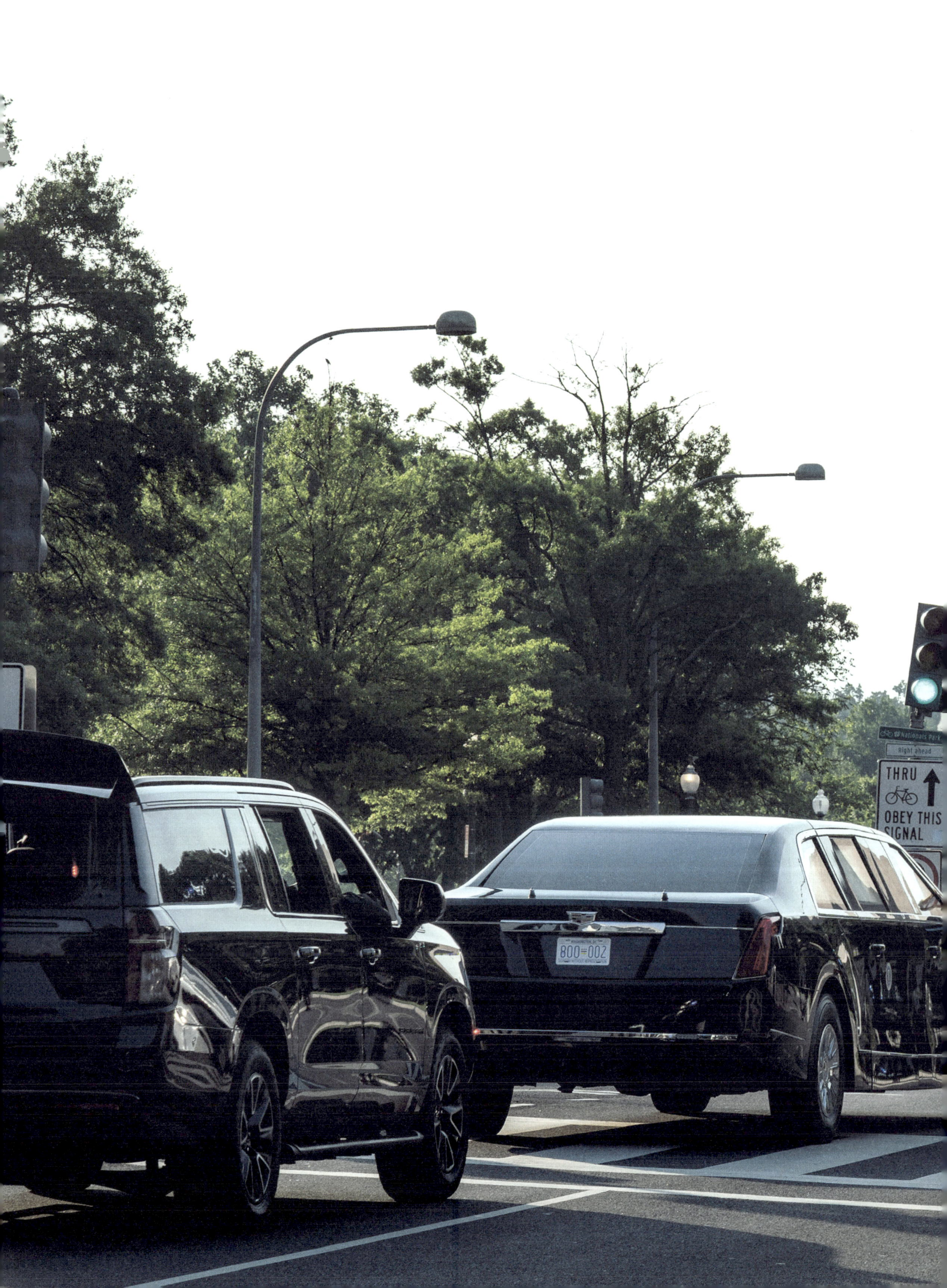
THRU
OBEY THIS
SIGNAL

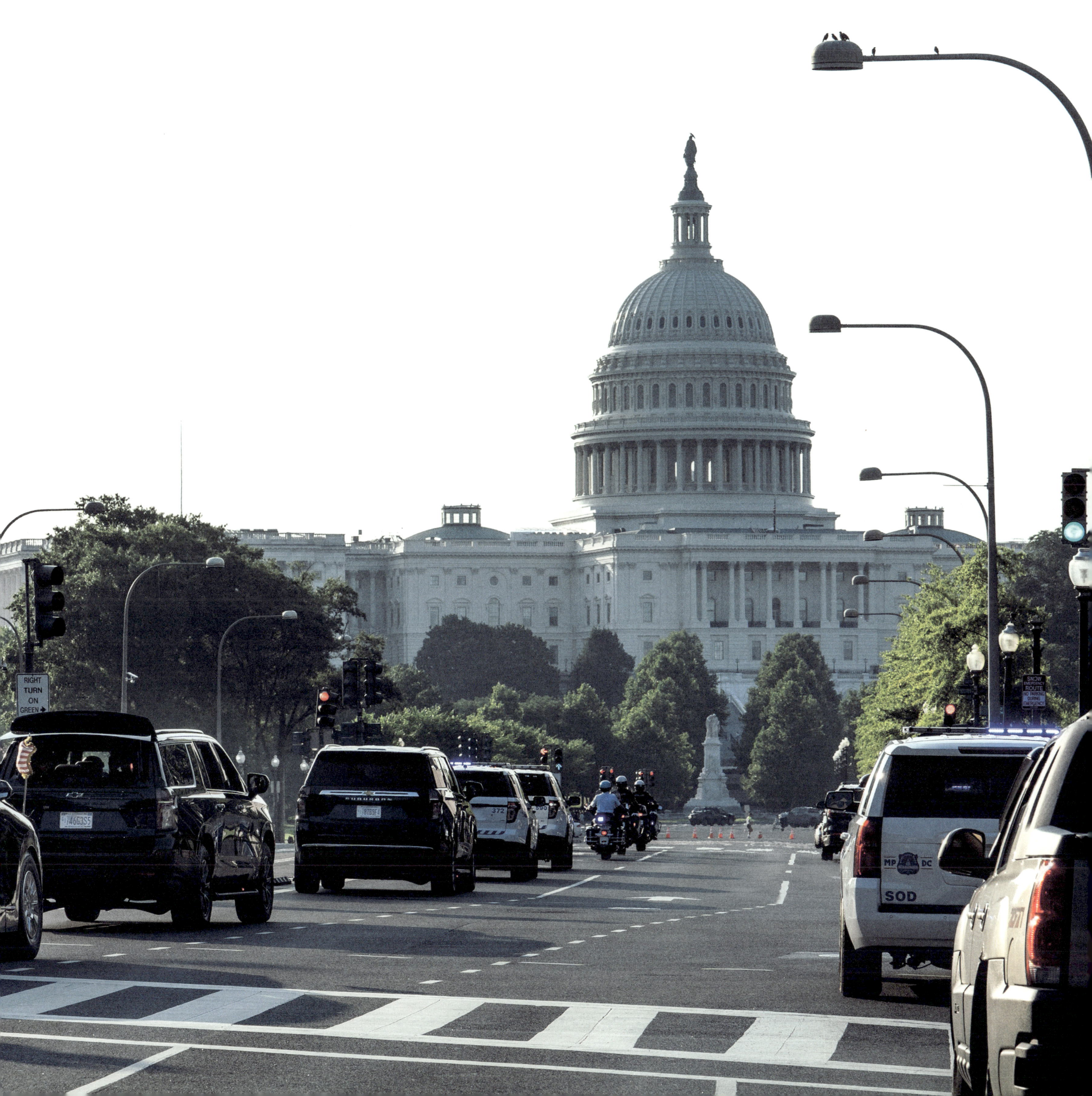
RIGHT
TURN
ON
GREEN
MP DC
SOD

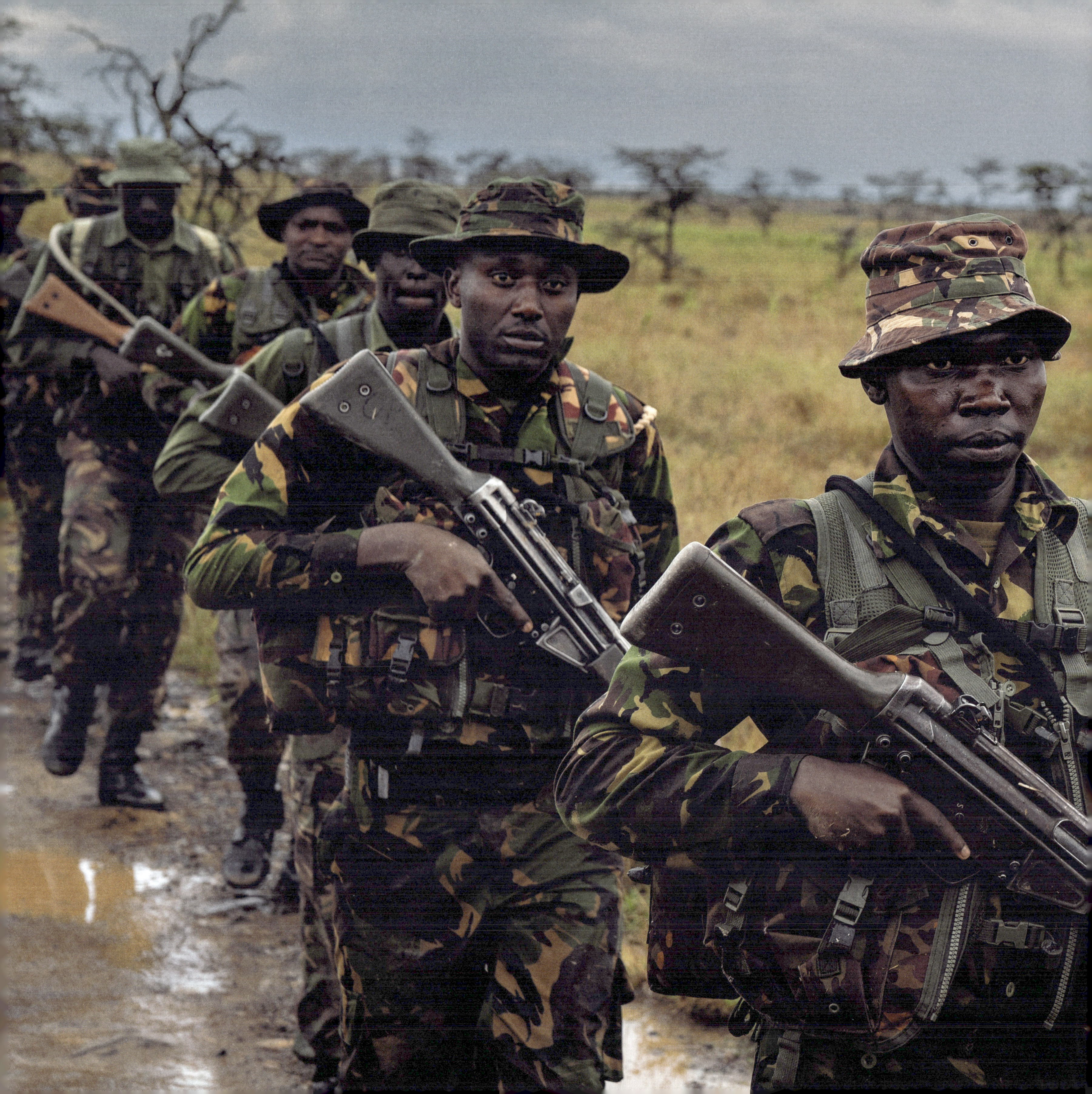

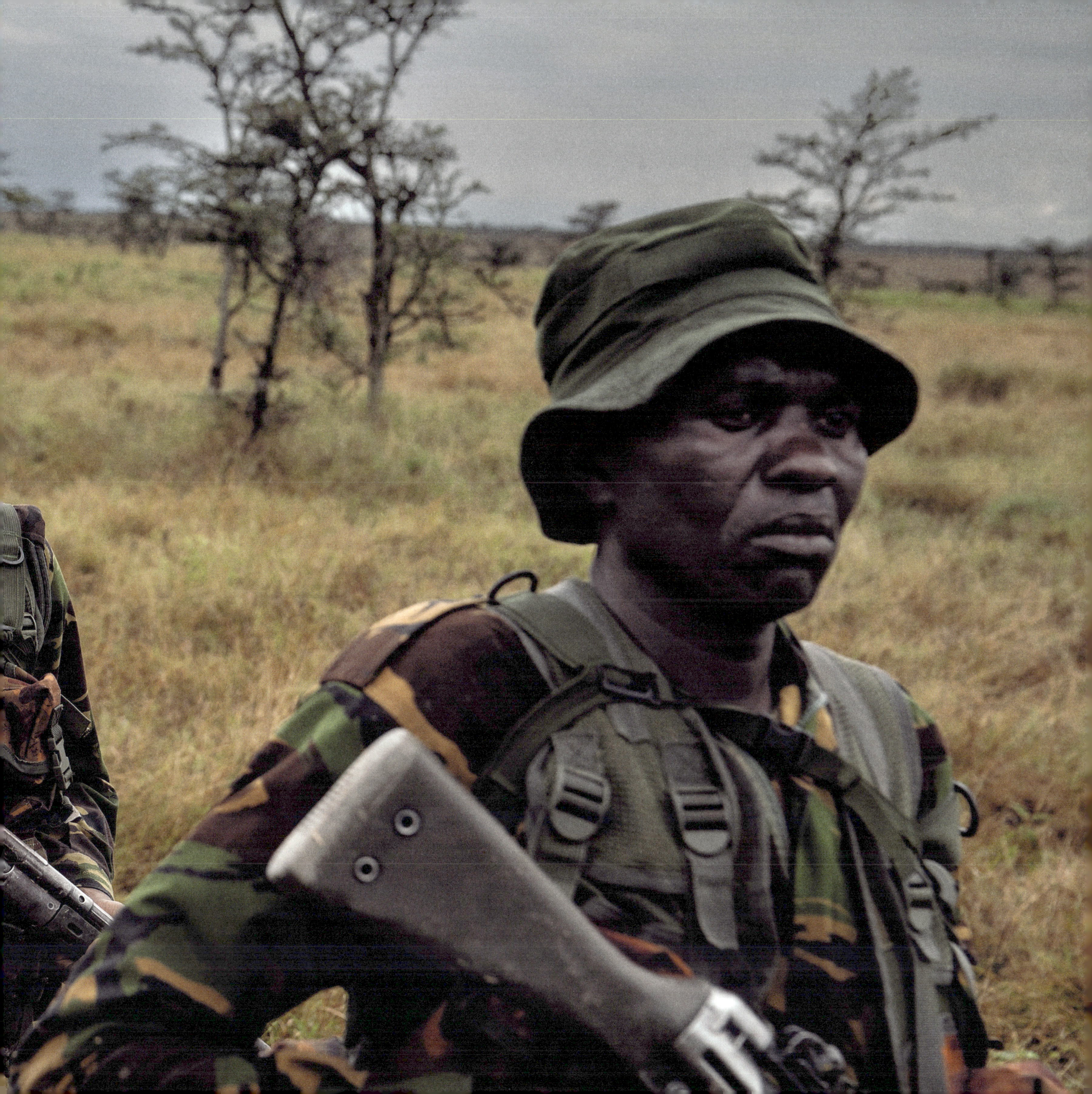

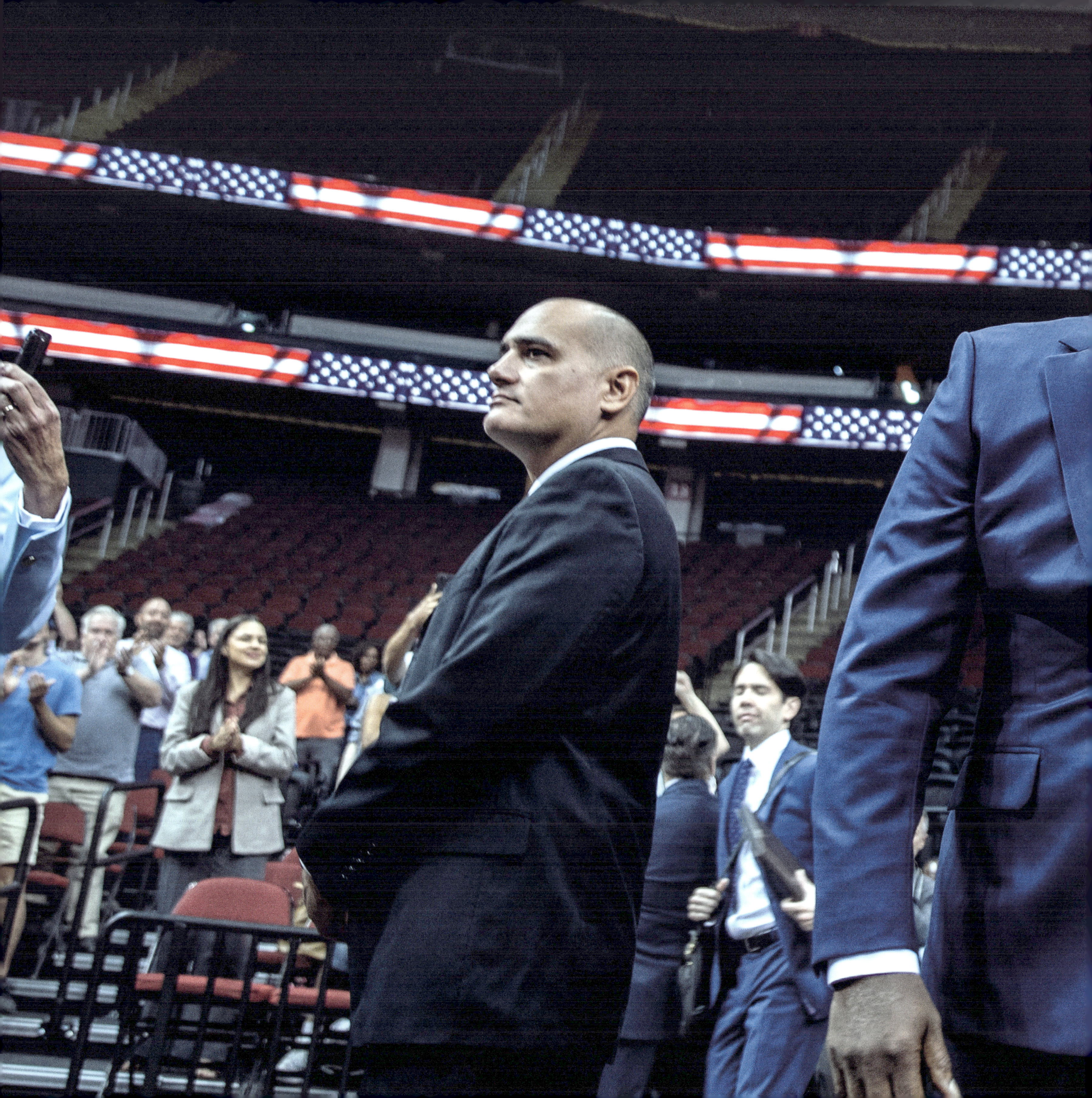

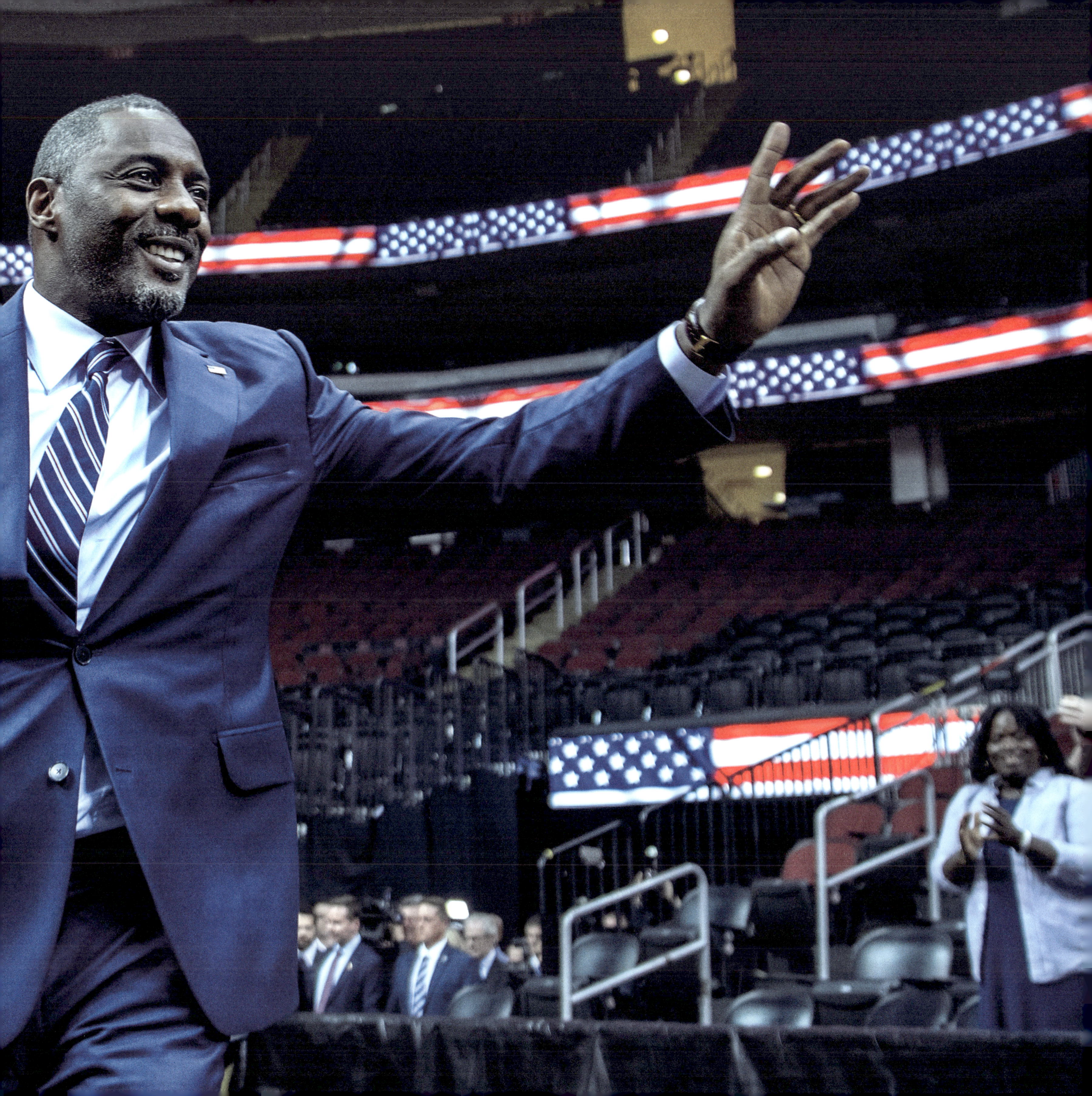

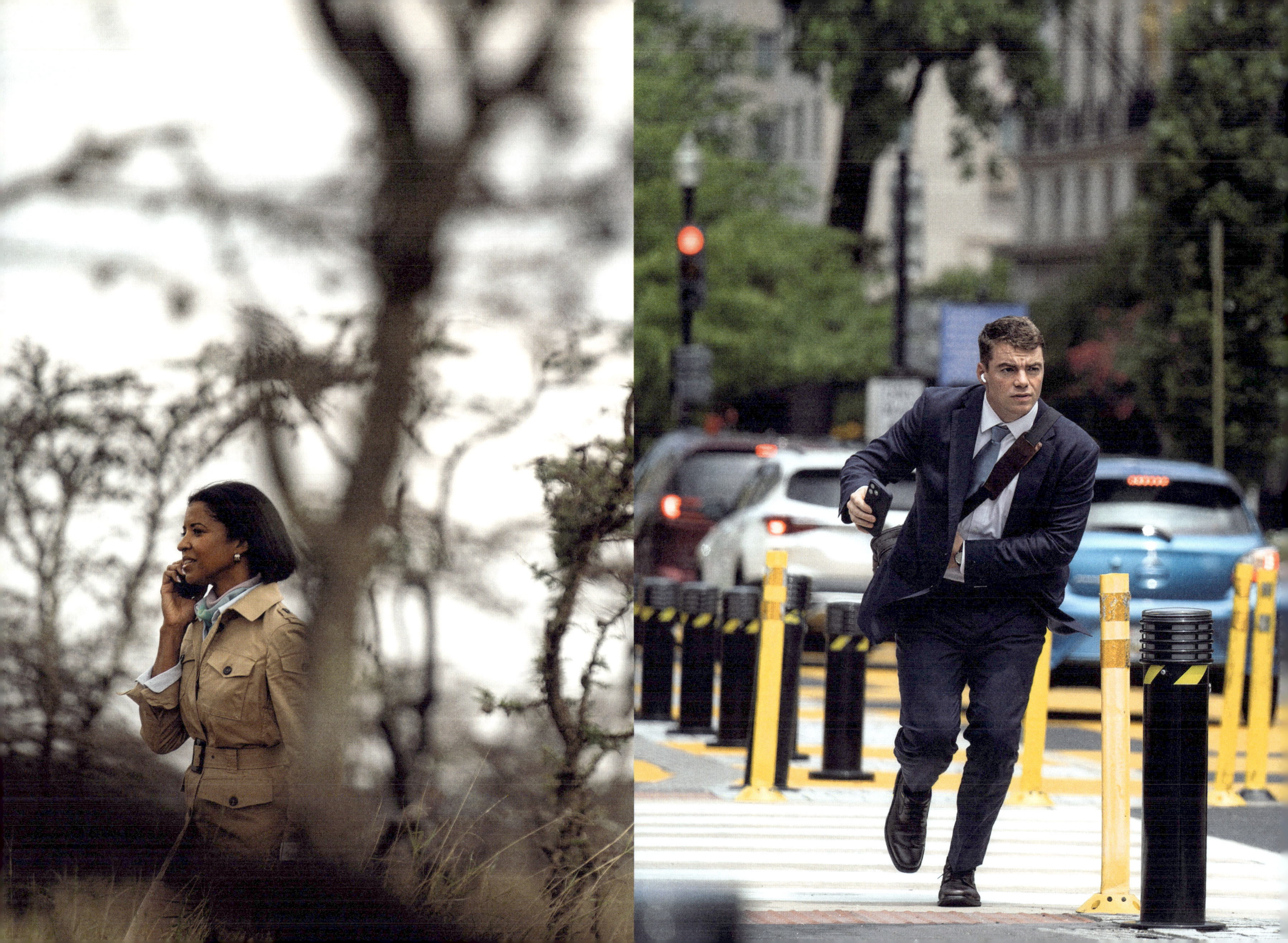

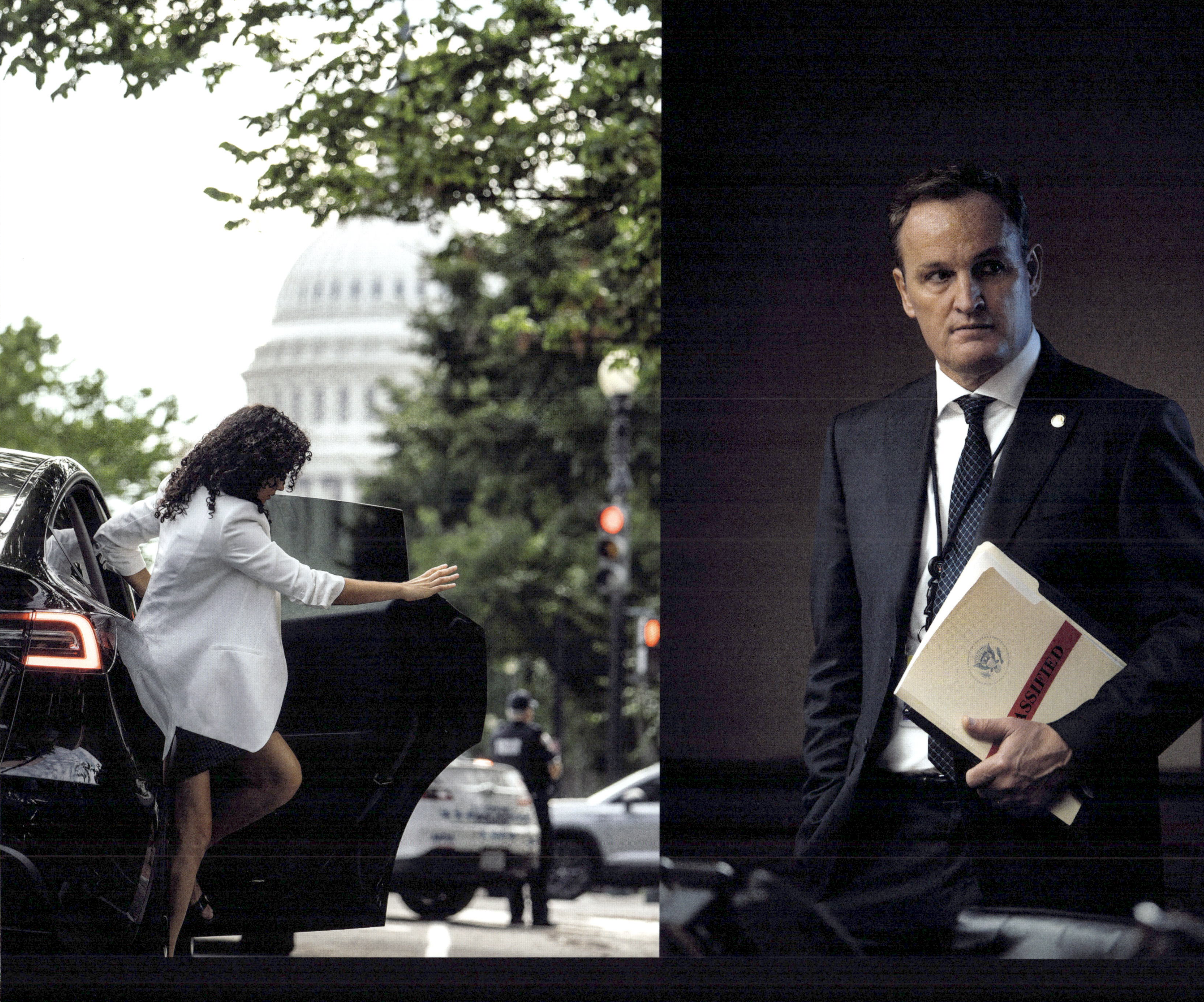
ASSIFIED

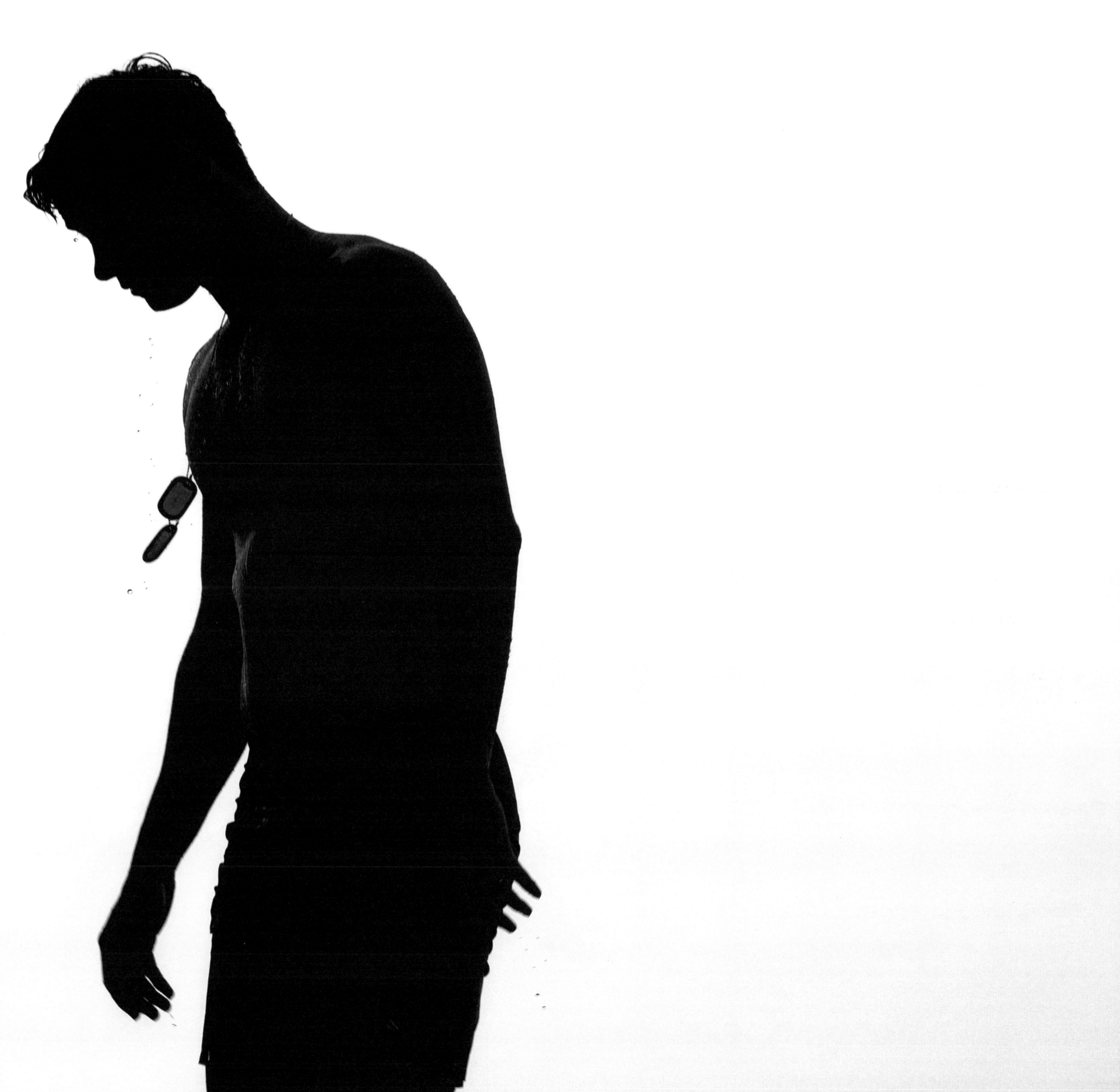

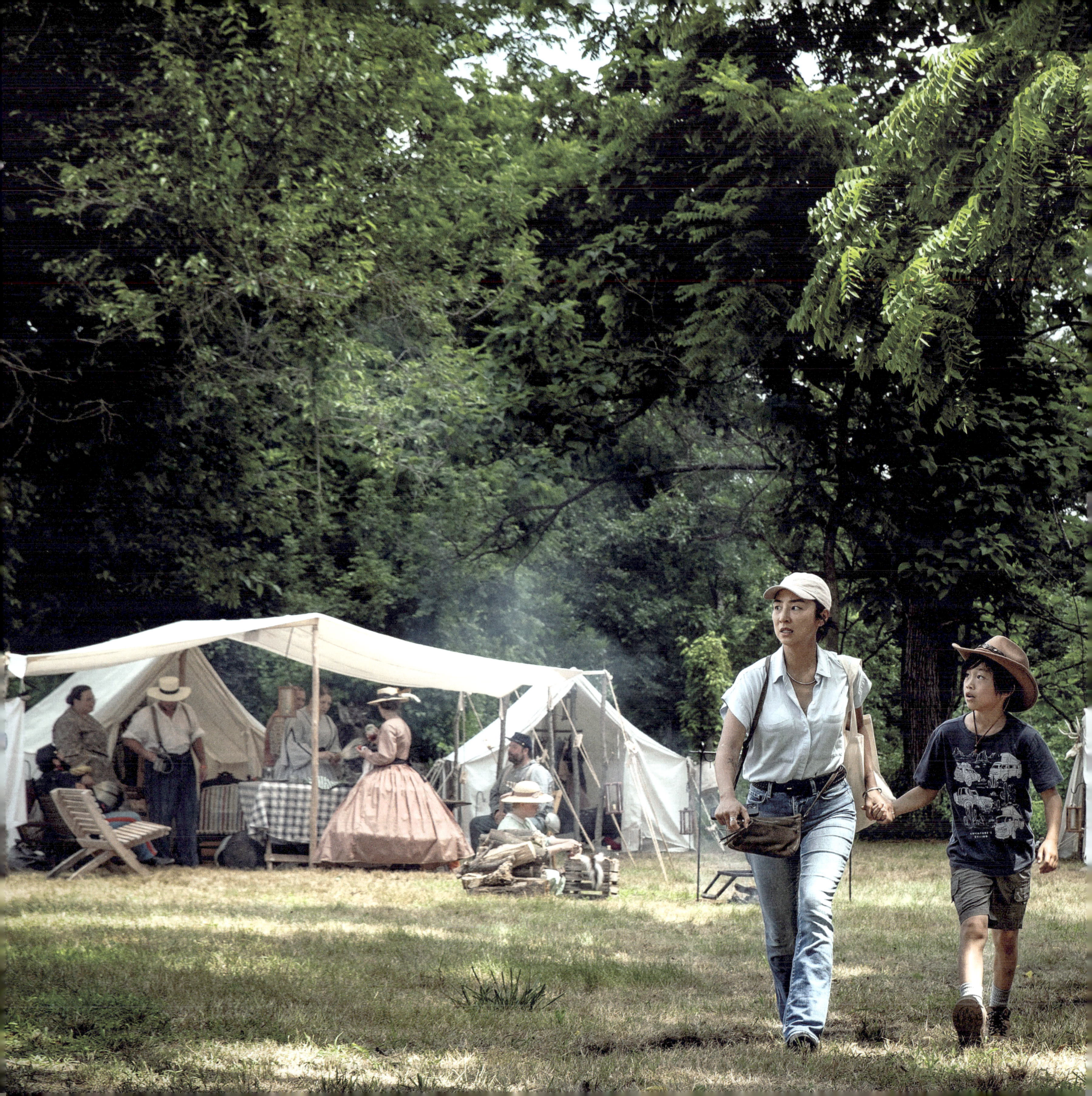

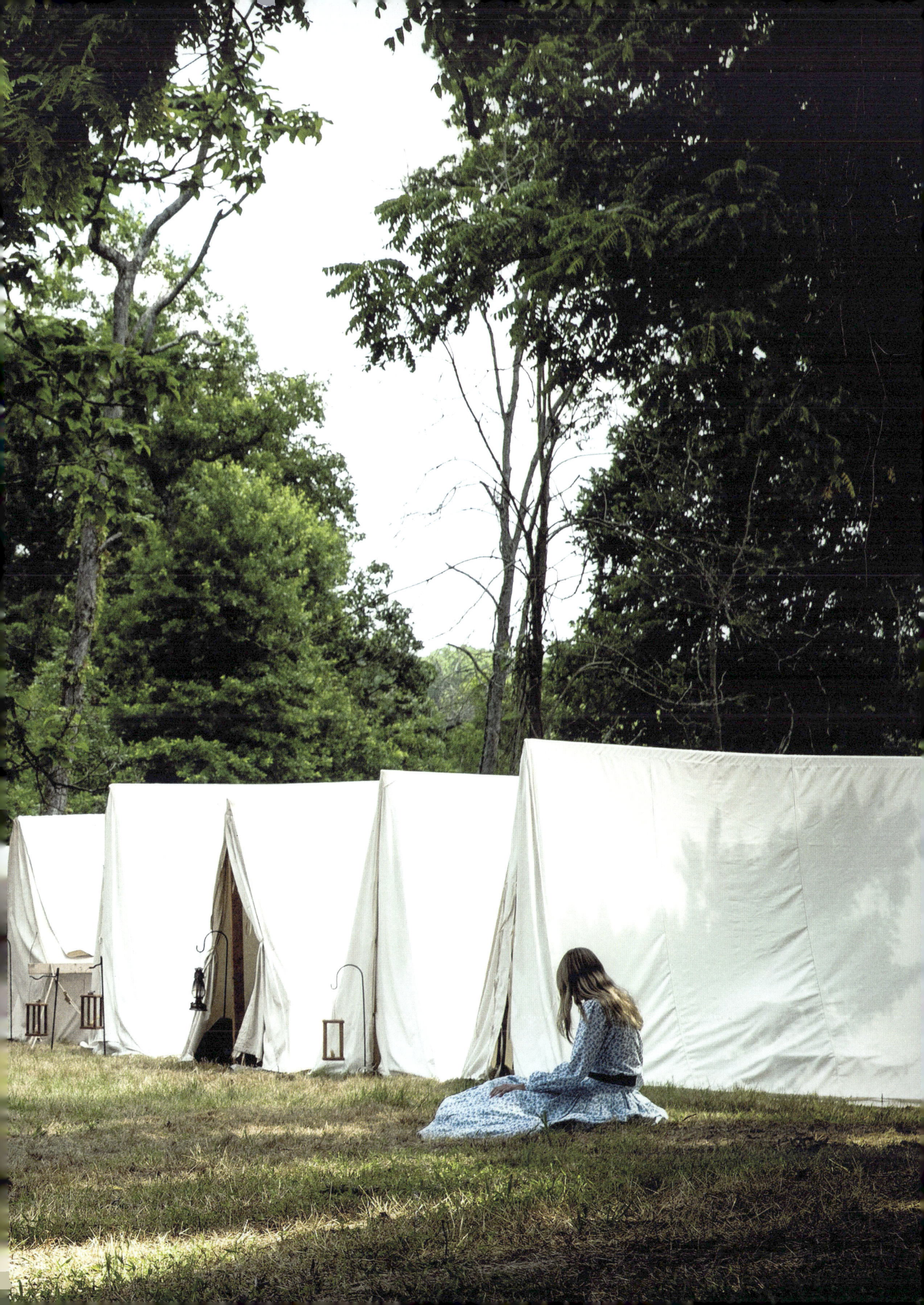

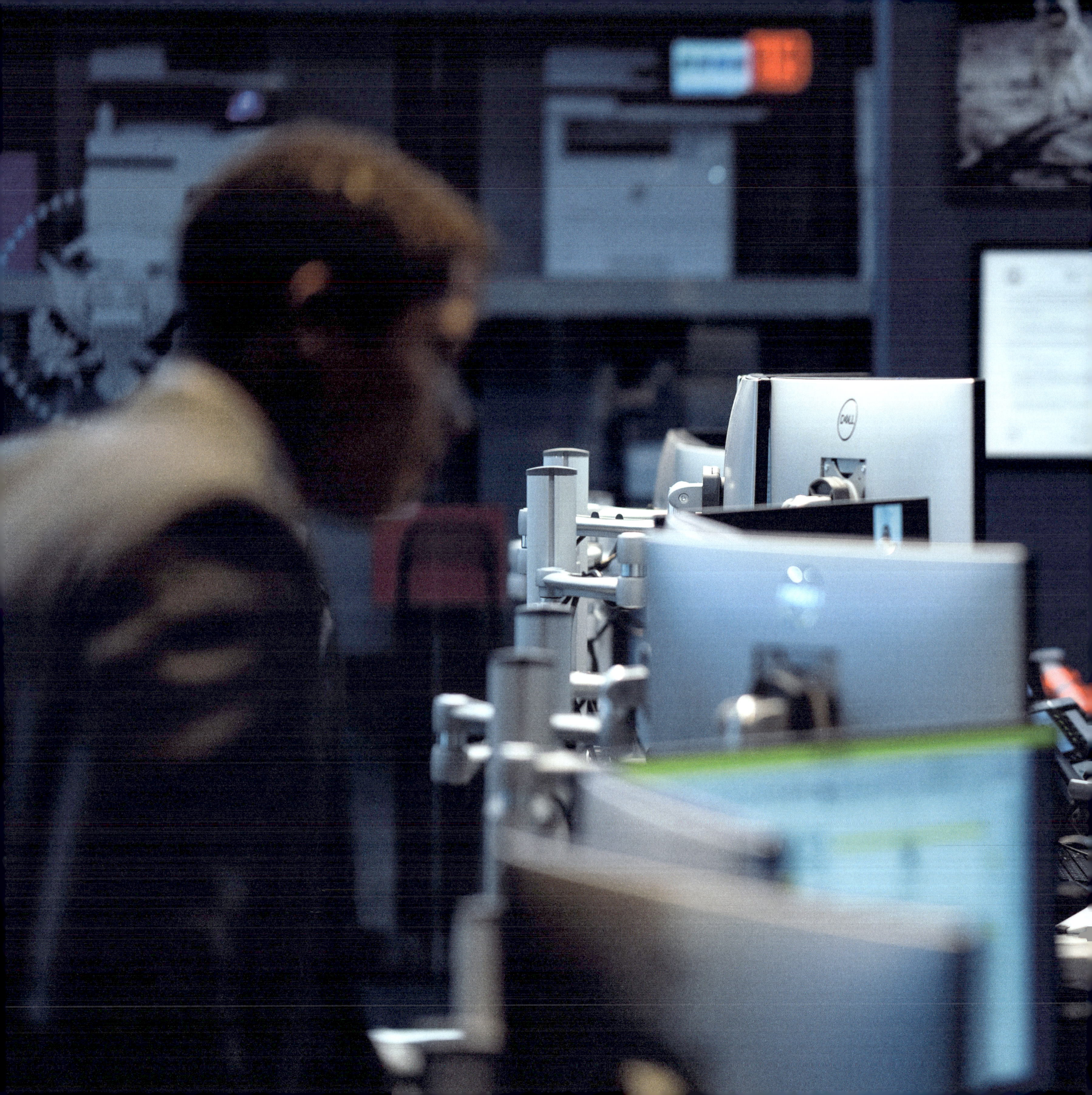
DELL

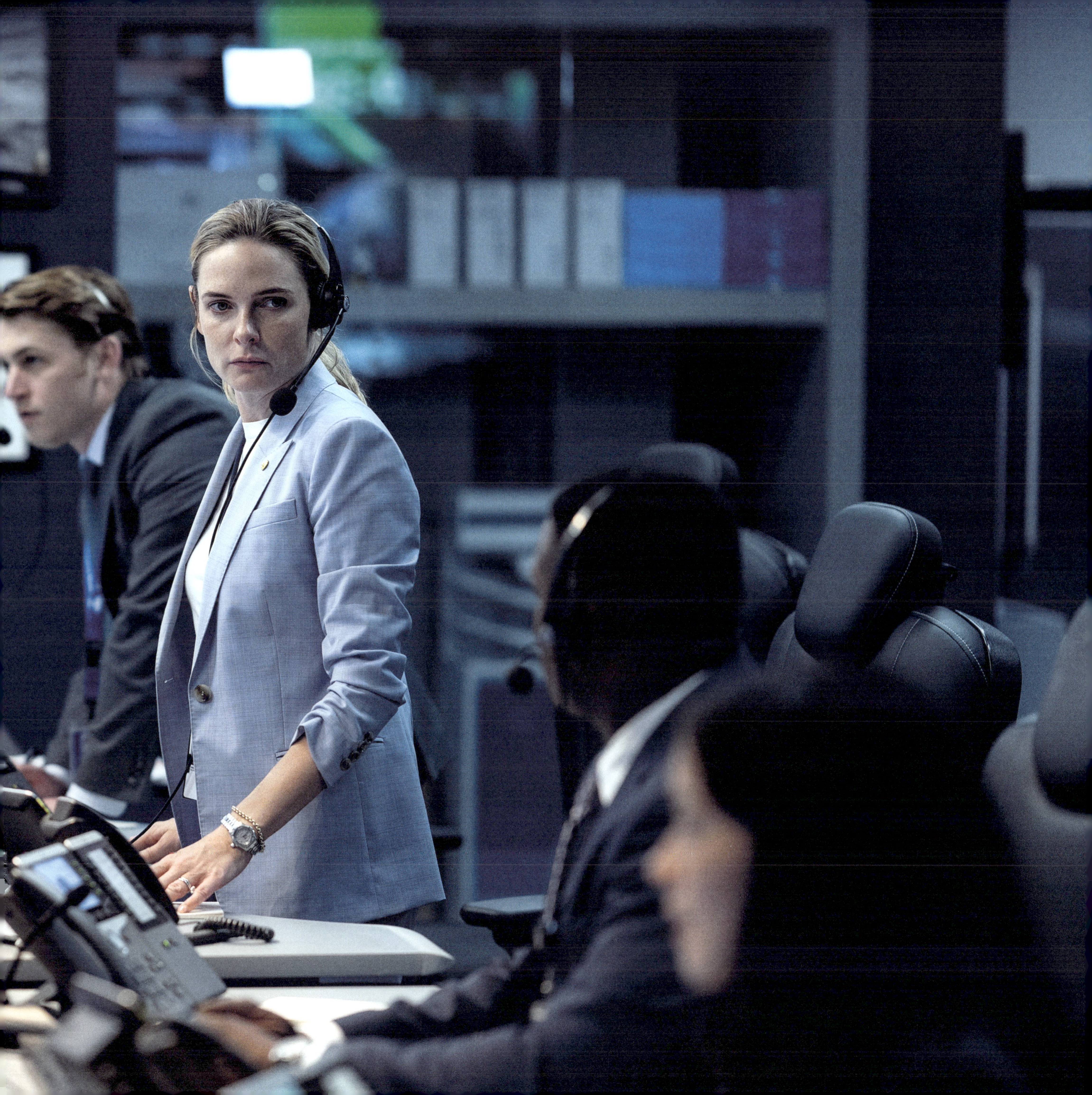

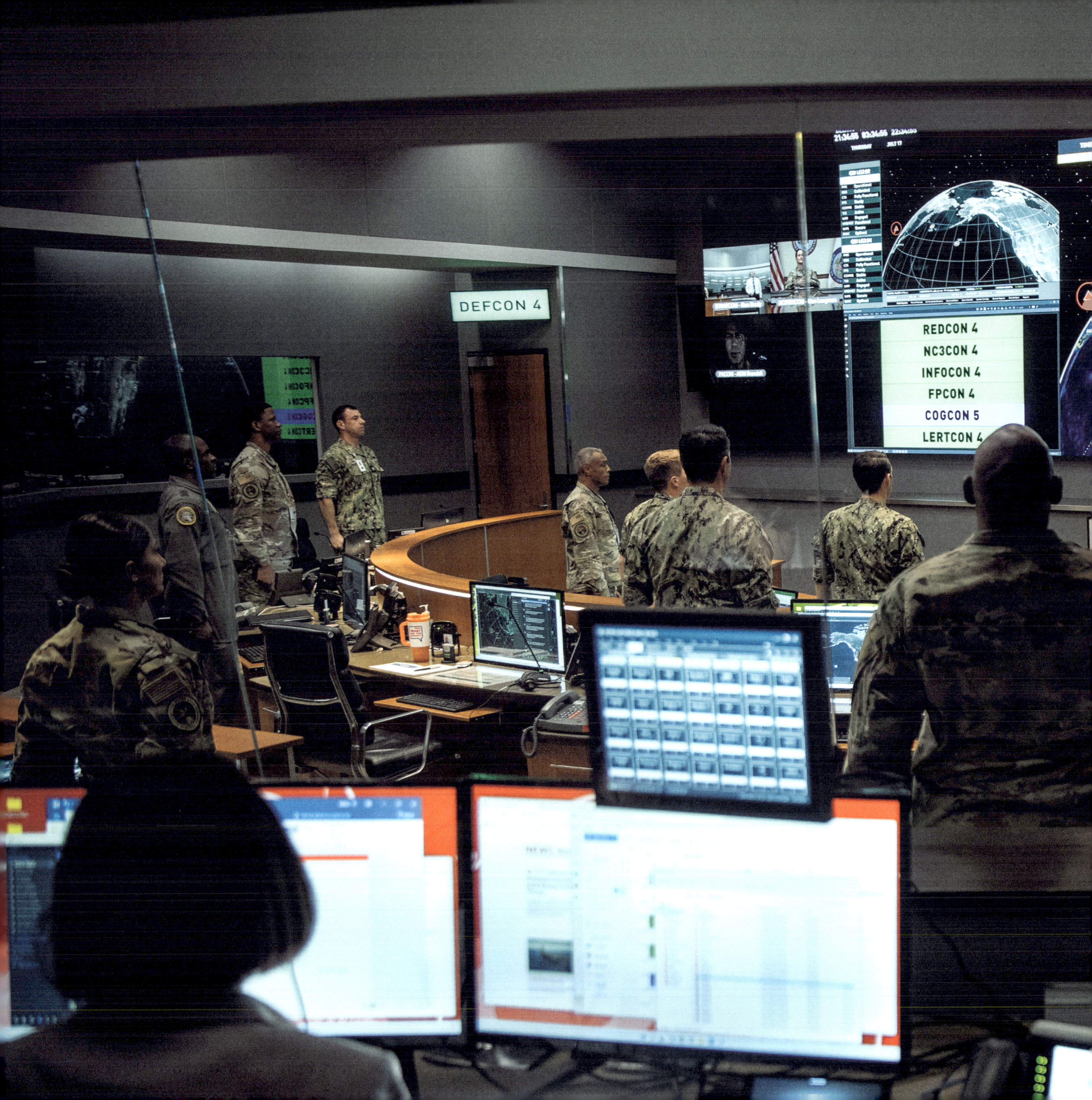
DEFCON 4
REDCON 4
NC3CON 4
INFOCON 4
FPCON 4
COGCON 5
LERTCON 4

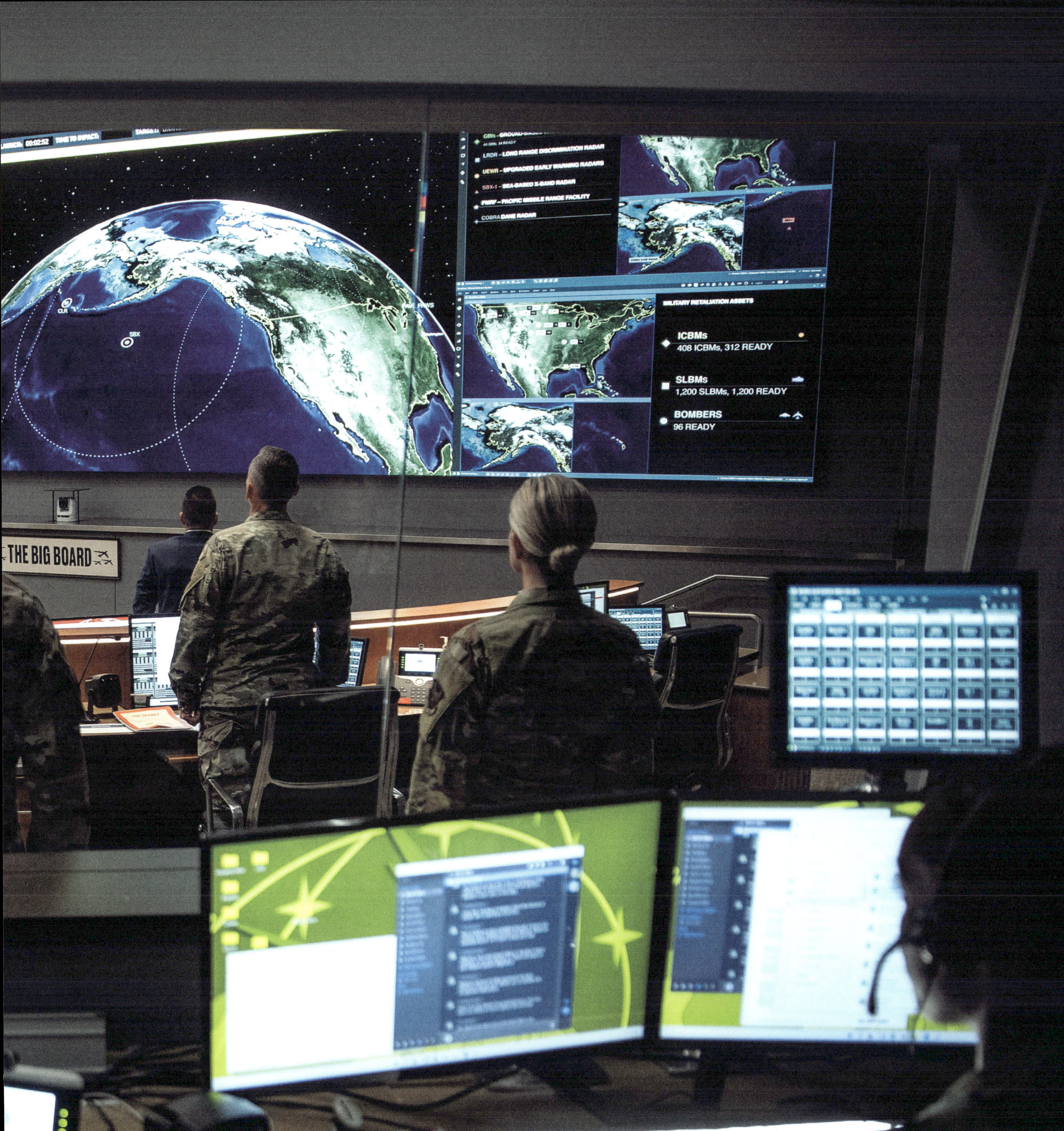

00:02:52
TIME TO IMPACT
LRDR – LONG RANGE DISCRIMINATION RADAR
UEWR – UPGRADED EARLY WARNING RADARS
SBX-1 – SEA-BASED X-BAND RADAR
PMRF – PACIFIC MISSILE RANGE FACILITY
COBRA DANE RADAR
CLR
SBX
MILITARY RETALIATION ASSETS
ICBMs
408 ICBMs, 312 READY
SLBMs
1,200 SLBMs, 1,200 READY
BOMBERS
96 READY
THE BIG BOARD

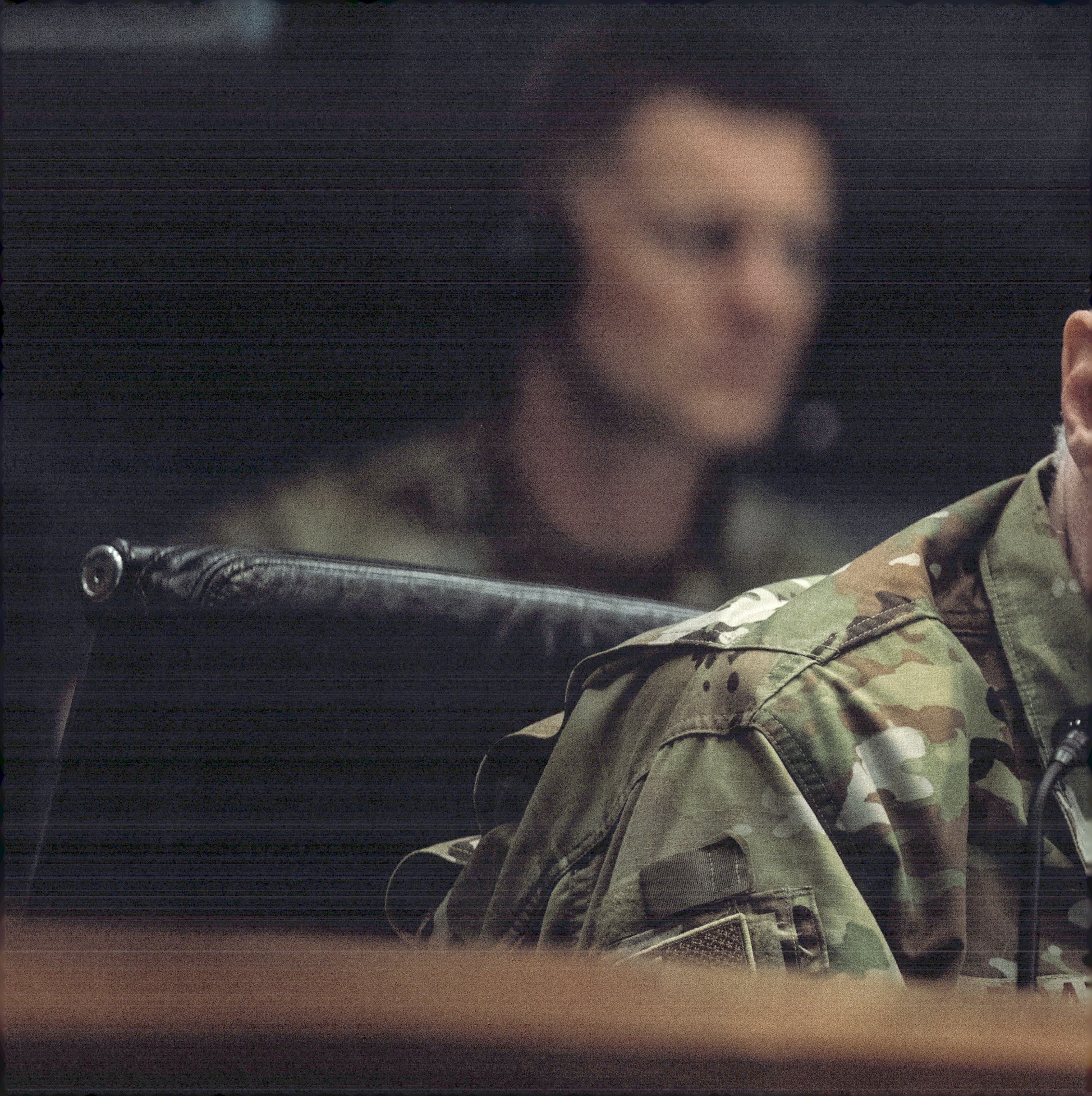

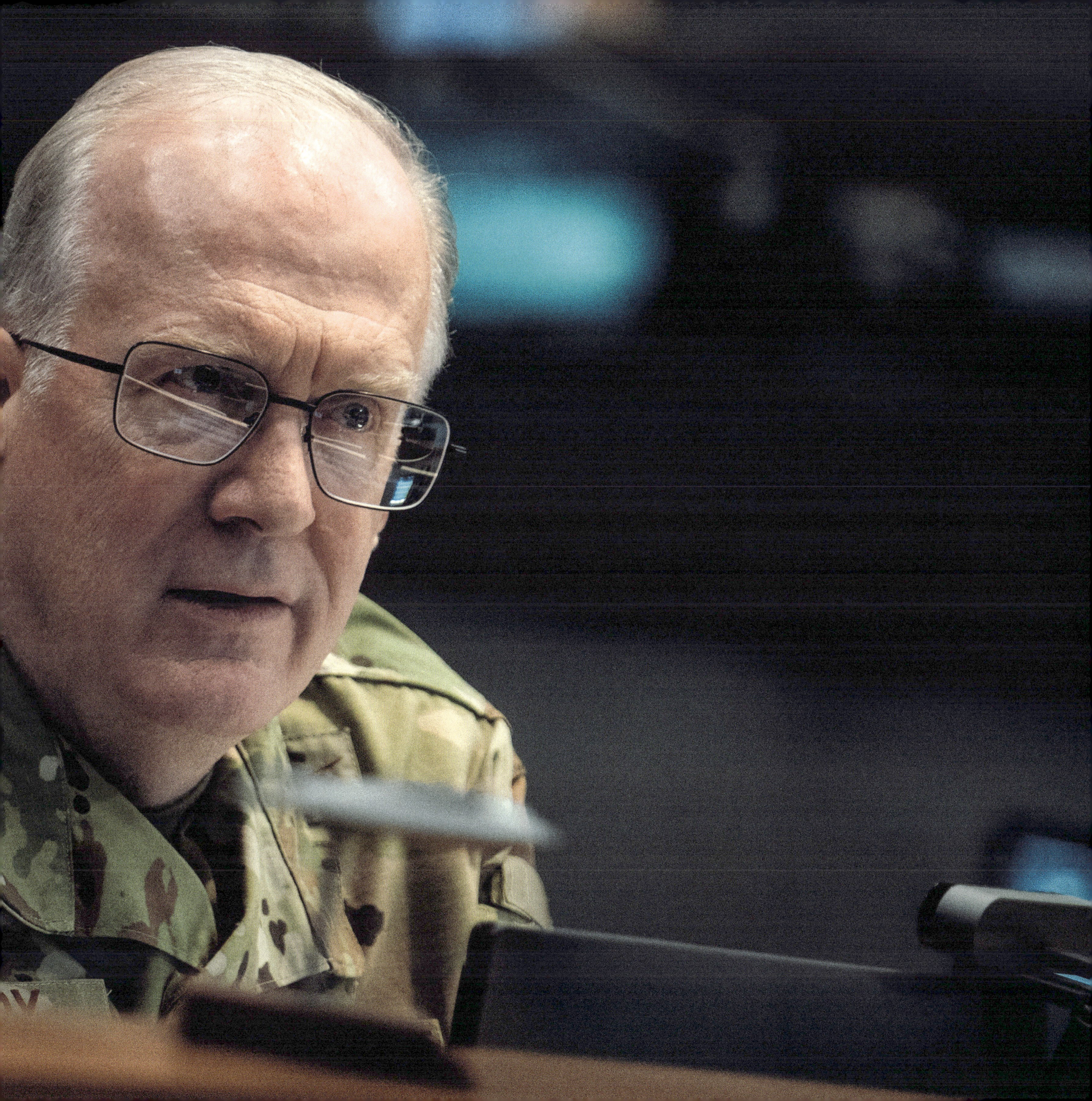

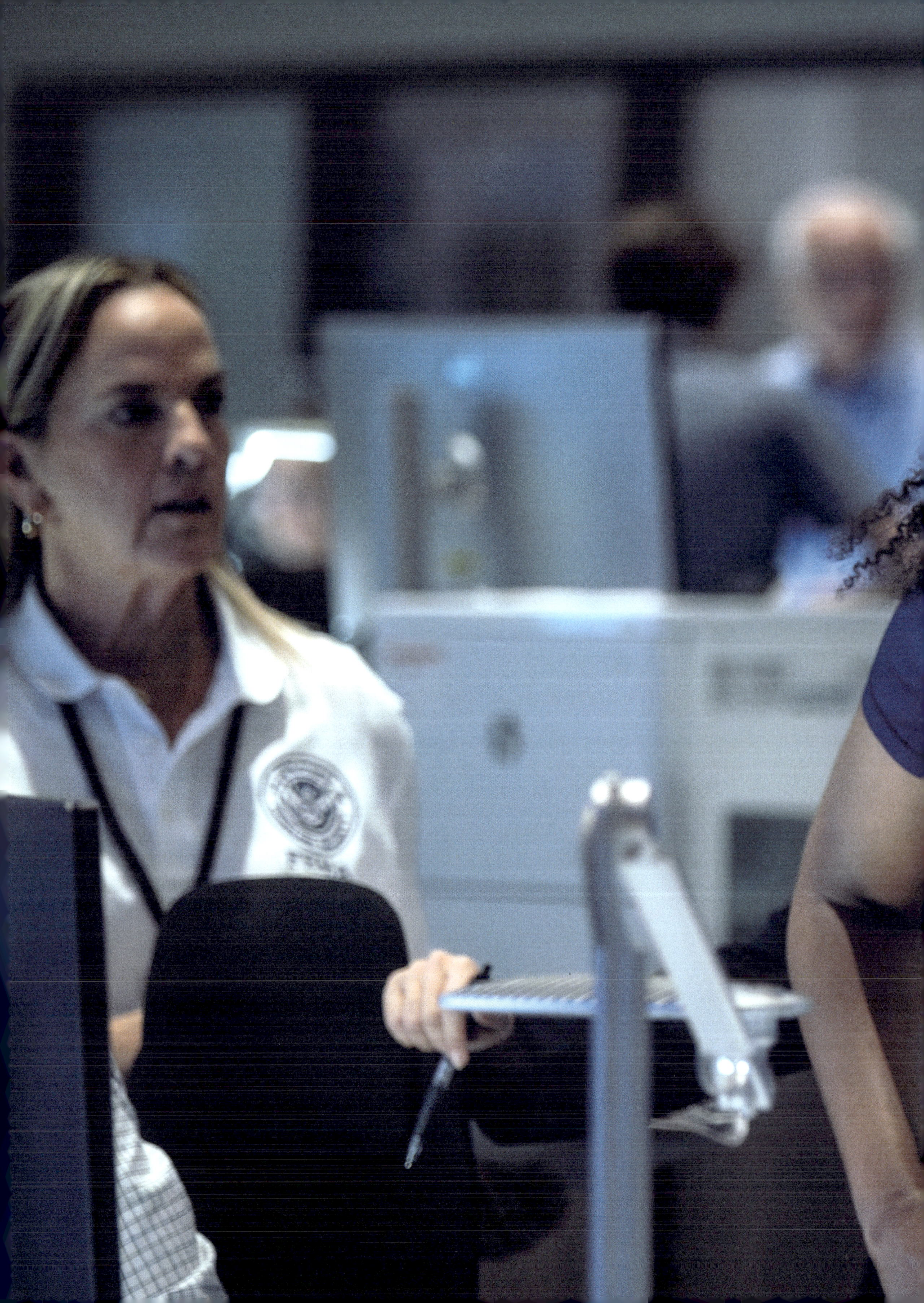

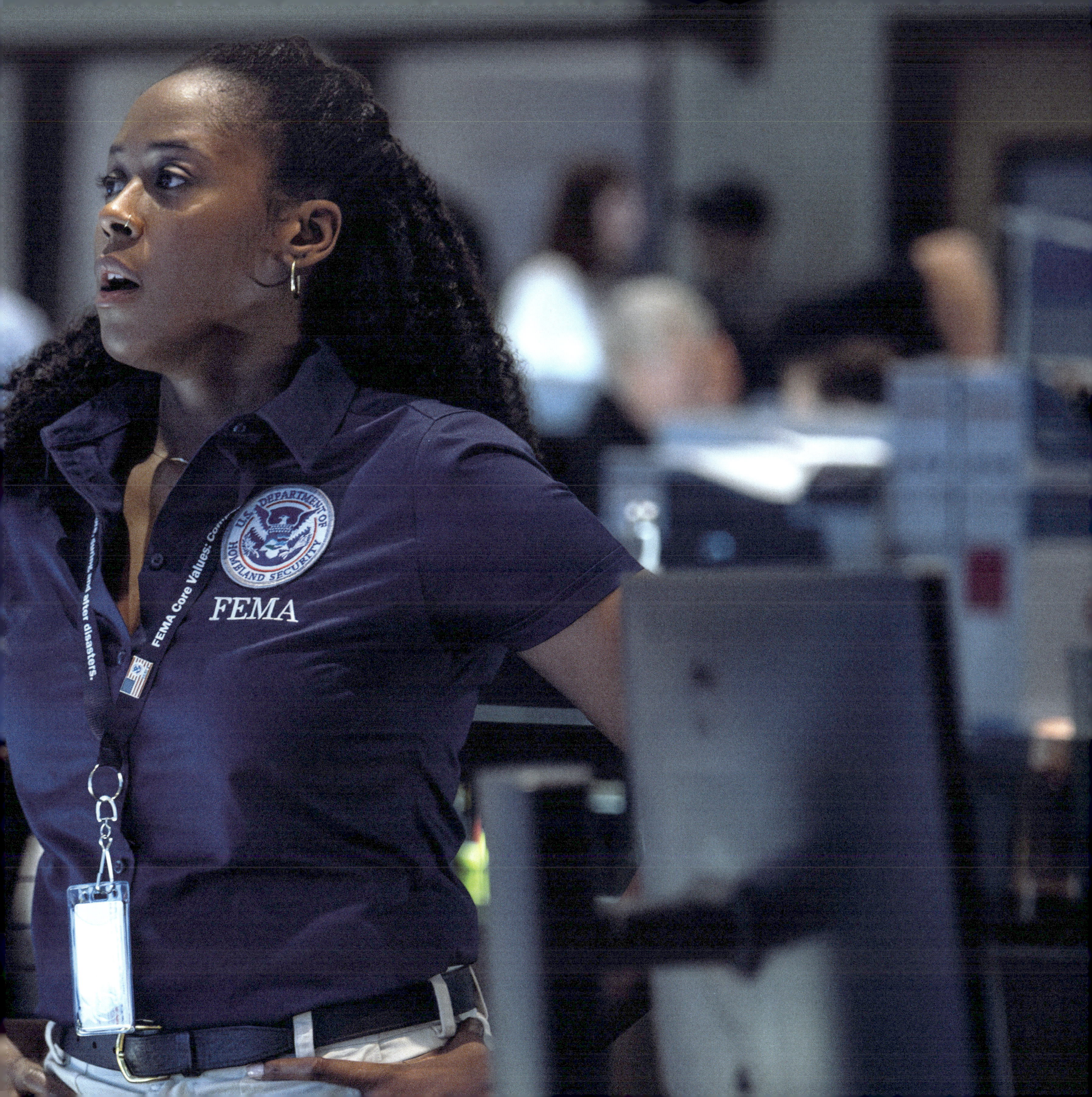
U.S. DEPARTMENT OF HOMELAND SECURITY
FEMA
FEMA Core Values:
after disasters.

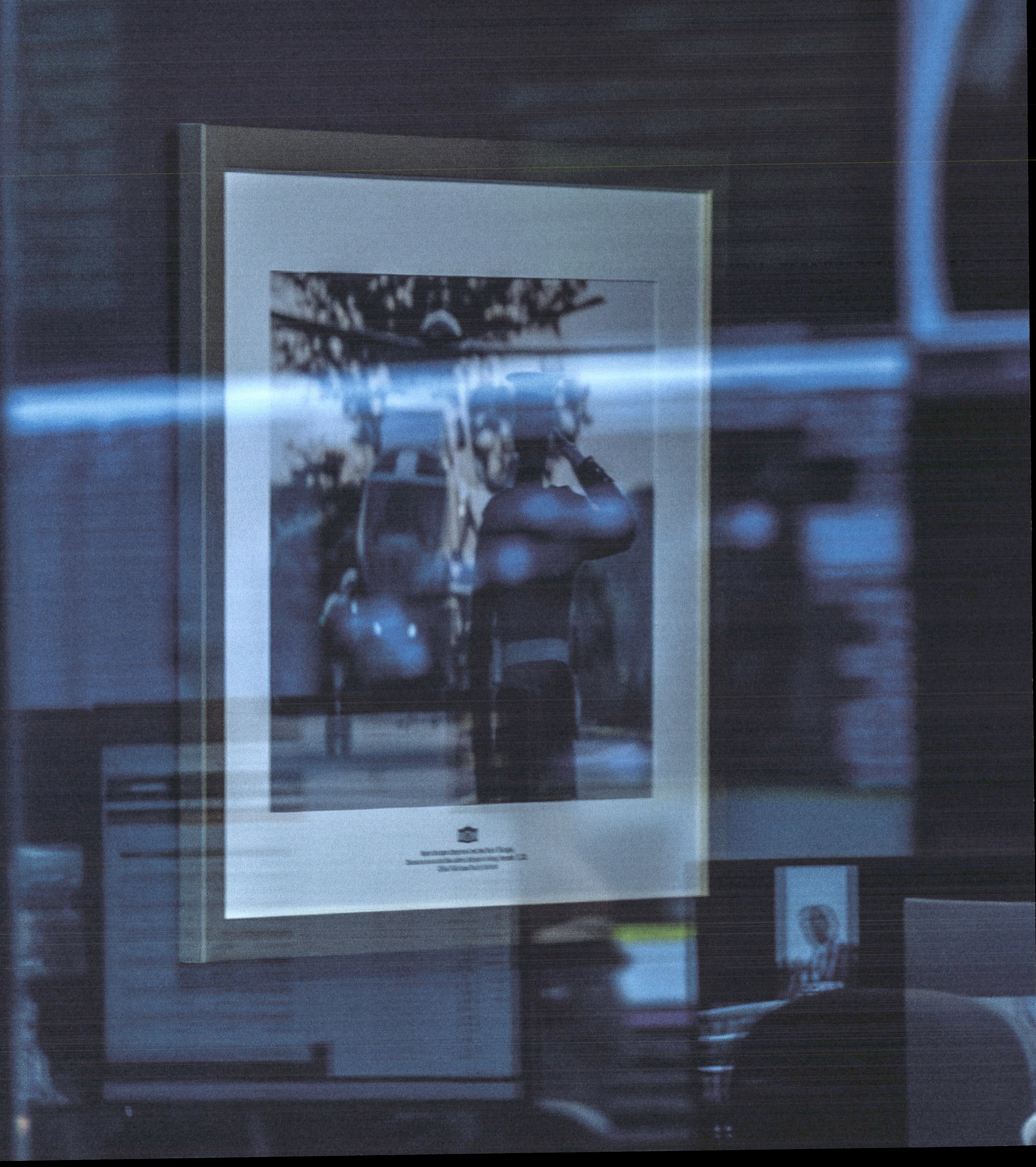

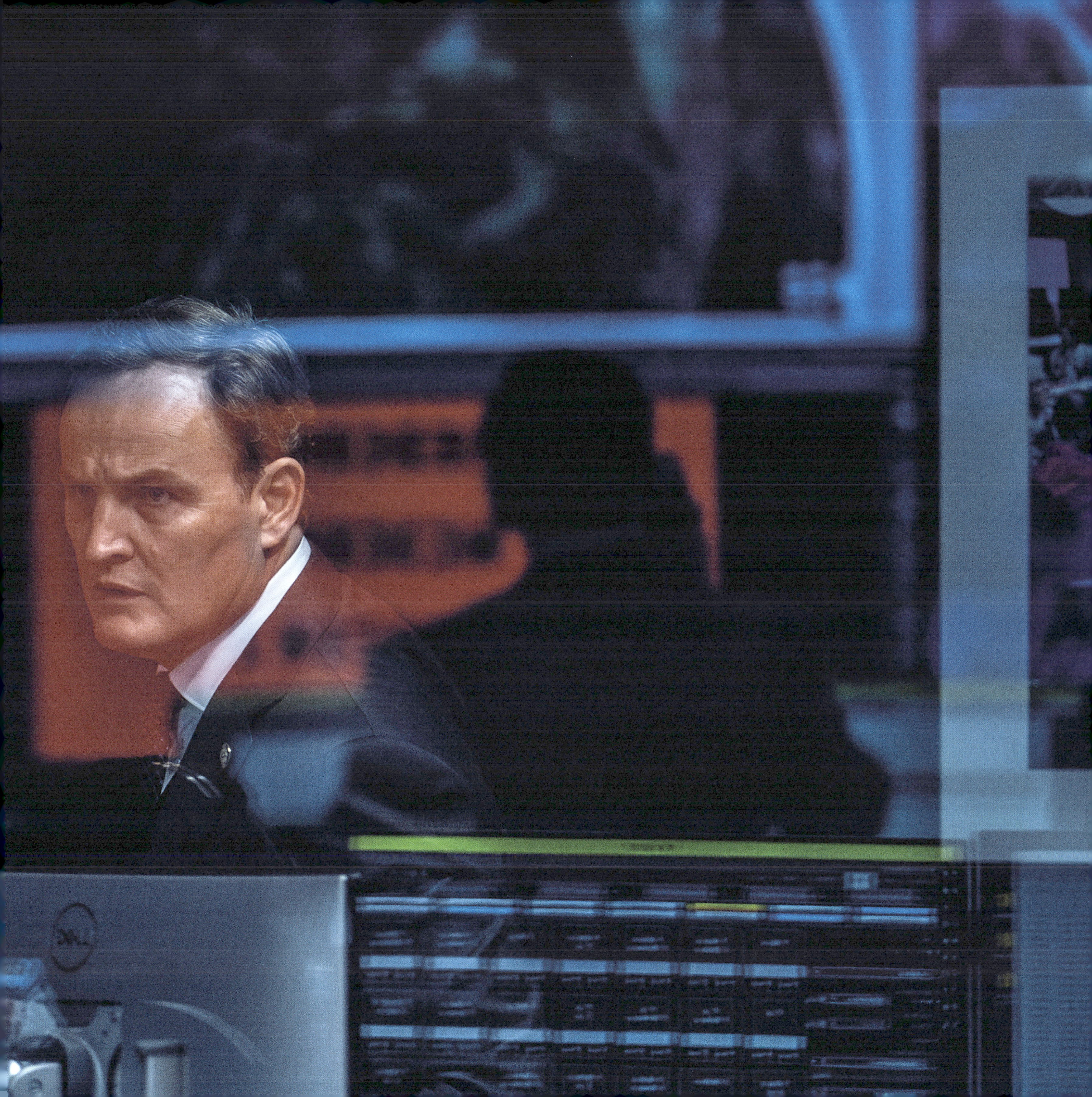

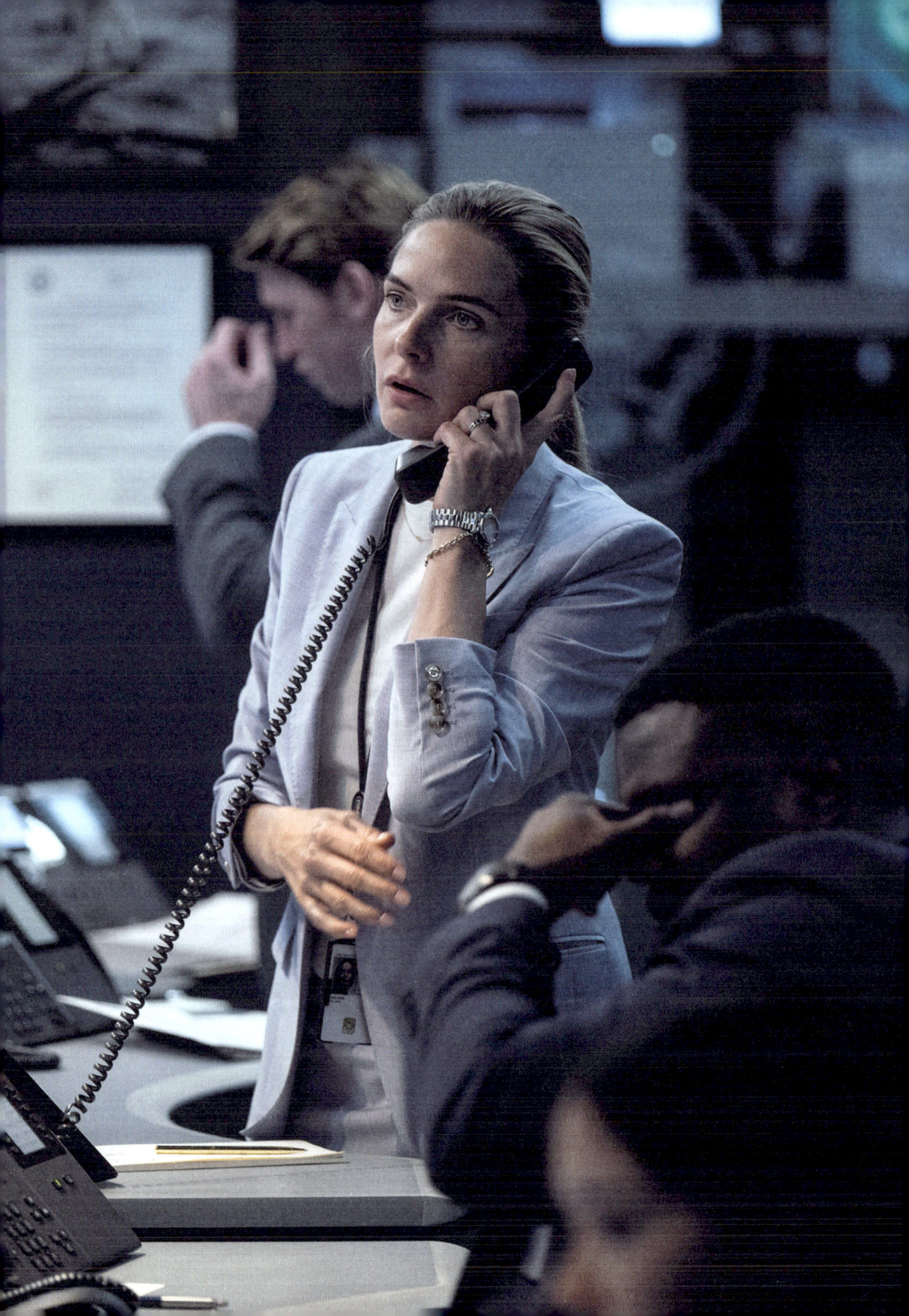

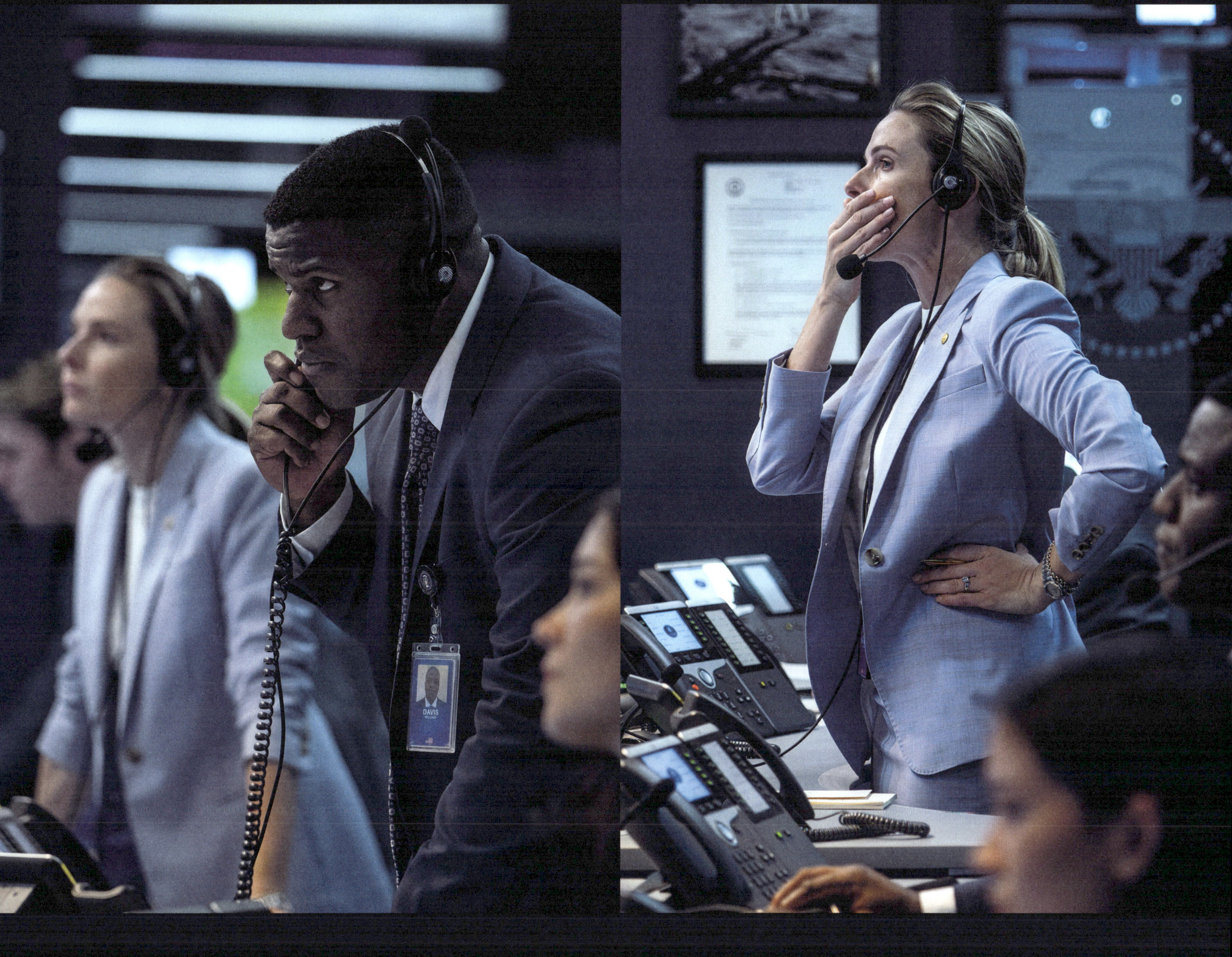
DAVIS

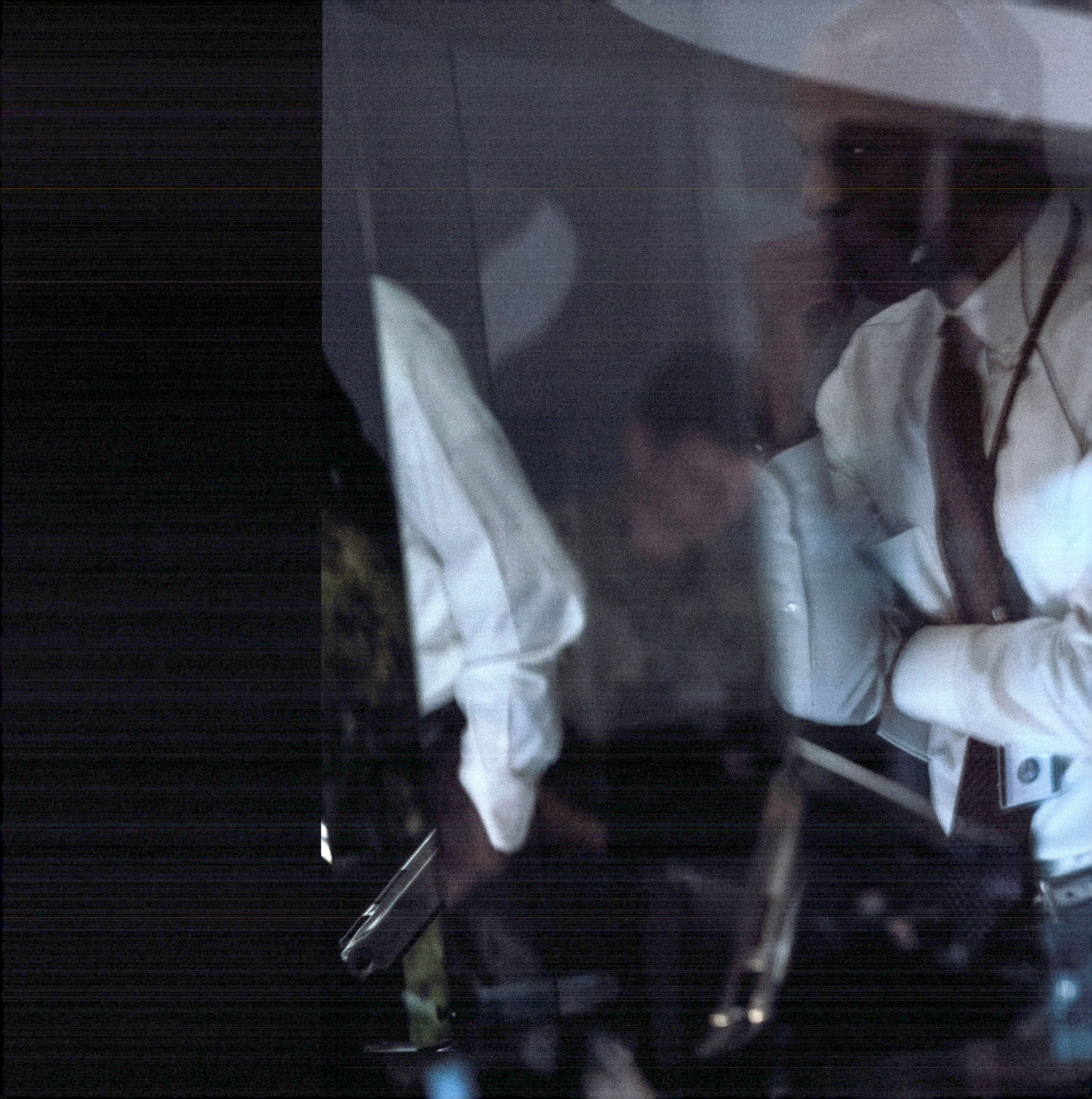

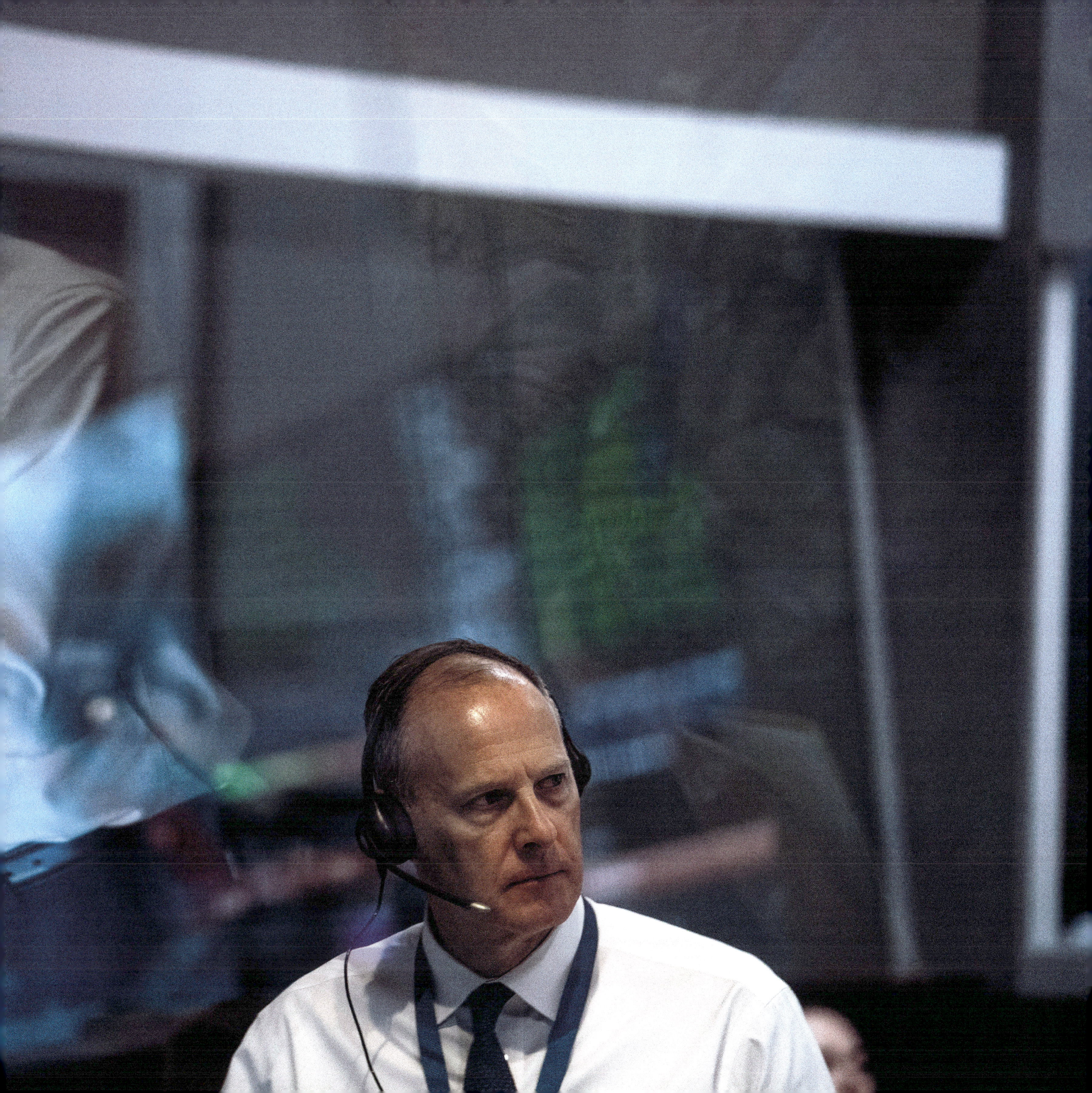

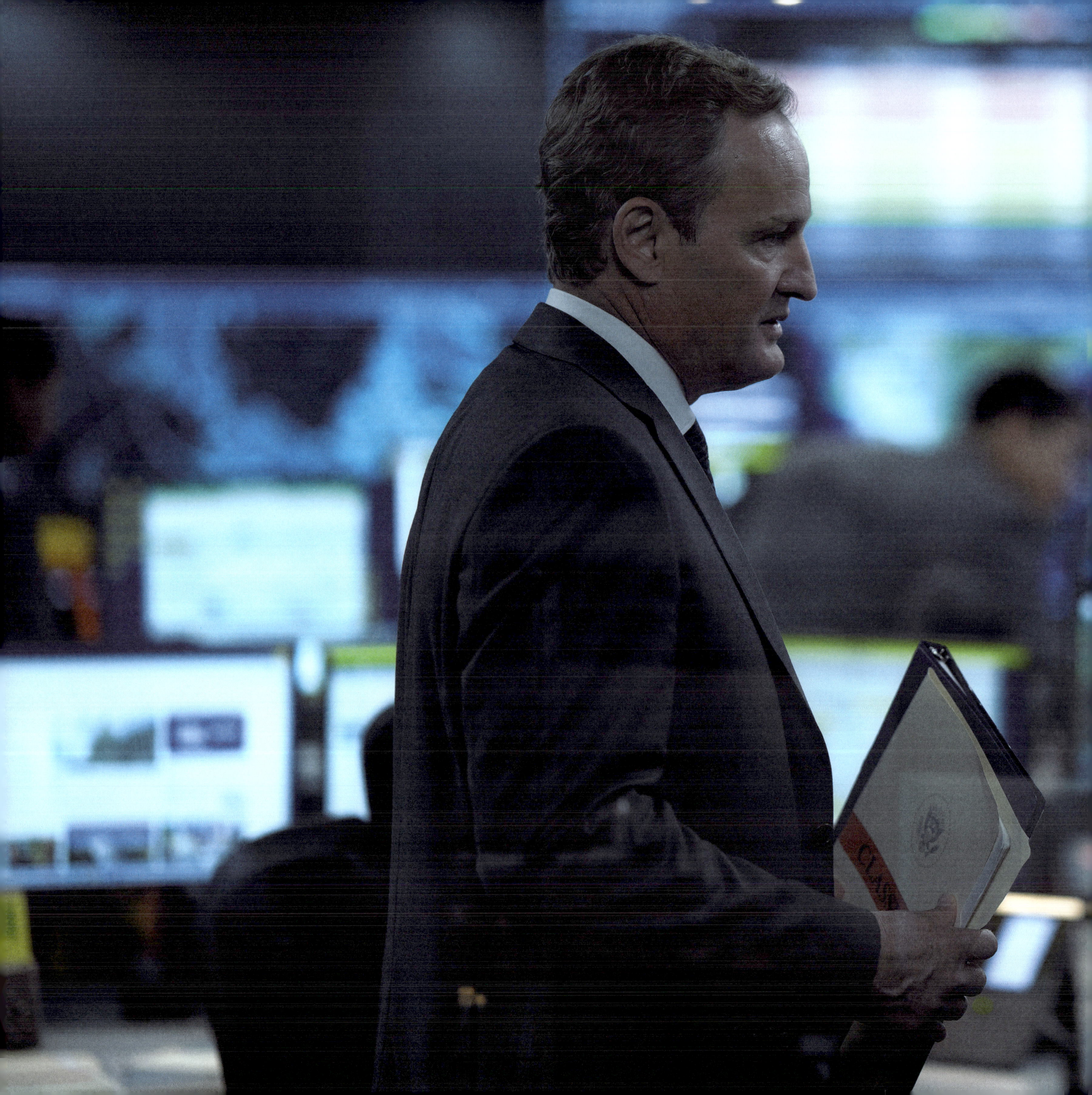

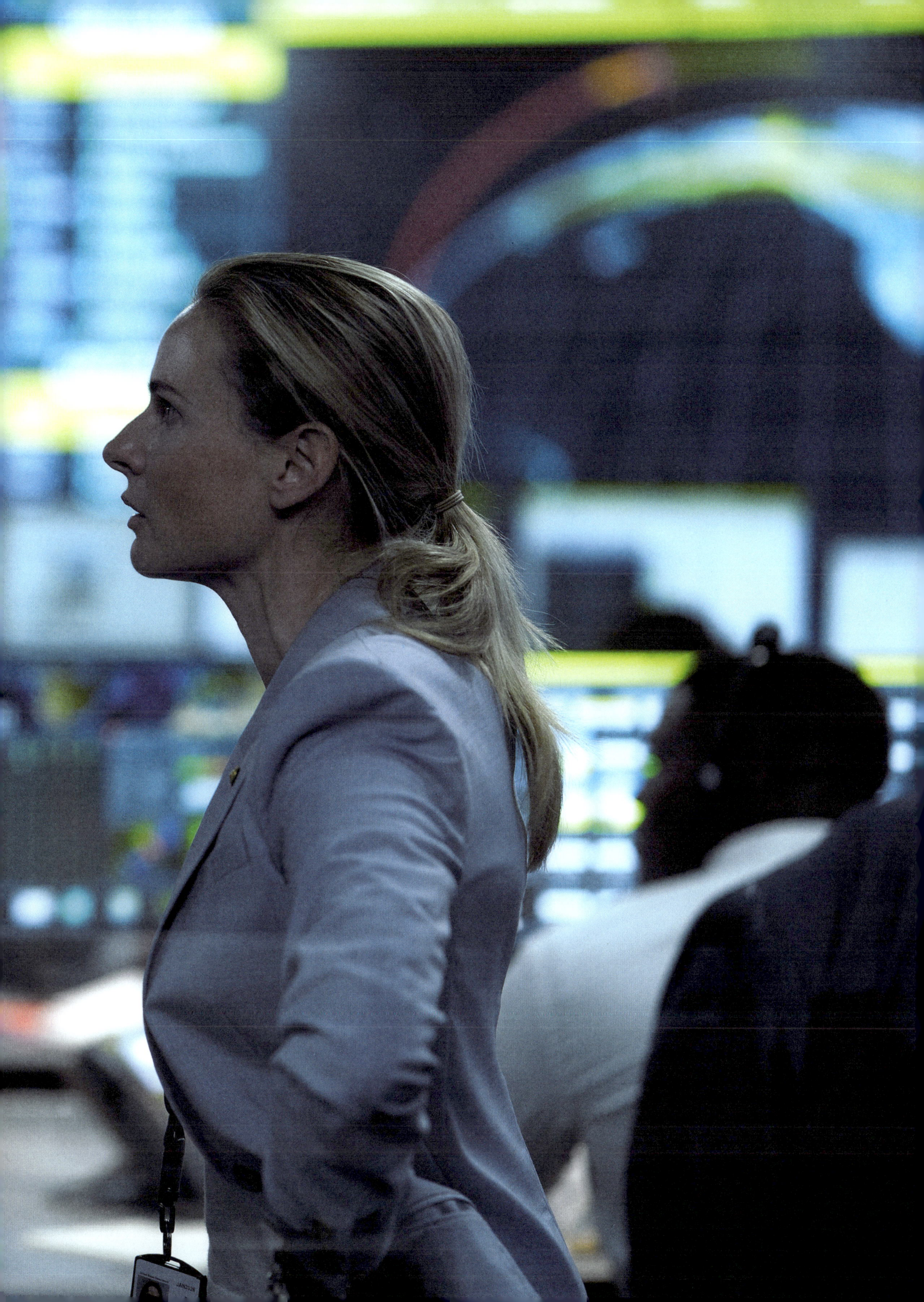

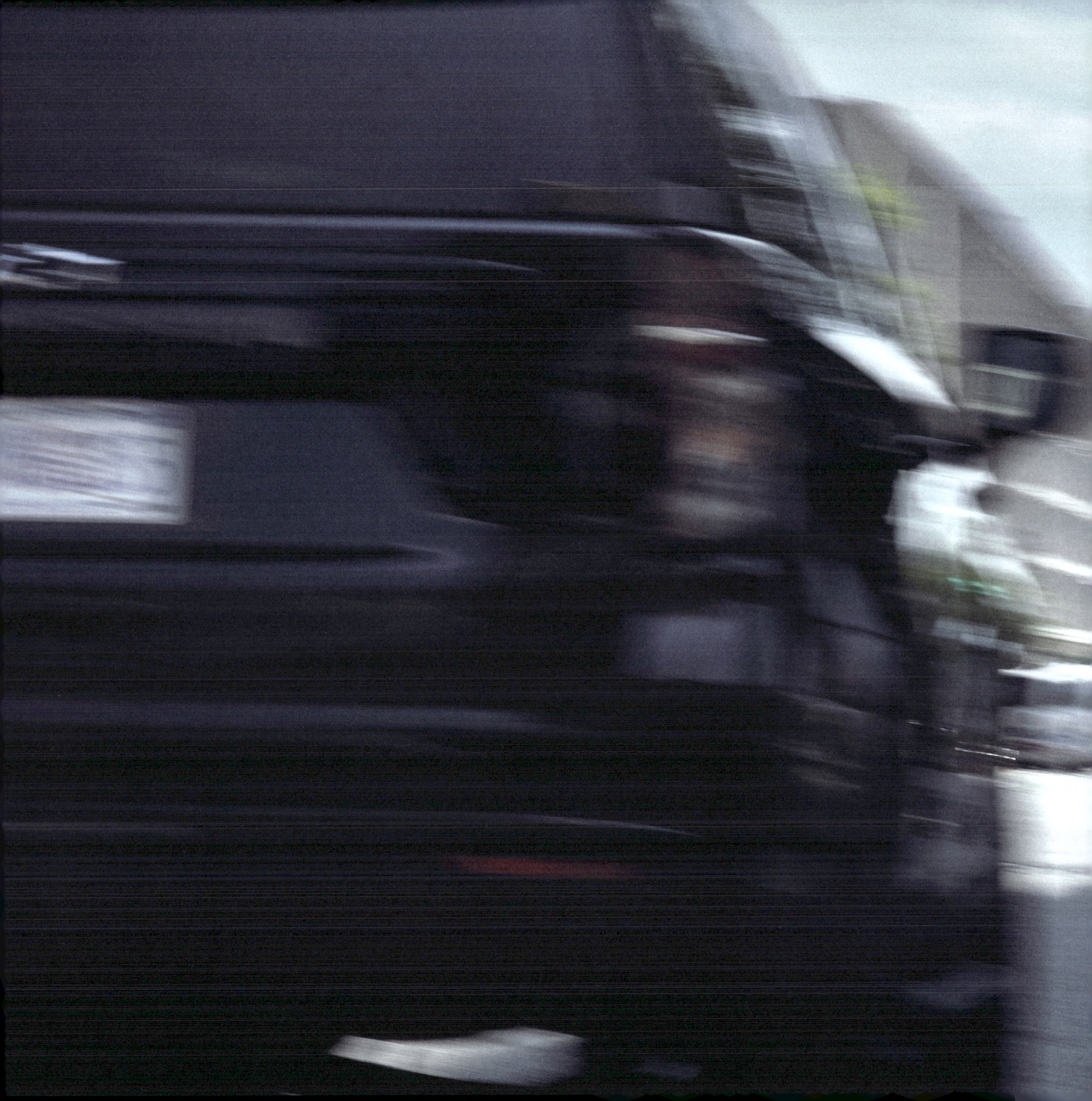

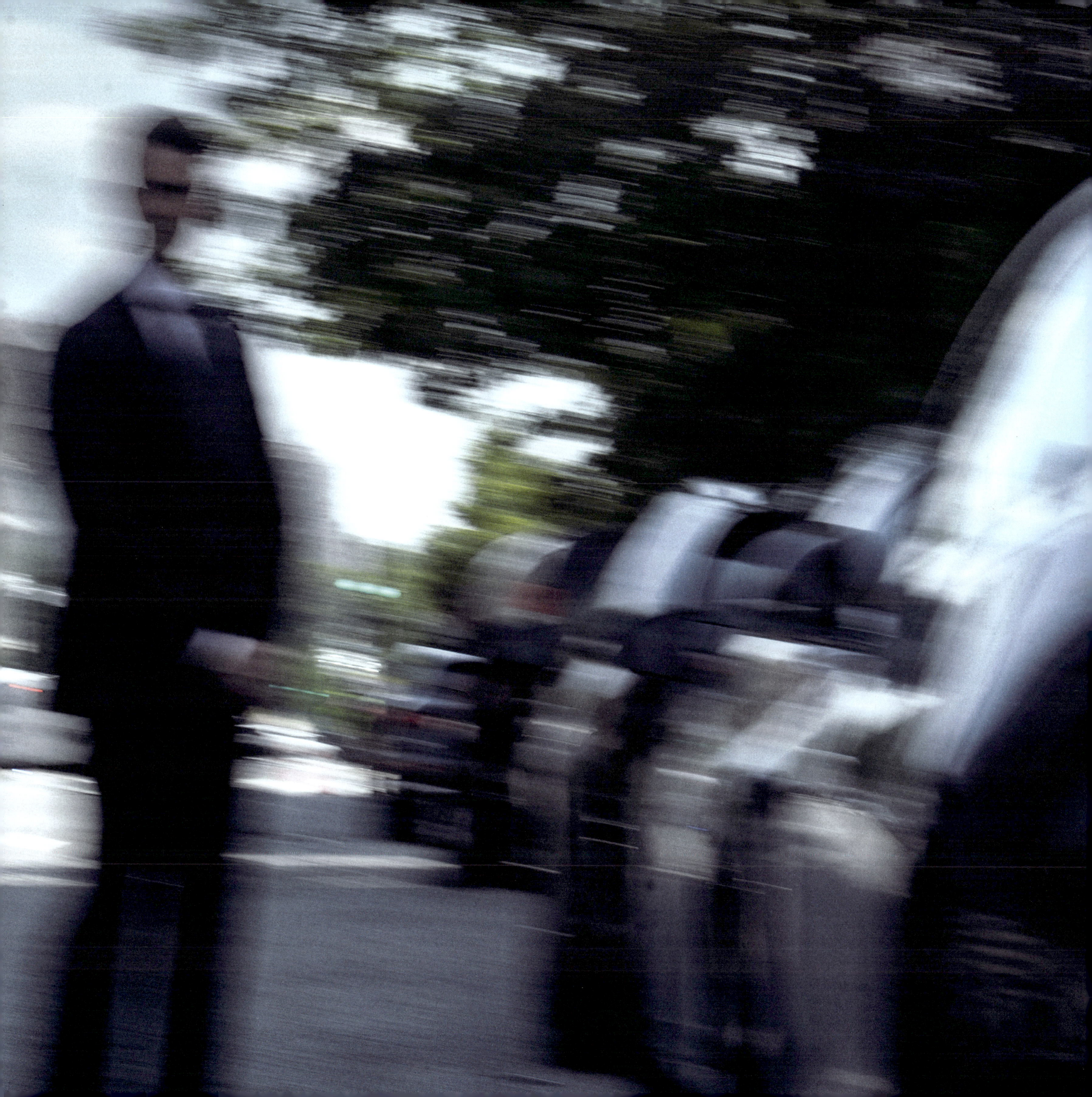

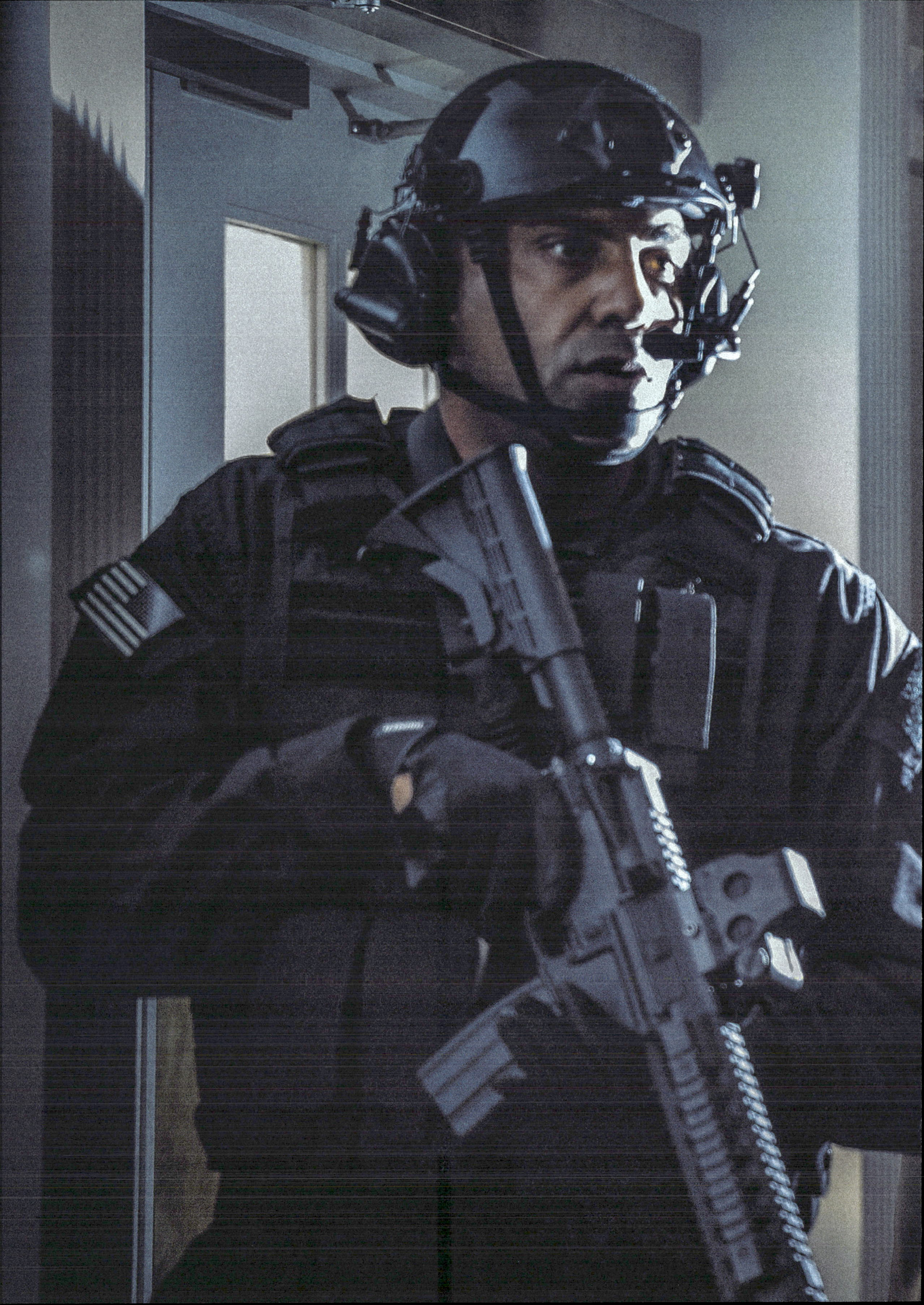

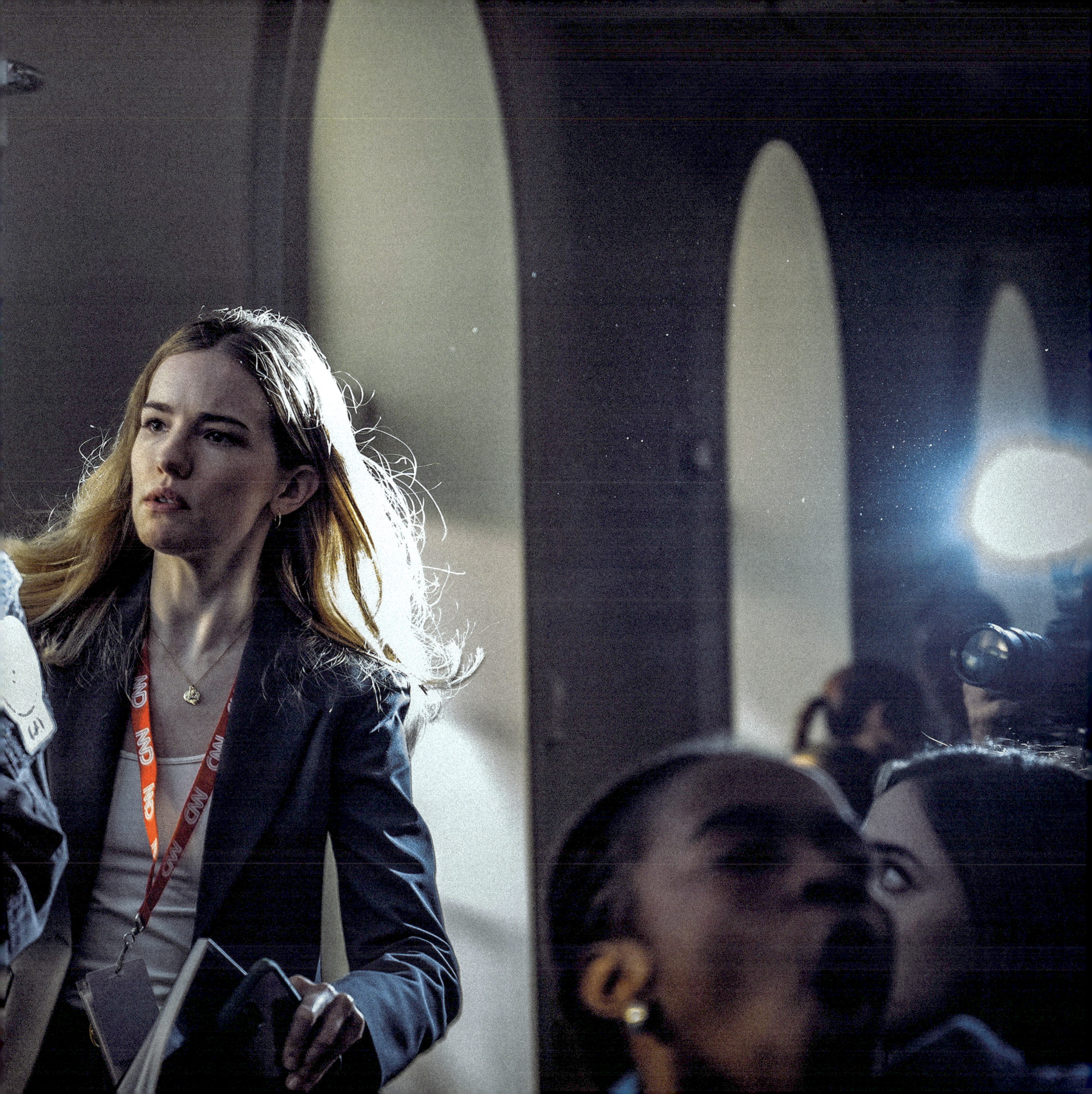
CNN

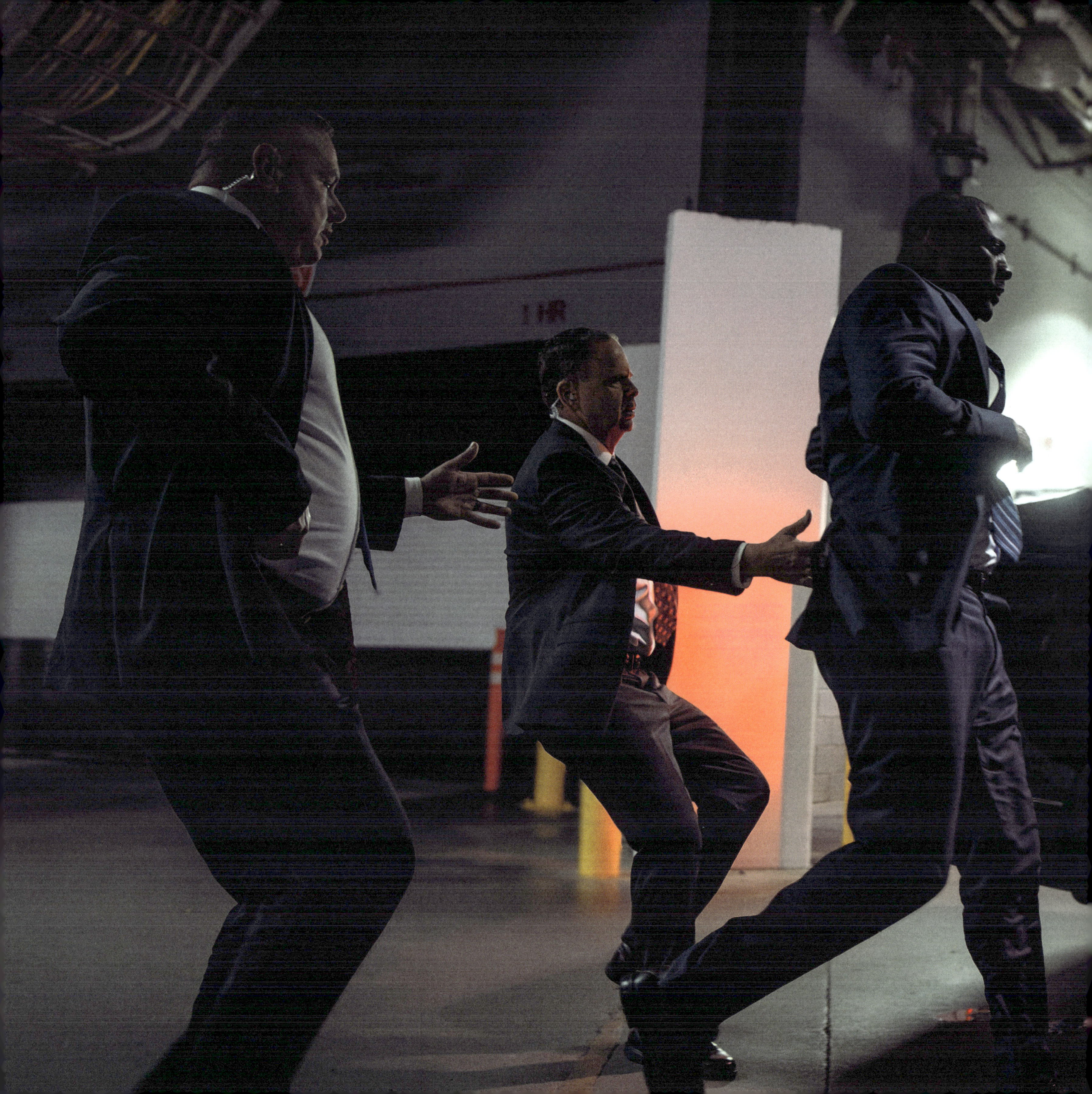
1 HR

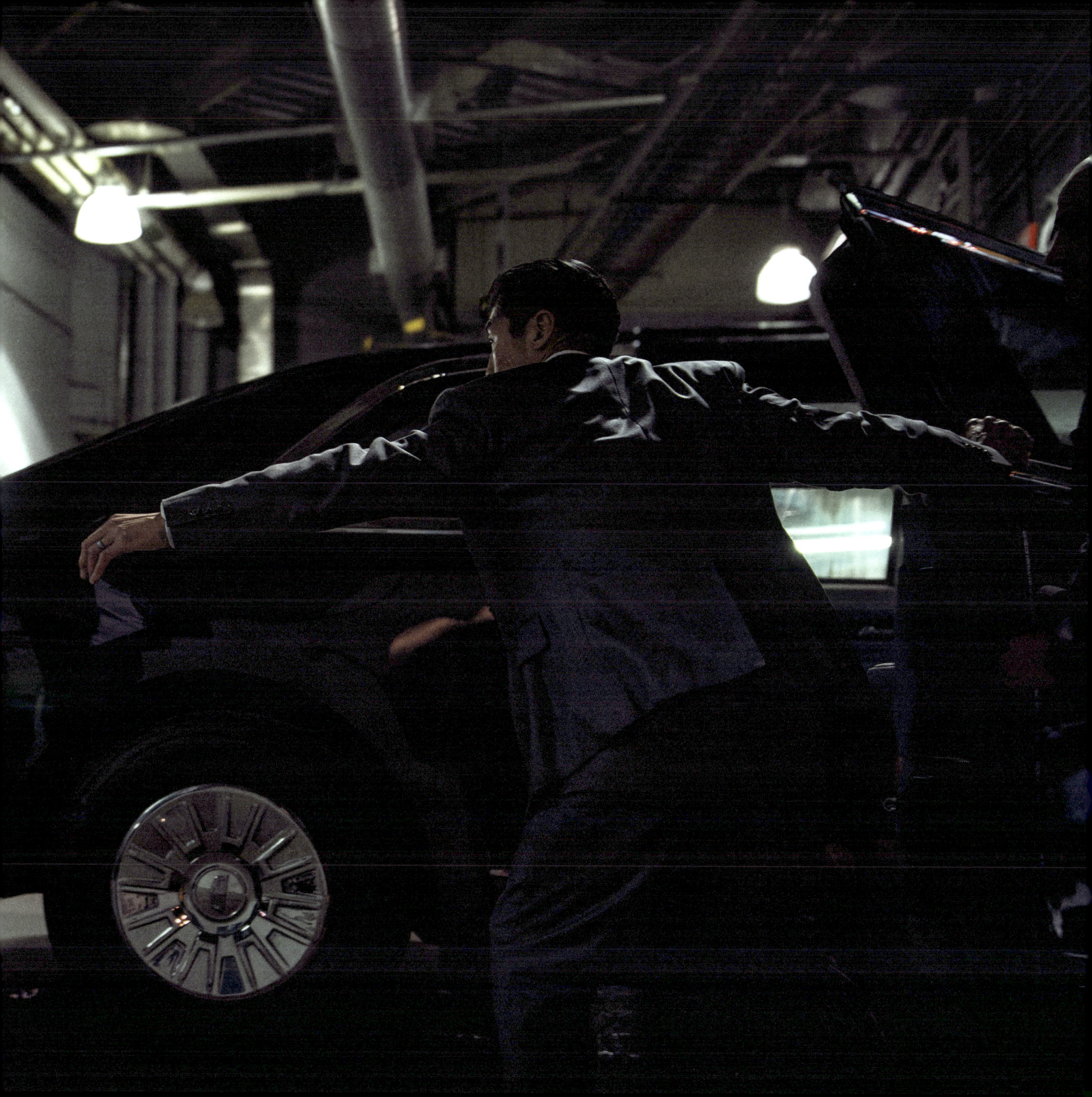

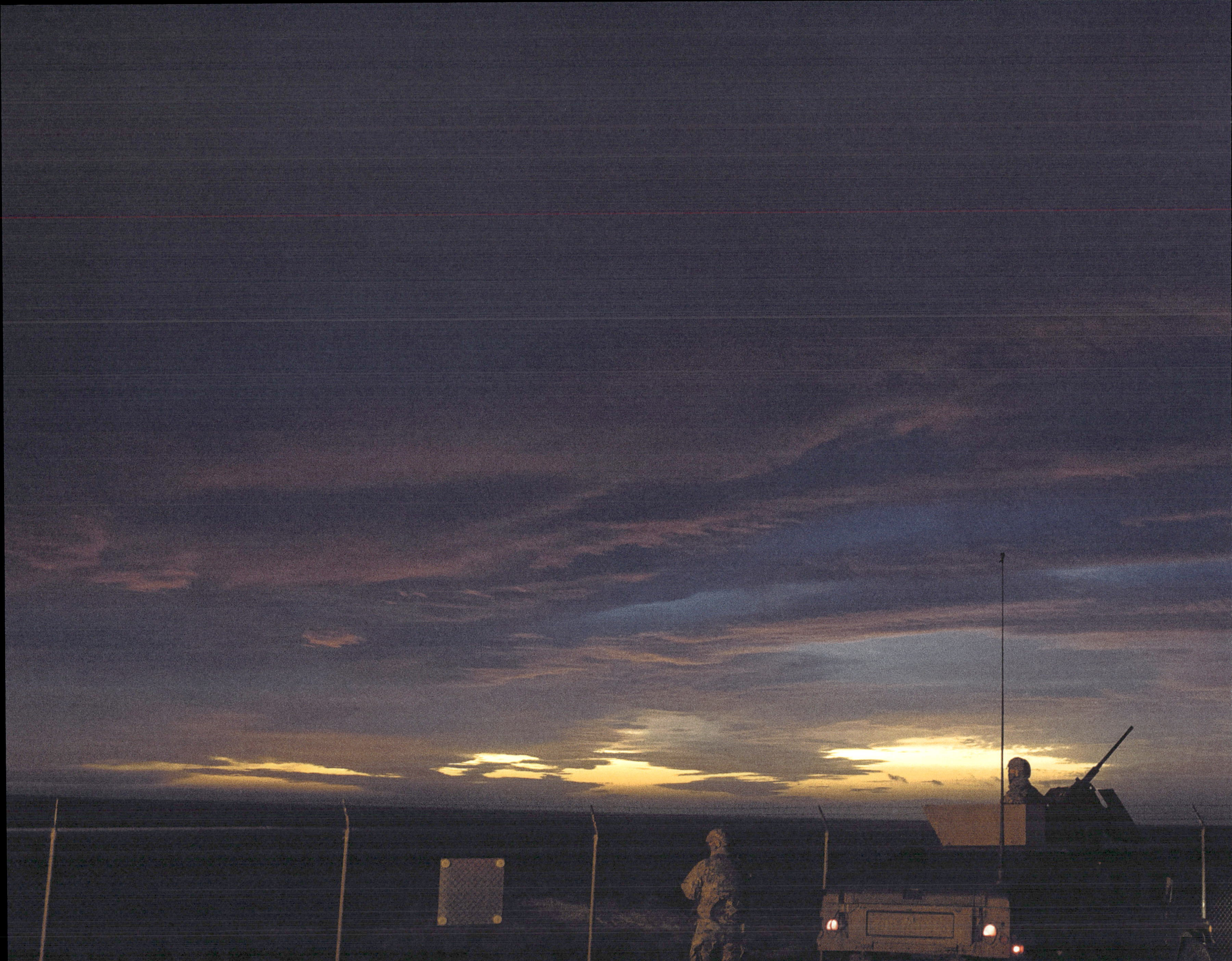

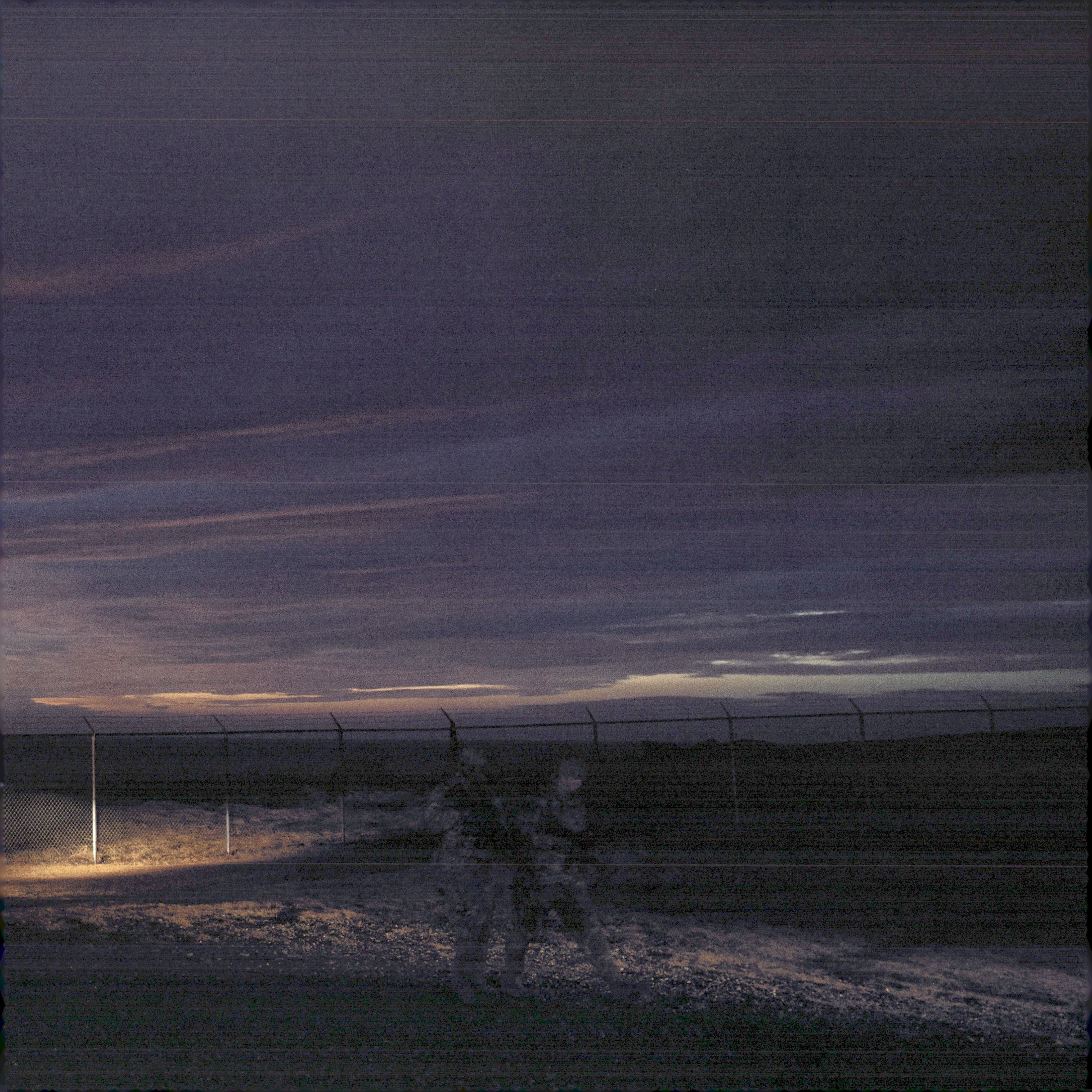

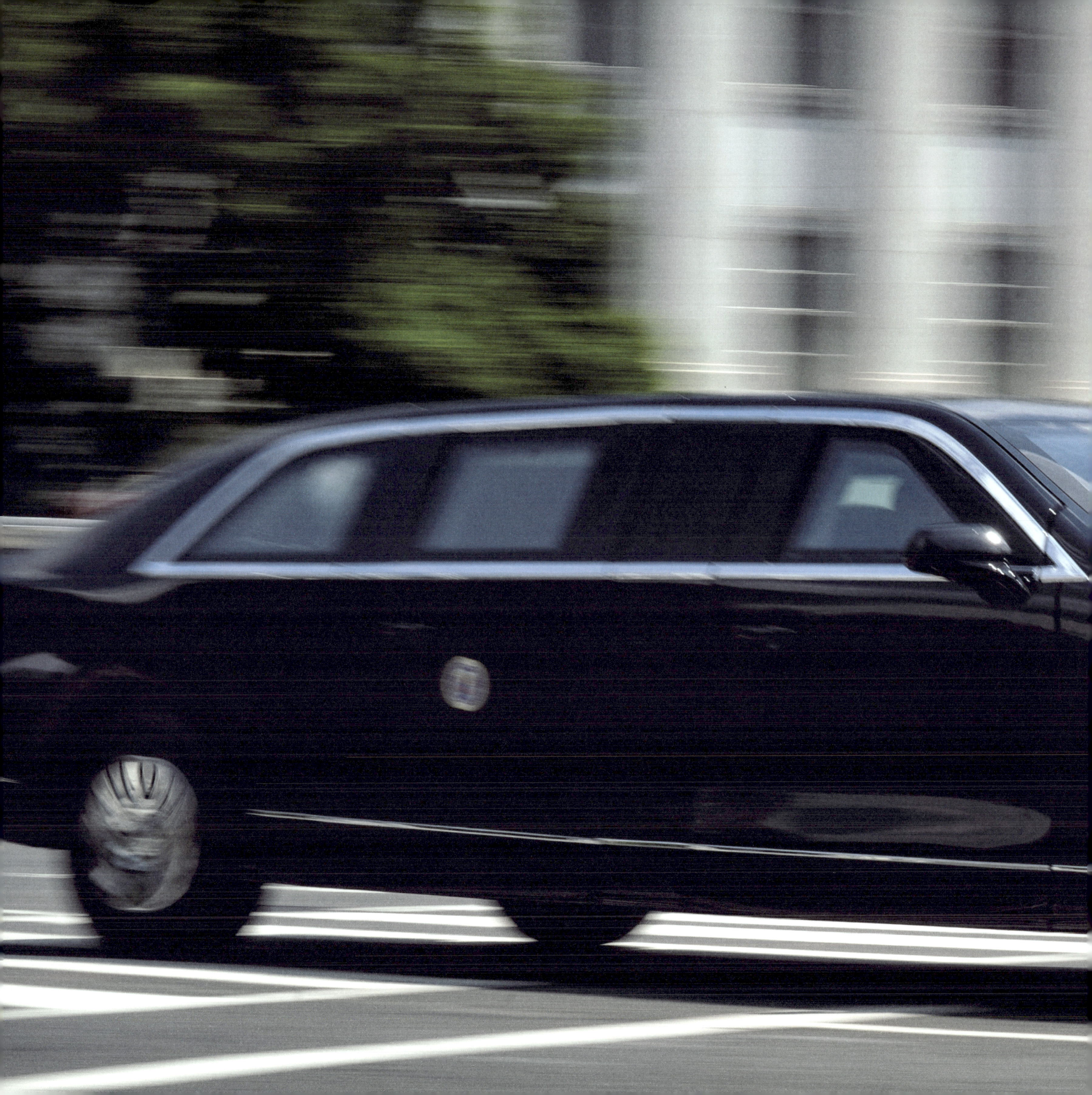

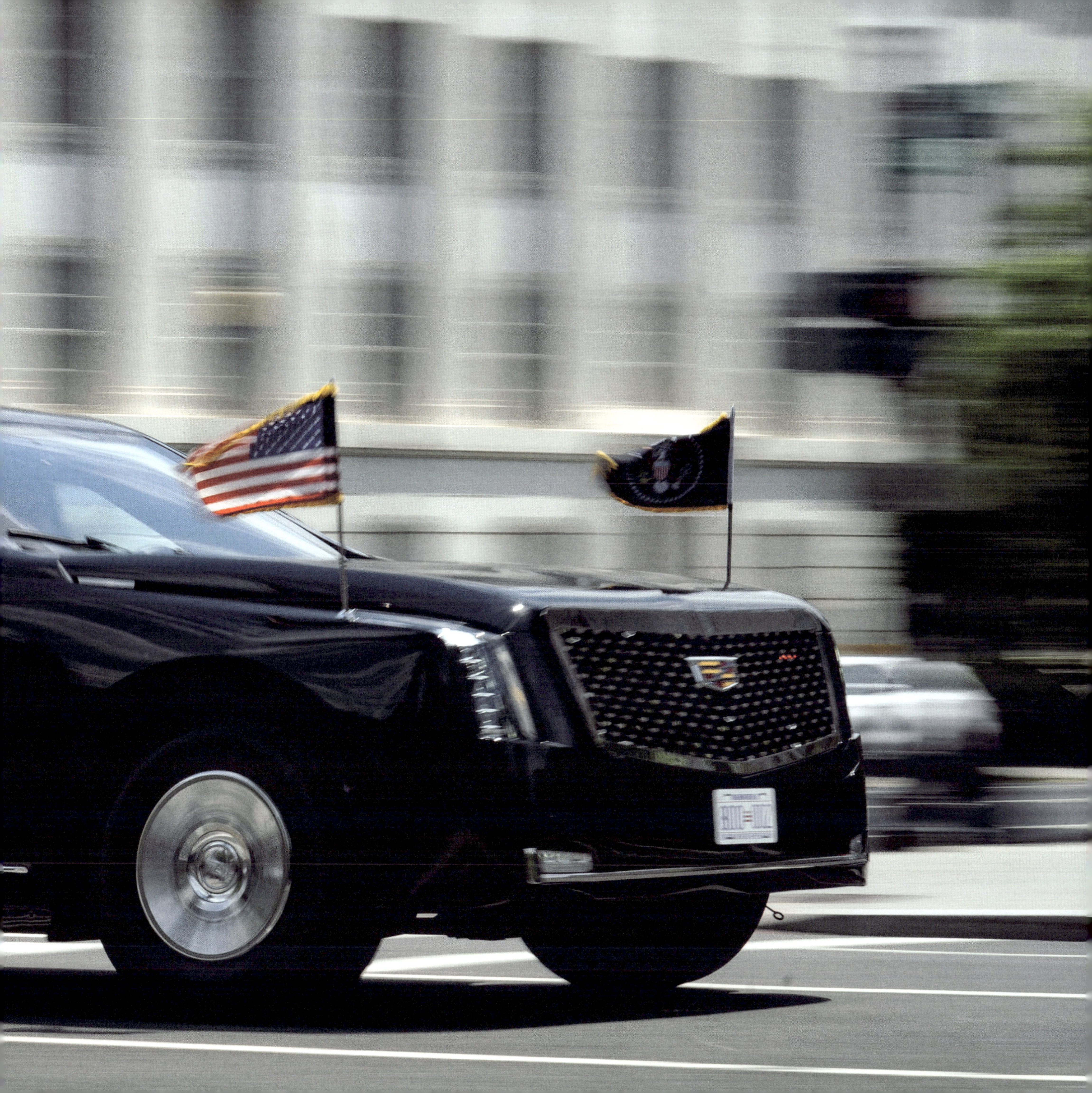

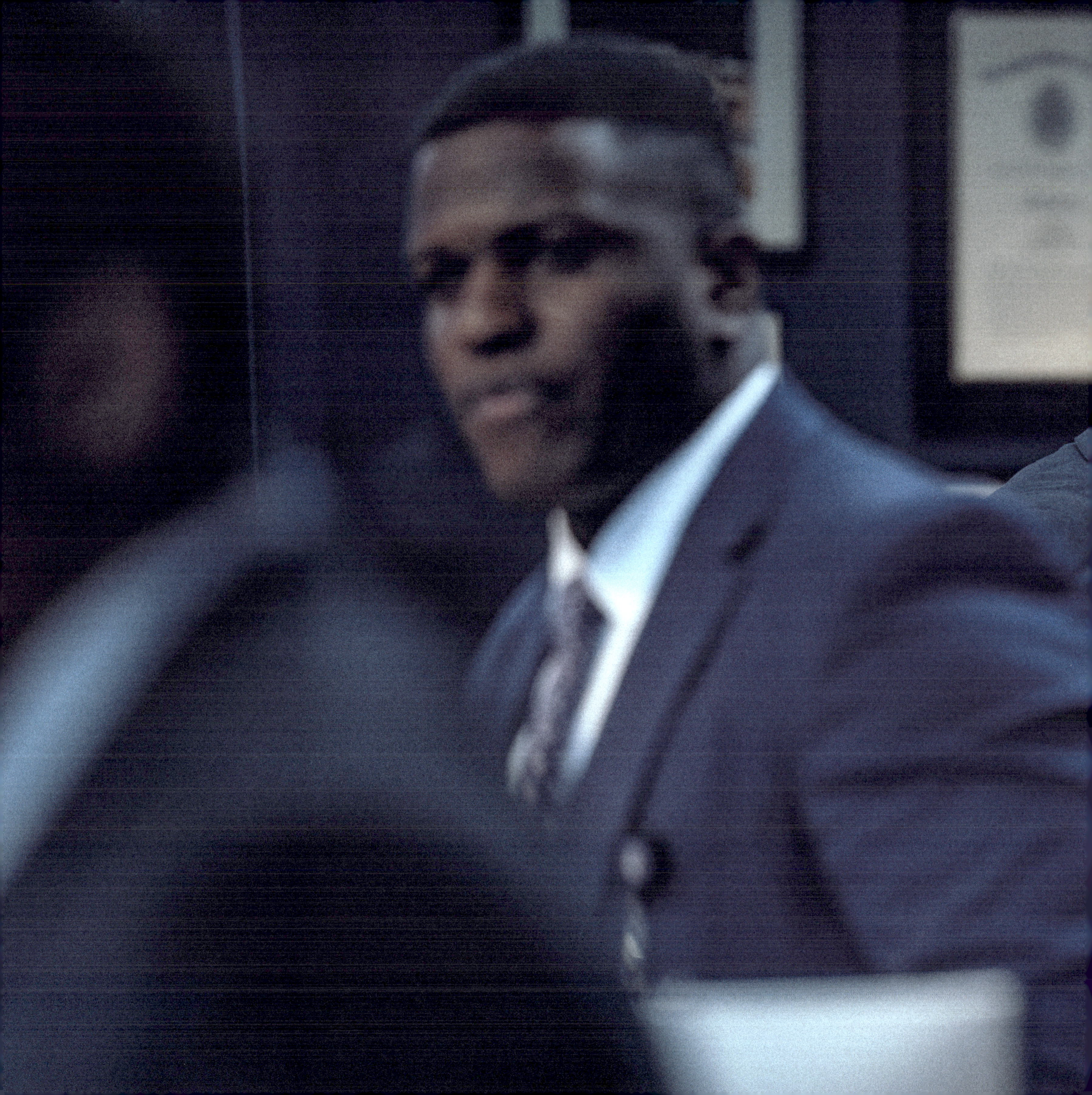

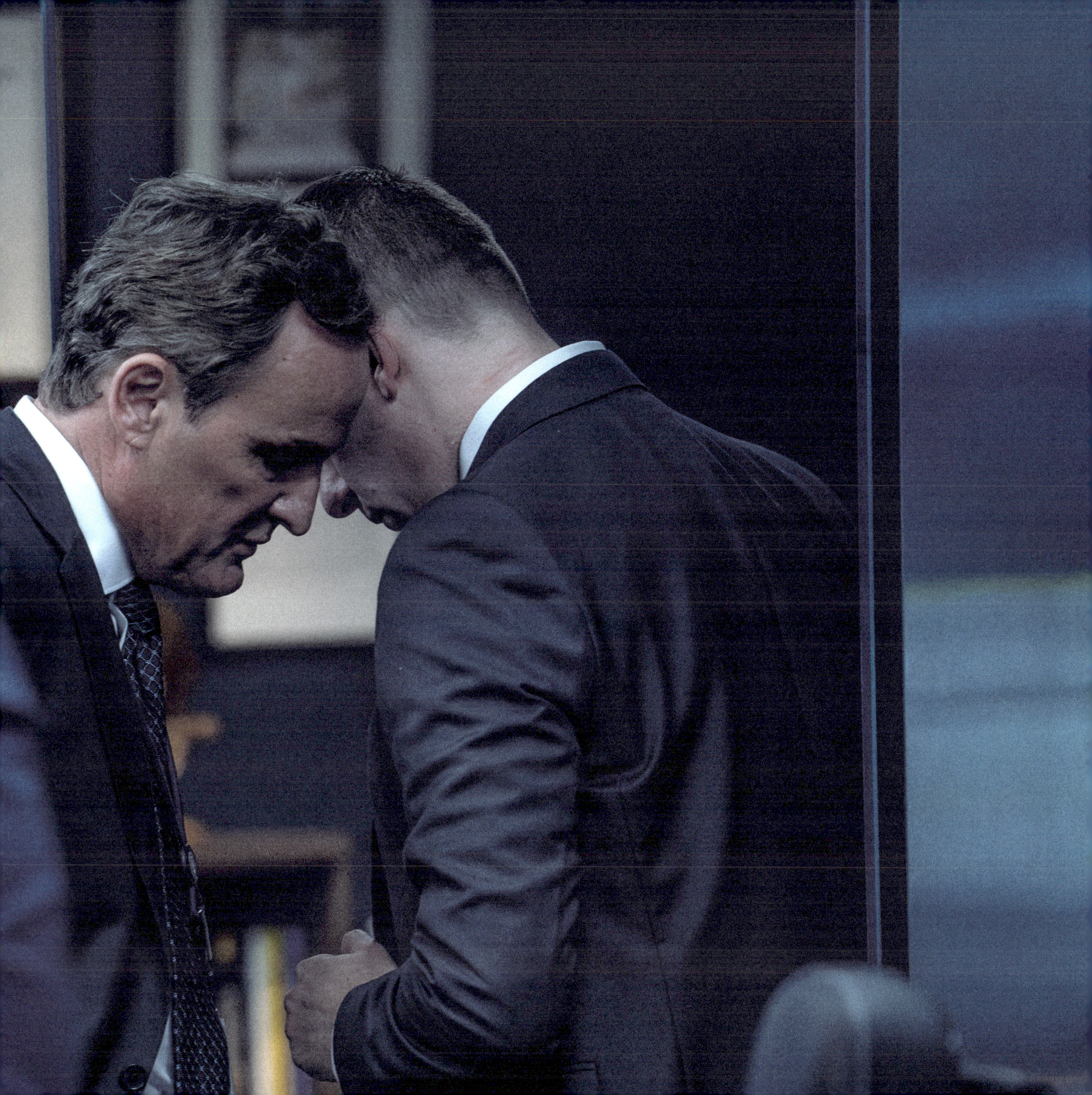

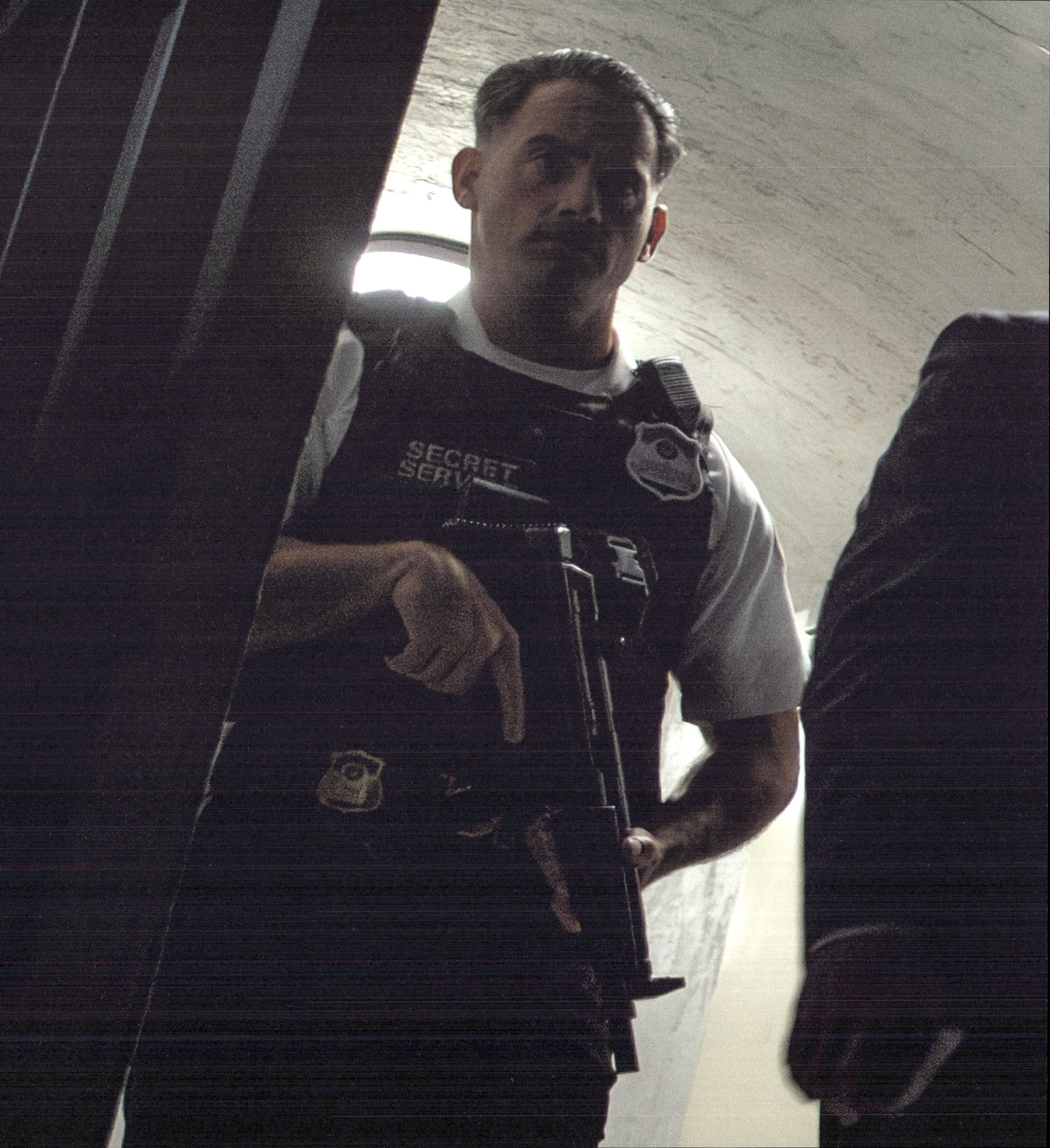
SECRET
SERV

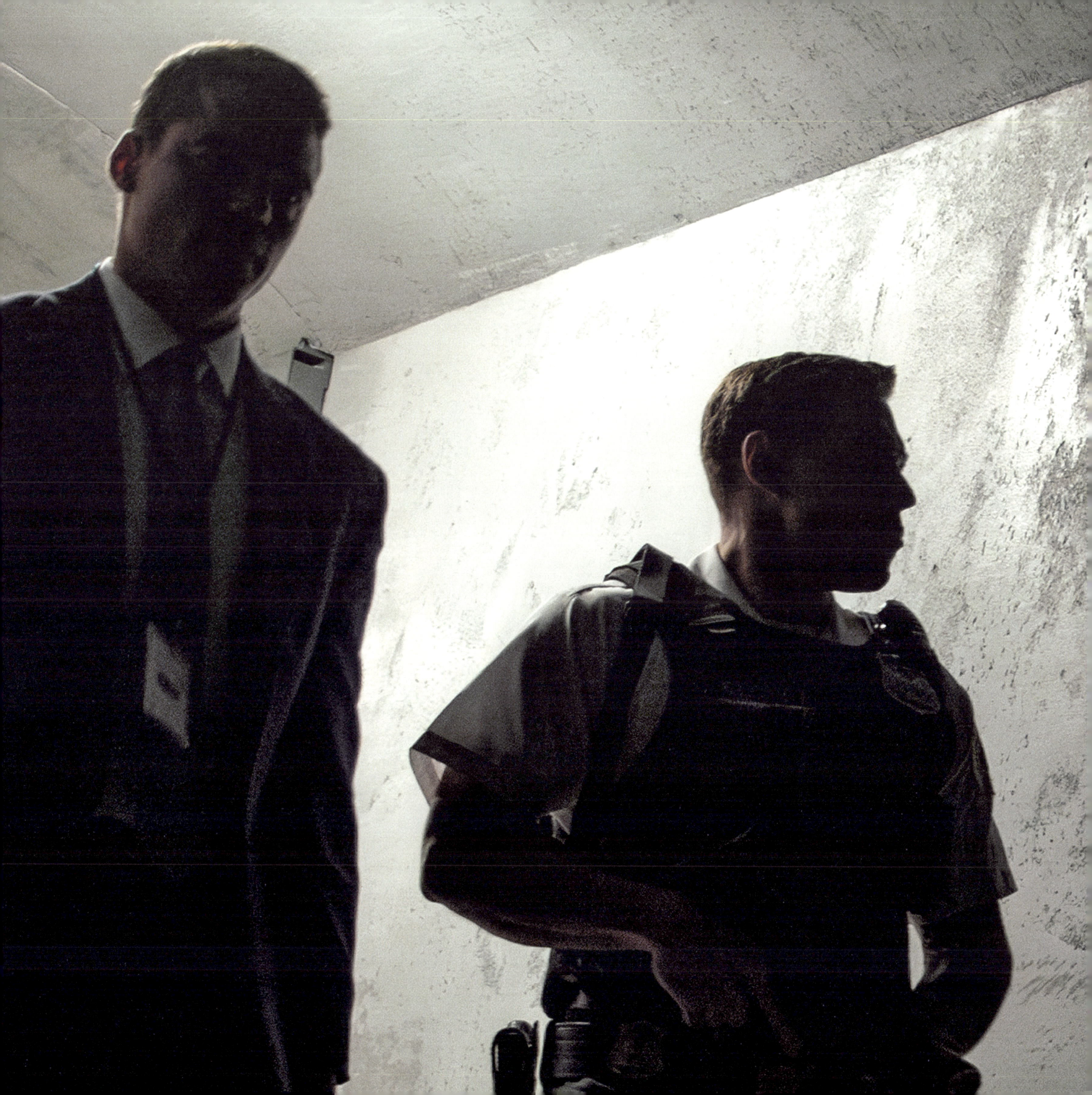

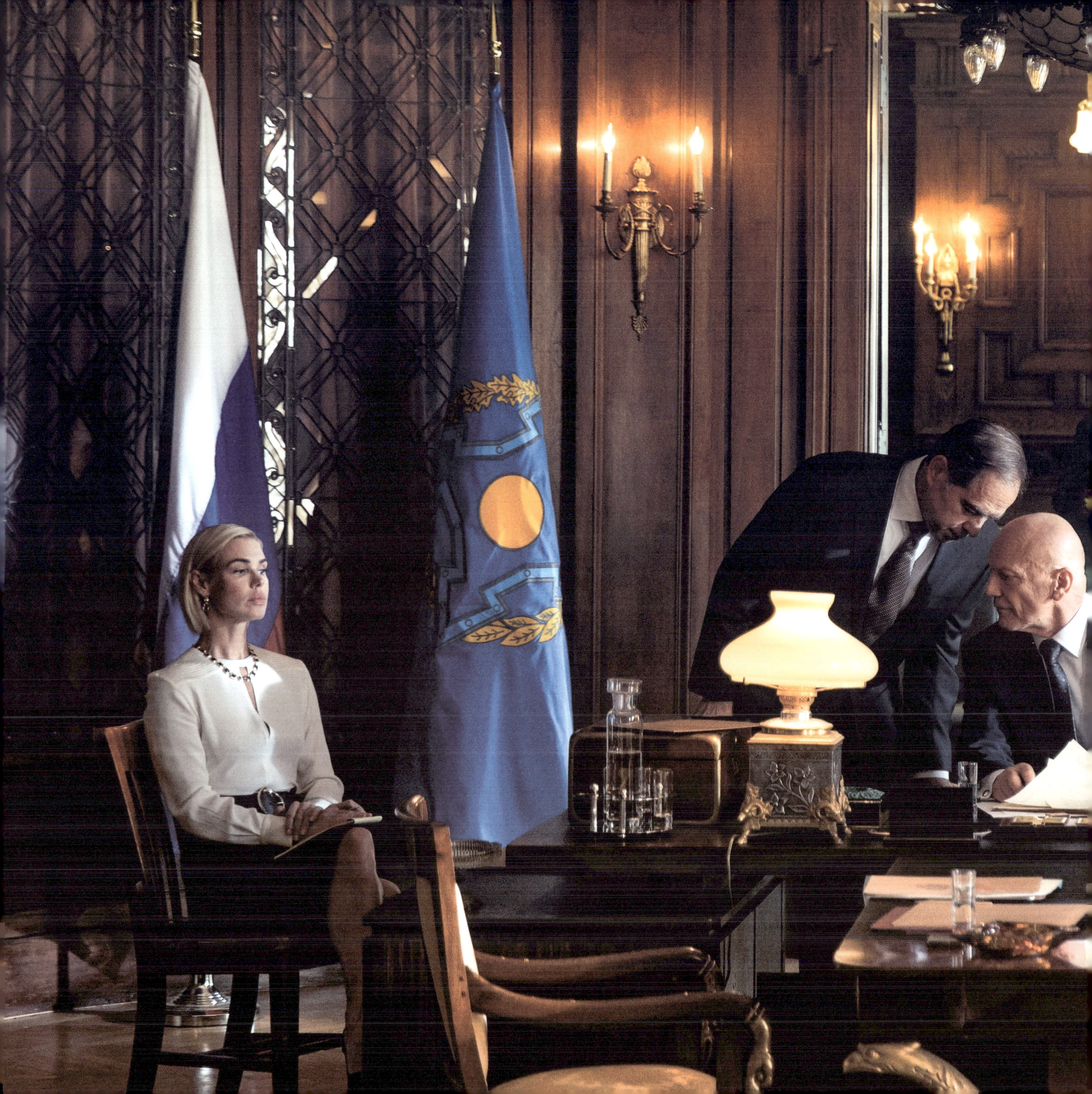

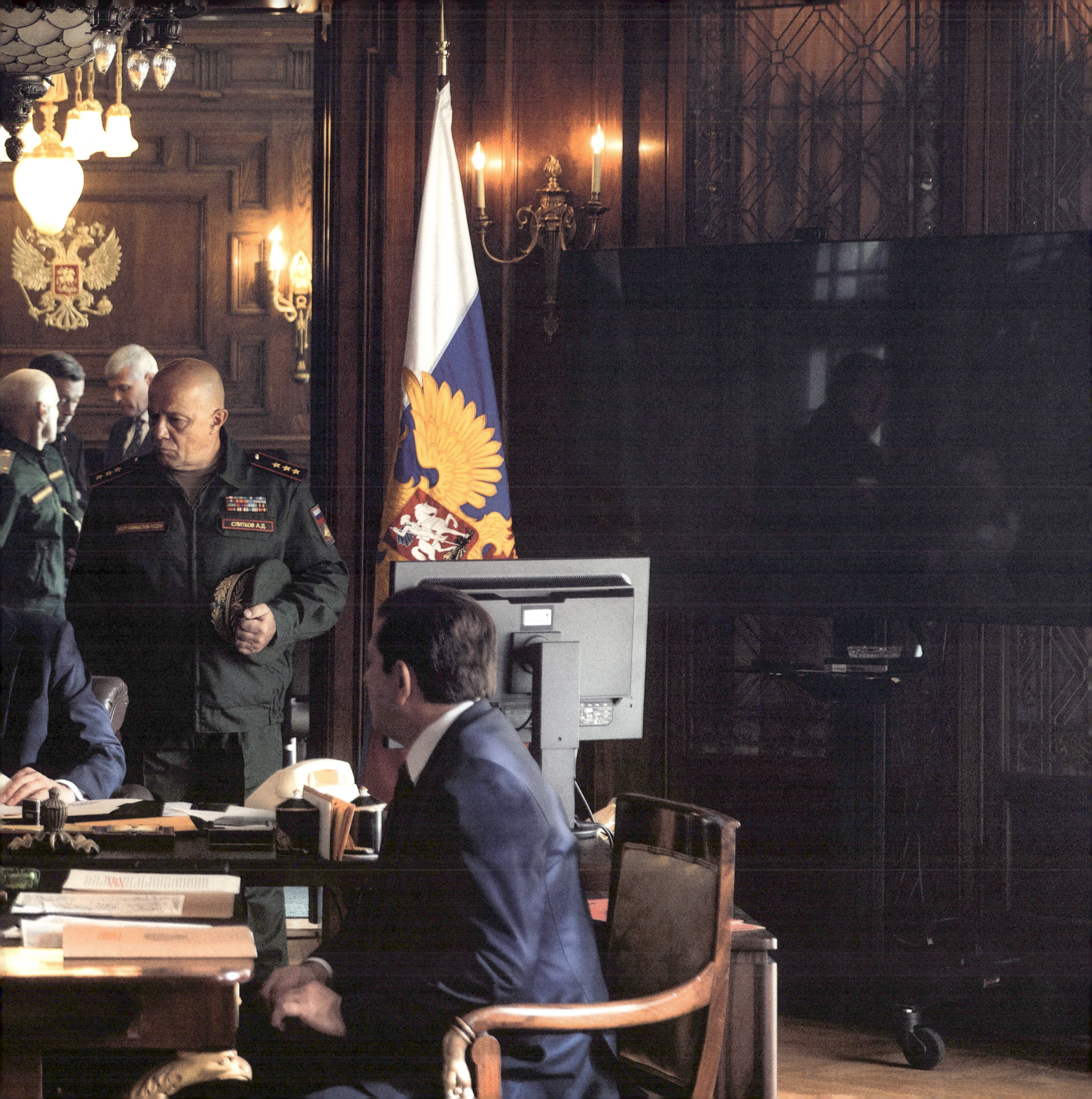
СЛИТКОВ А.Д.

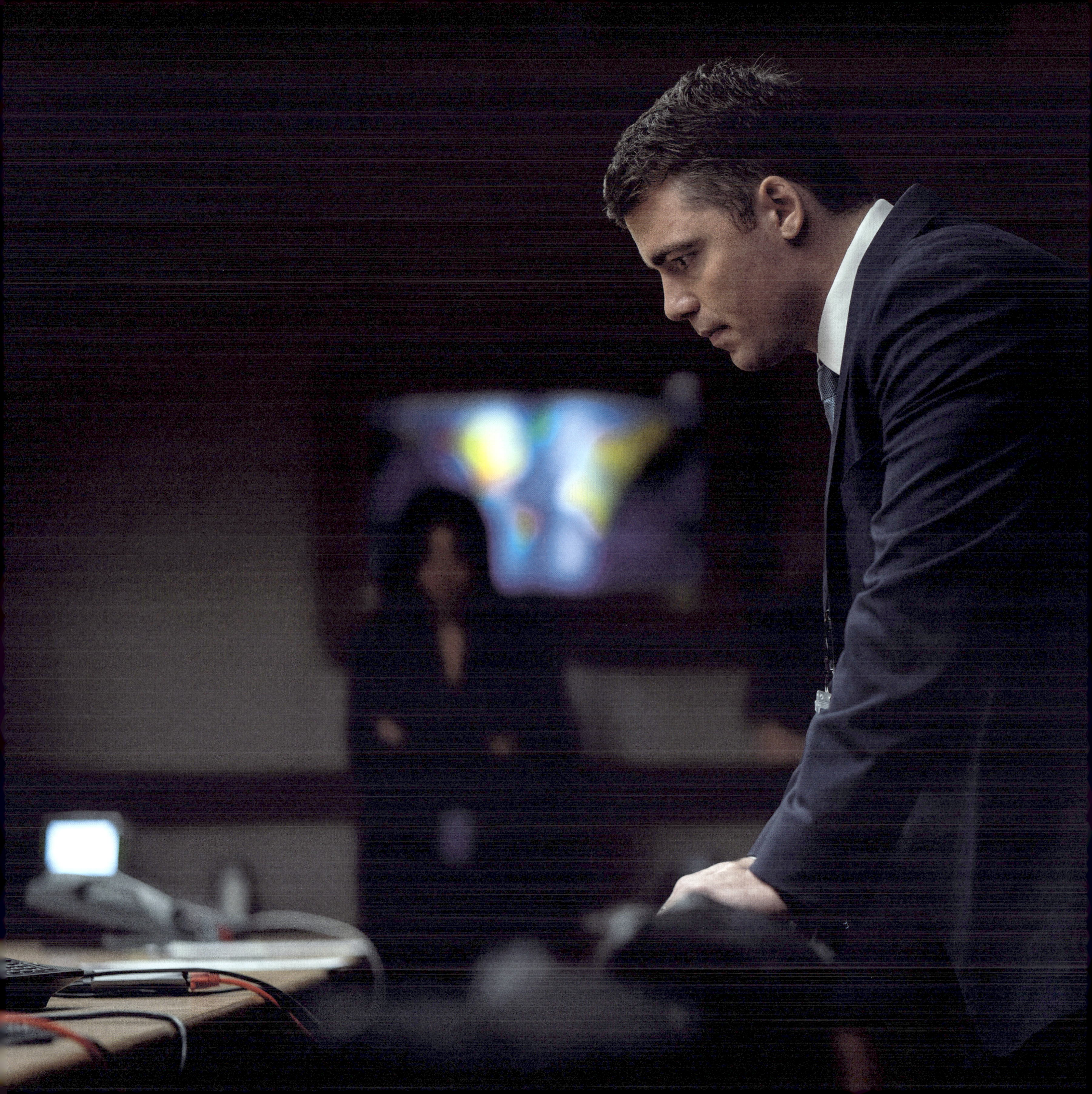

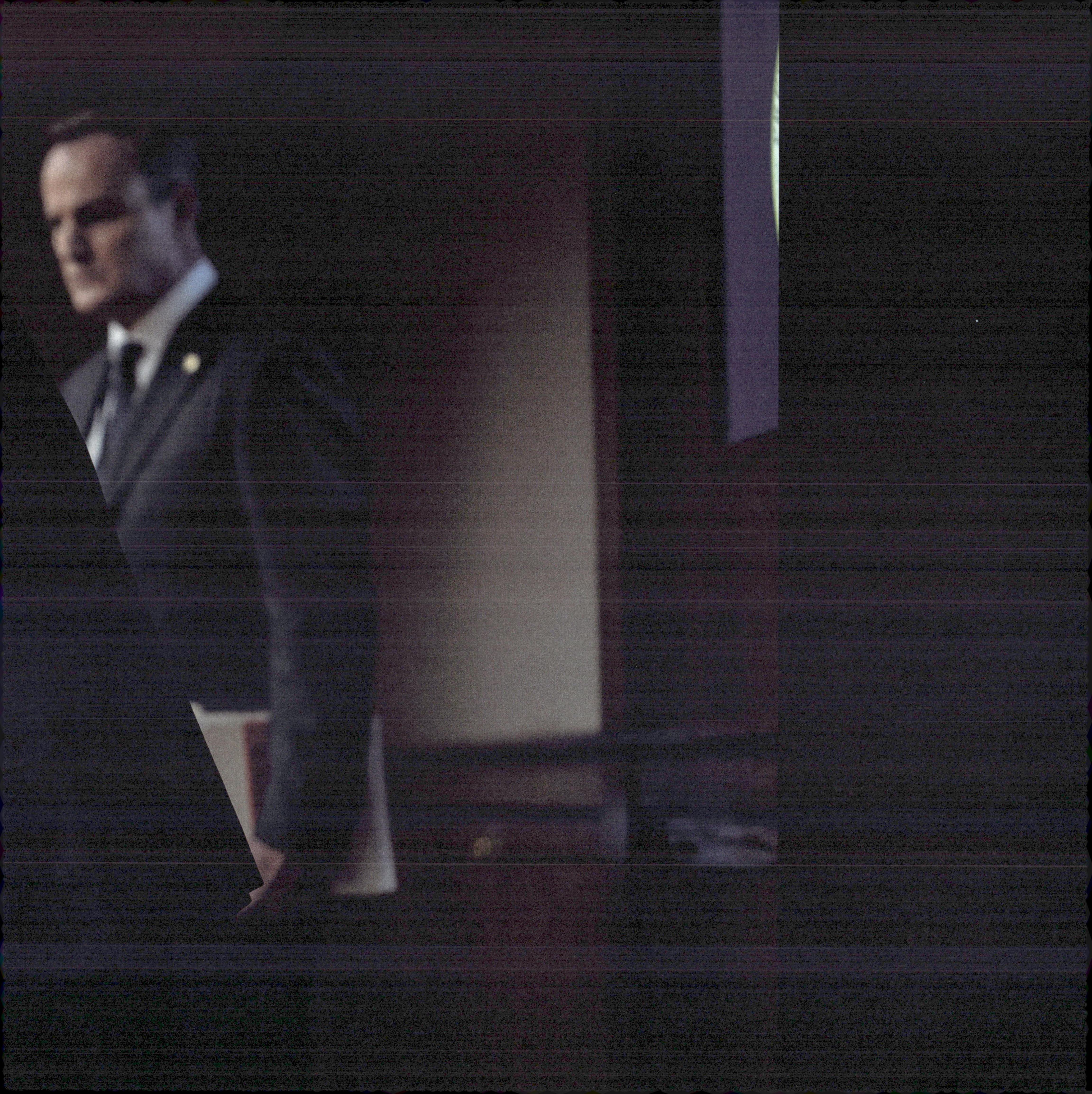

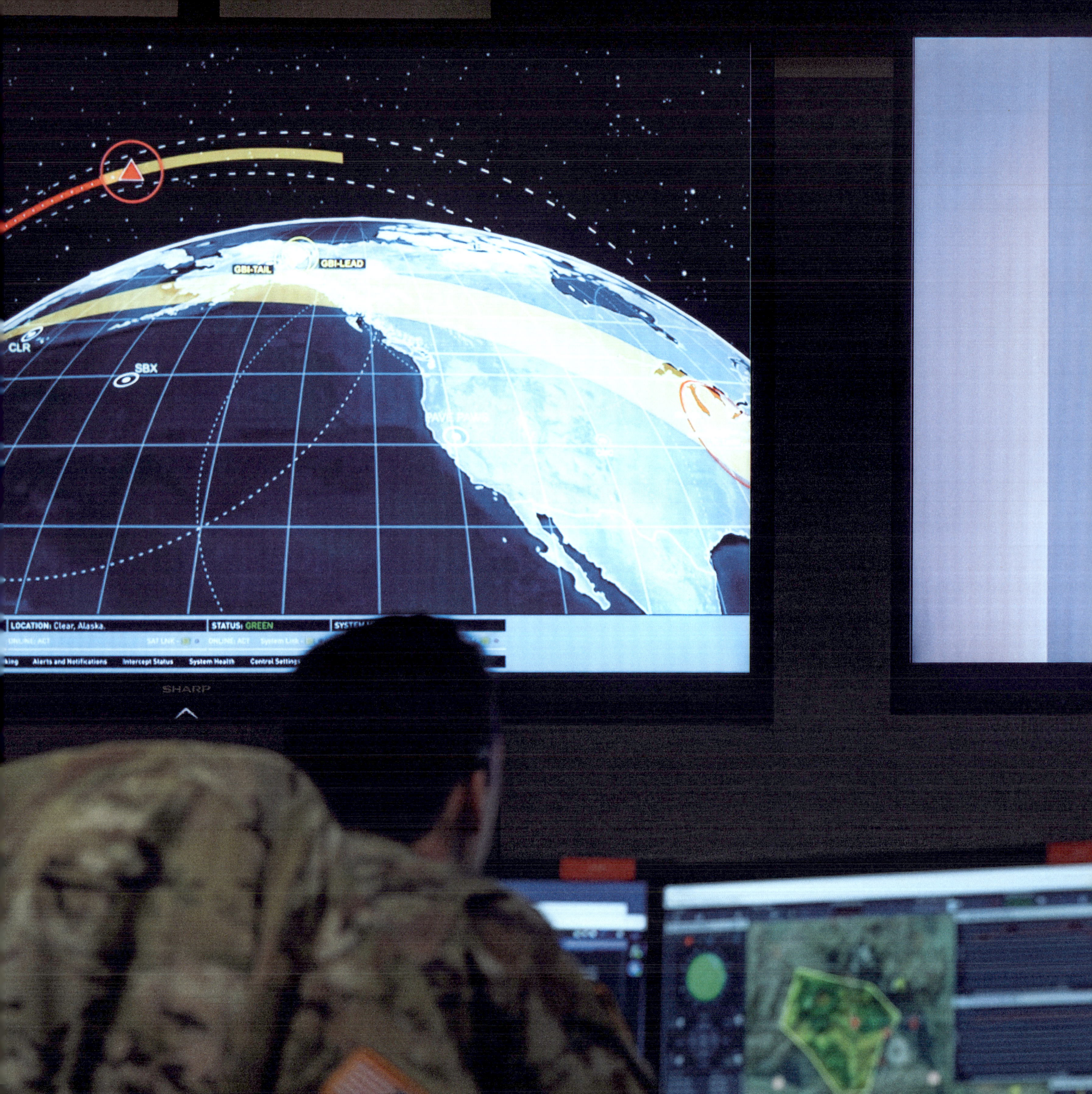

GBI-TAIL
GBI-LEAD
CLR
SBX
LOCATION: Clear, Alaska.
STATUS: GREEN
Alerts and Notifications
Intercept Status
System Health
Control Settings
SHARP

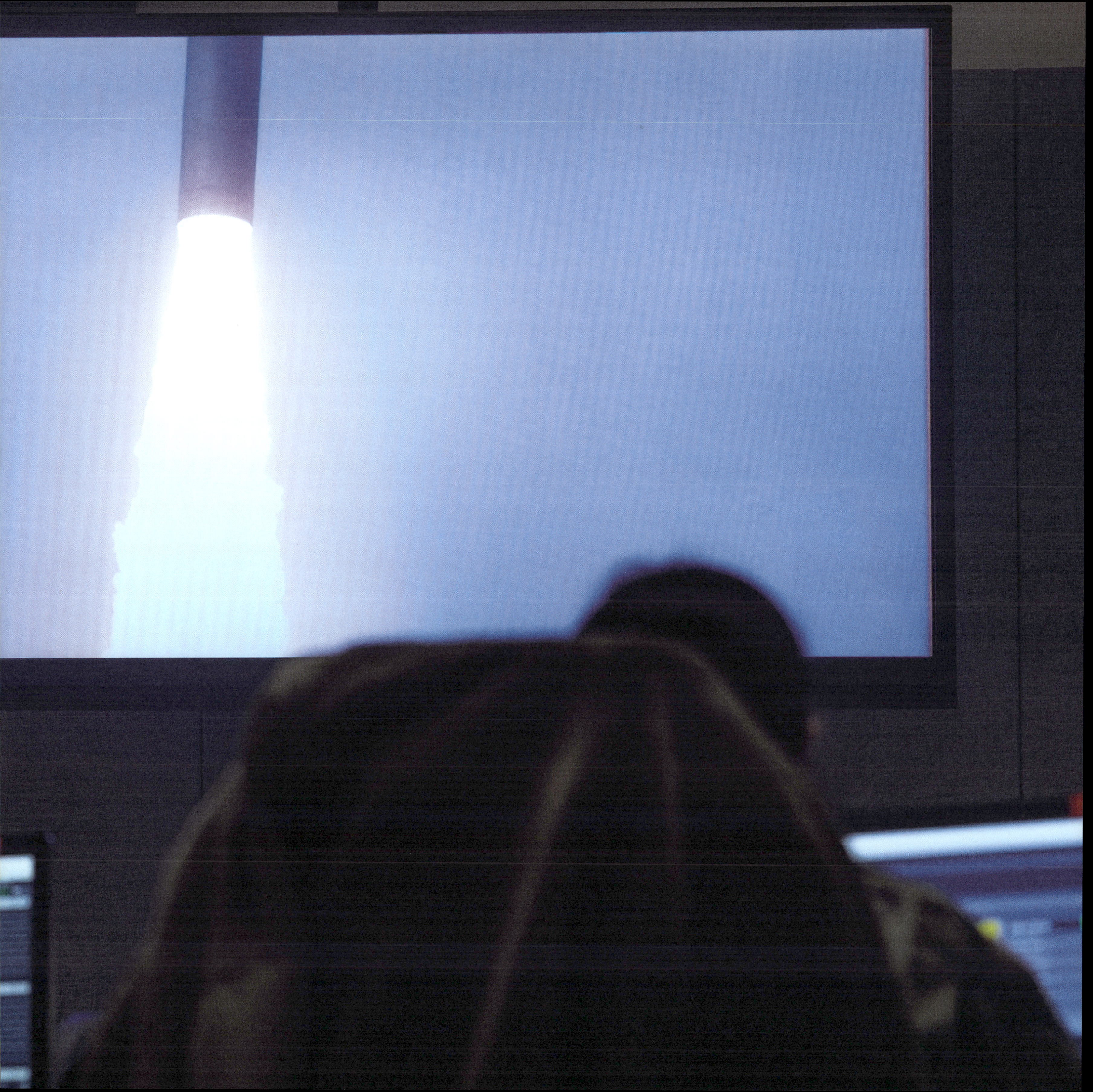

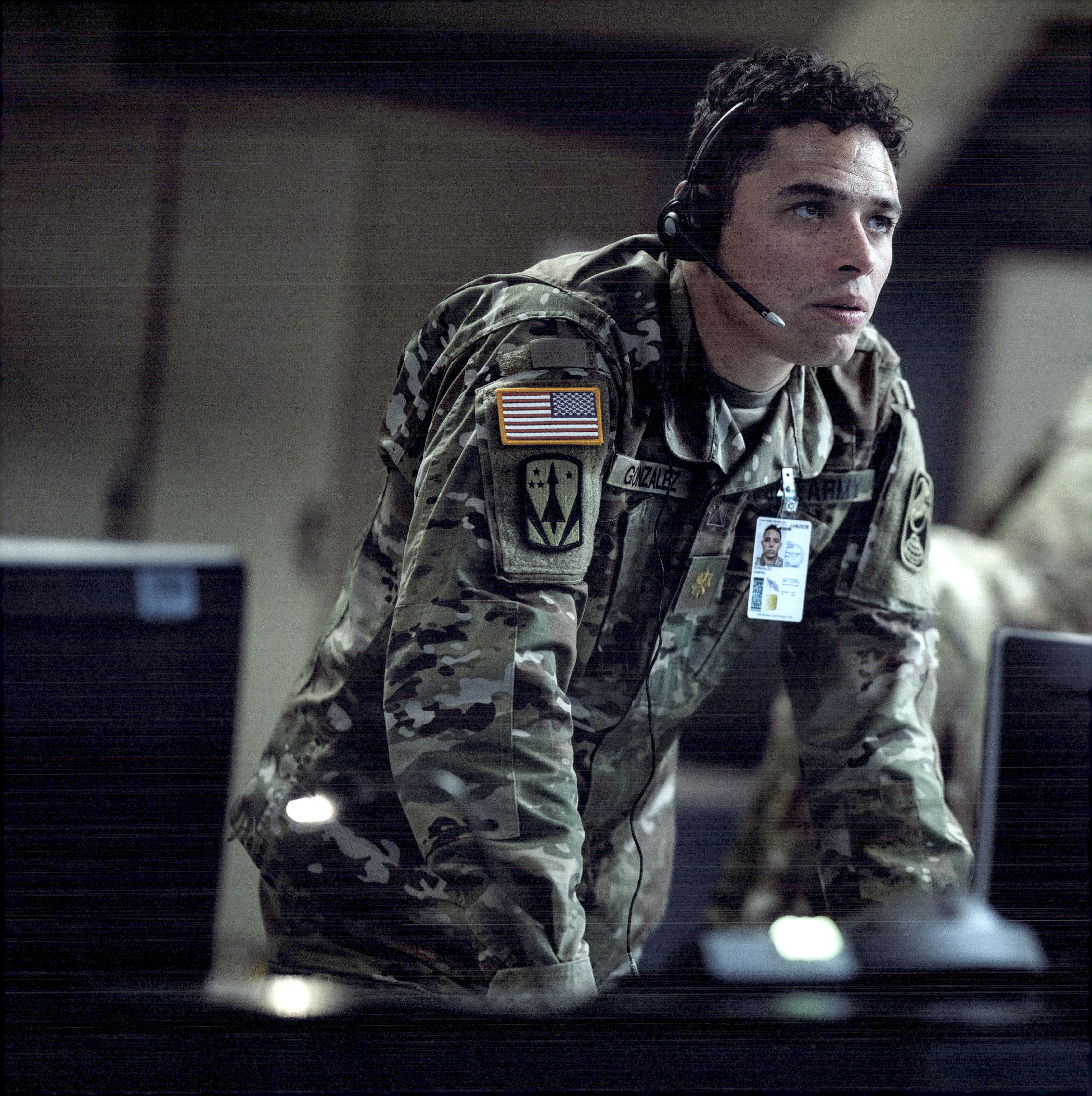
GONZALEZ
ARMY

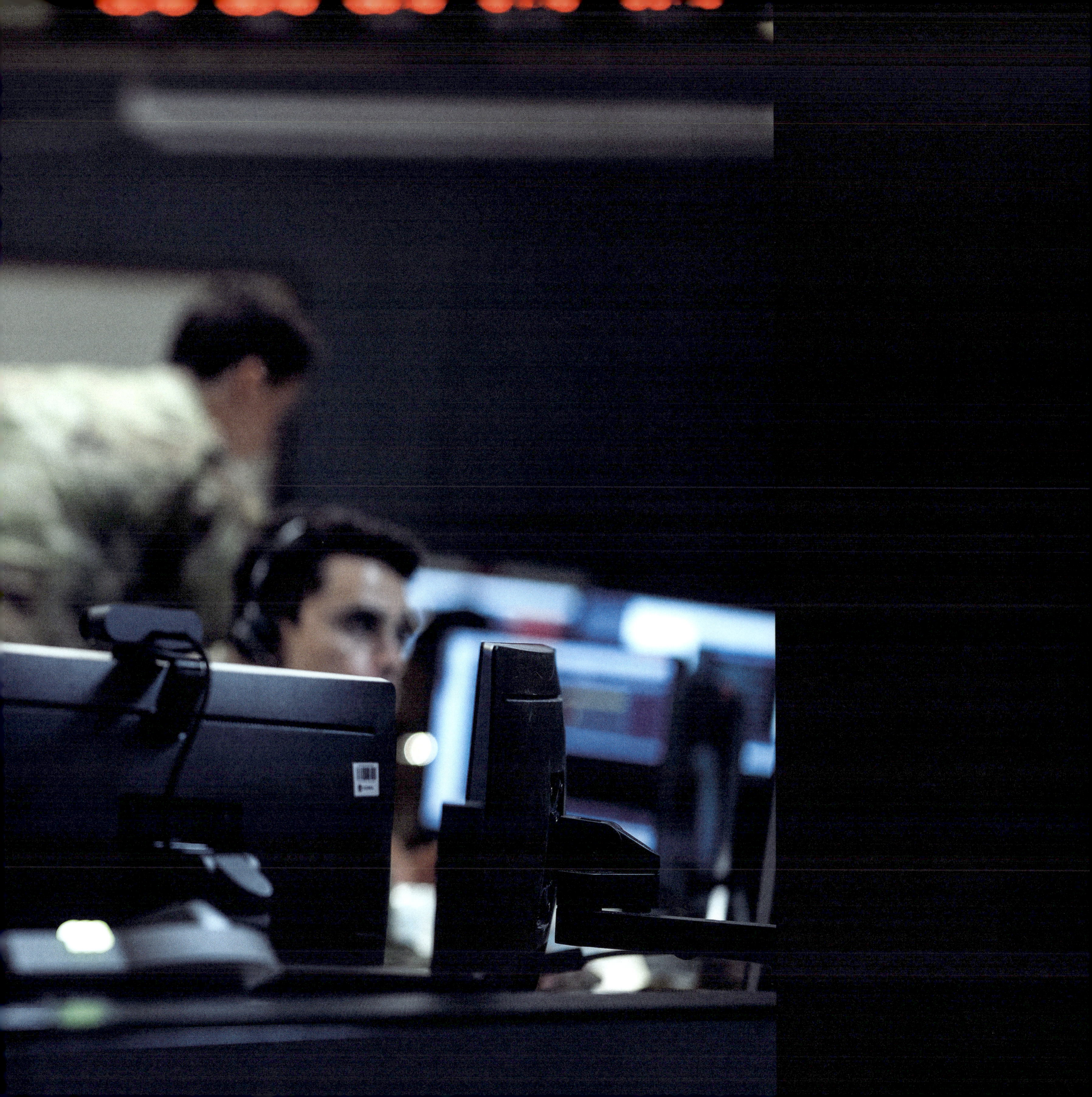

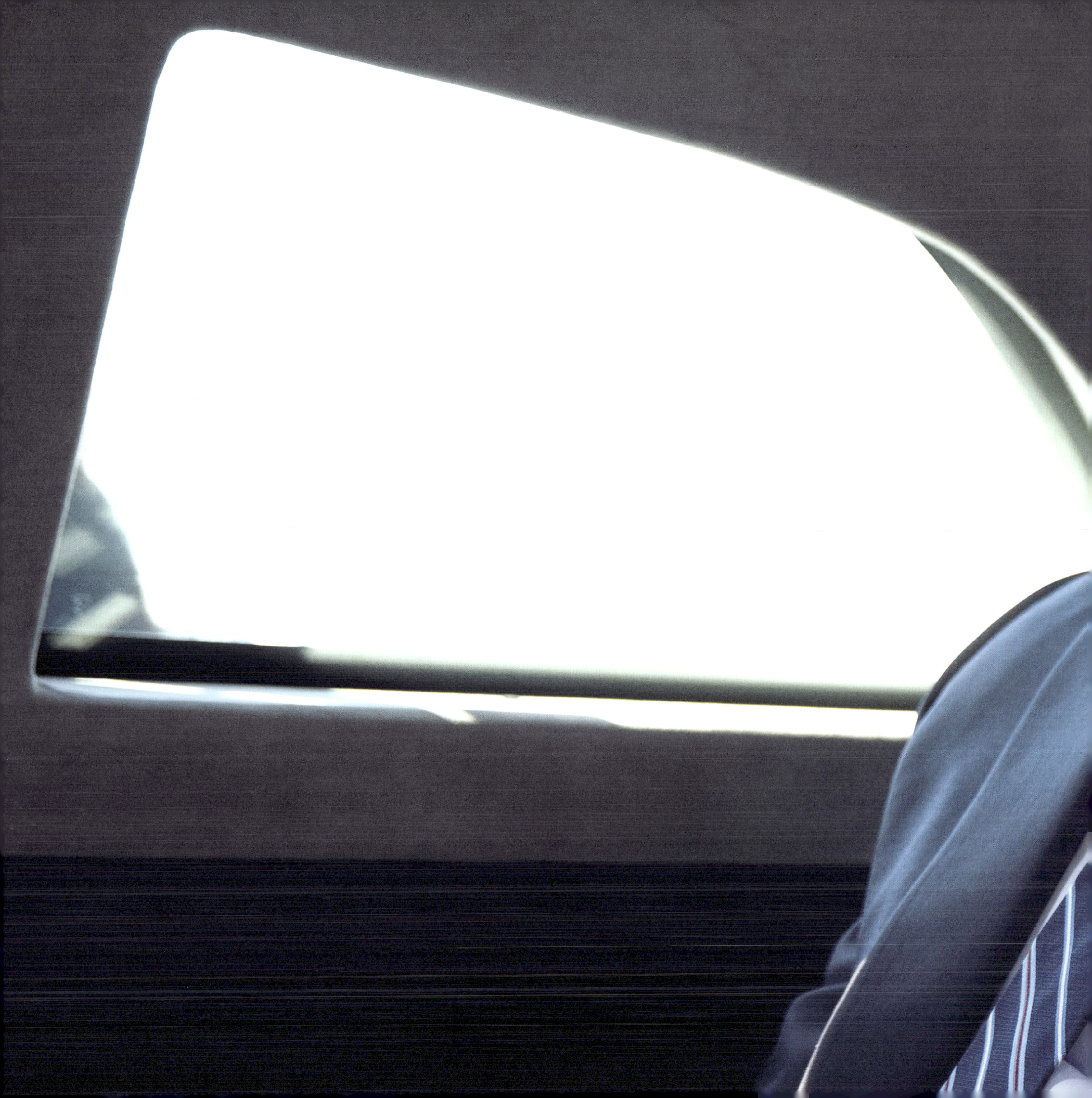

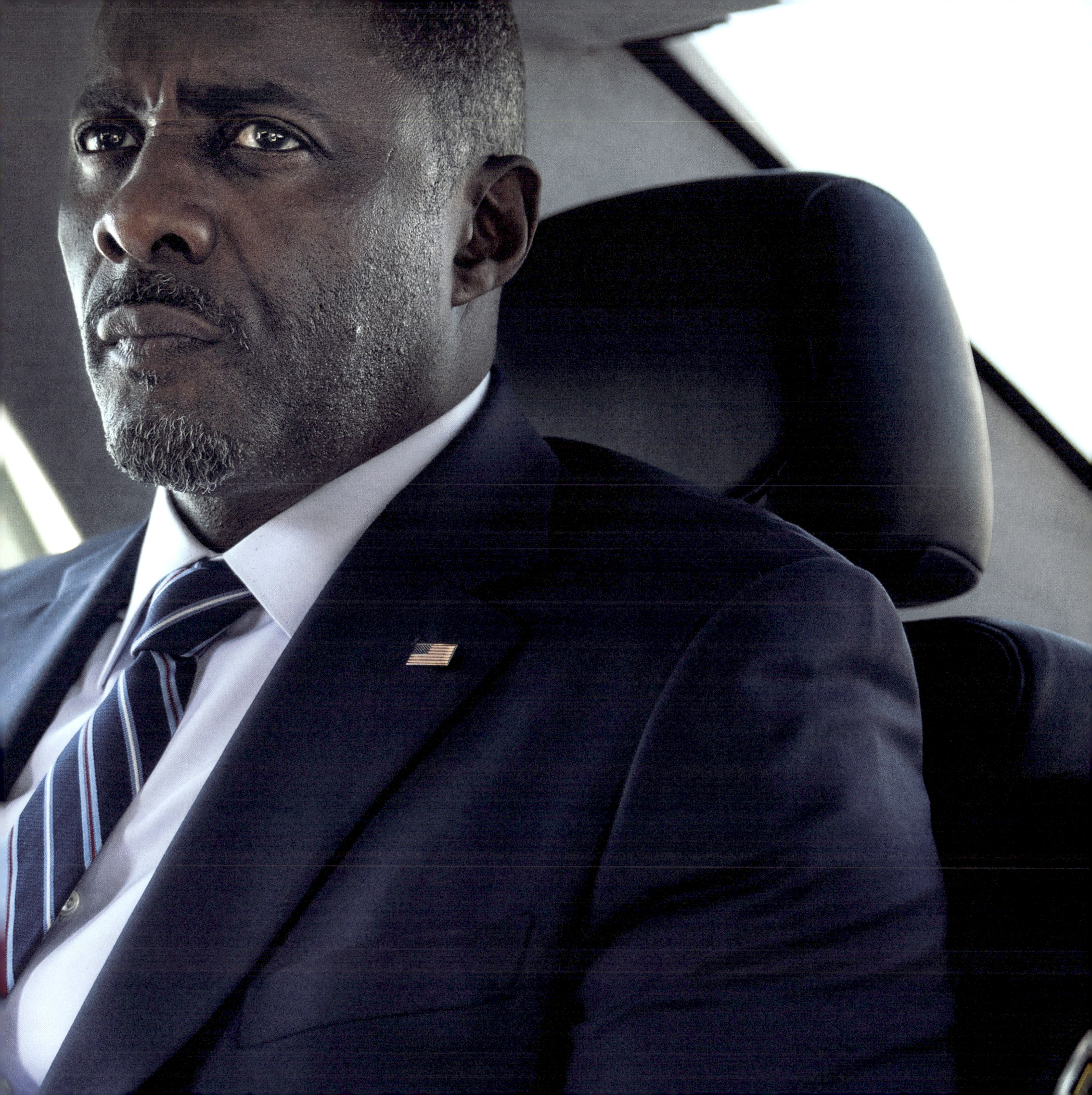

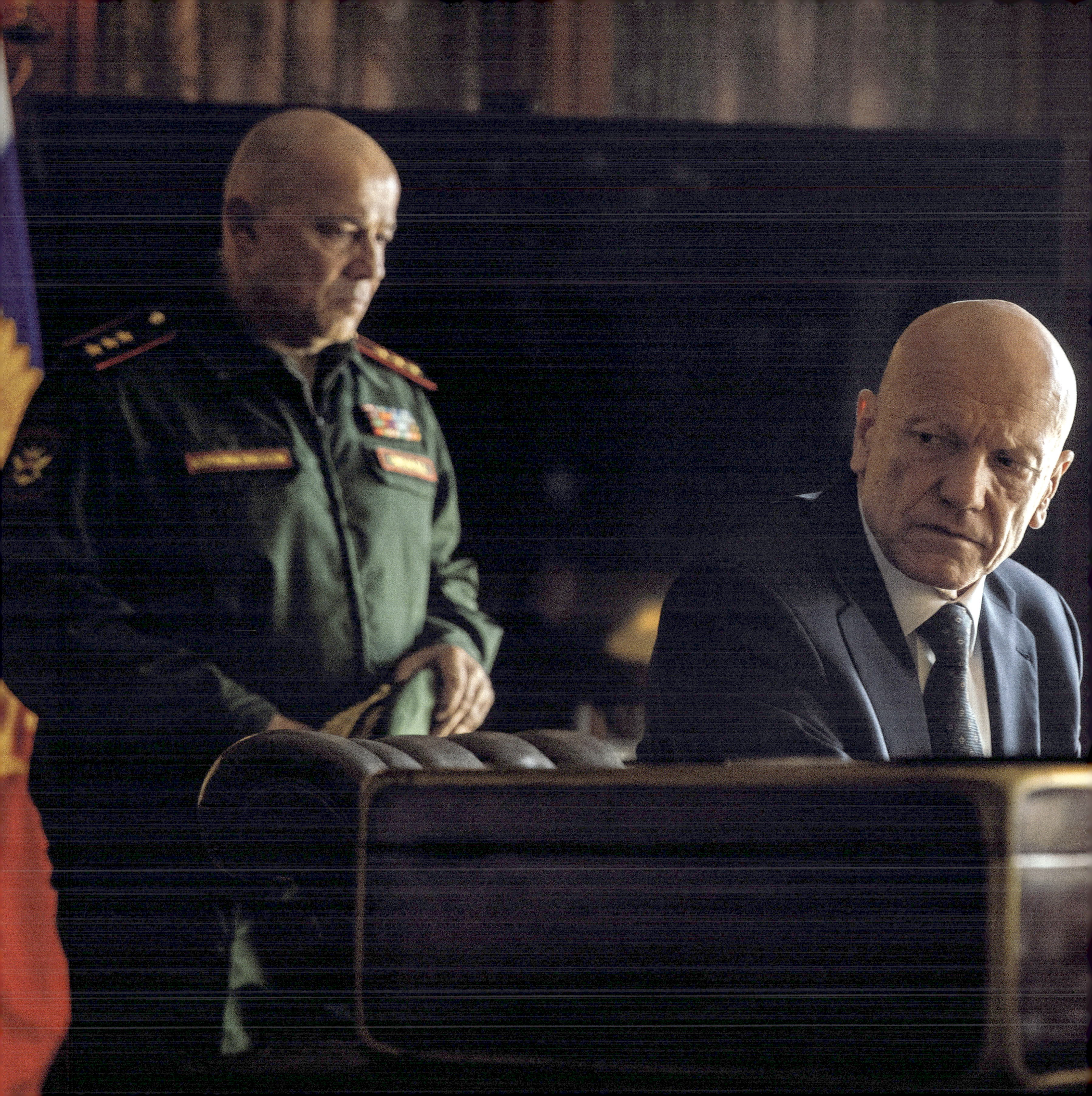

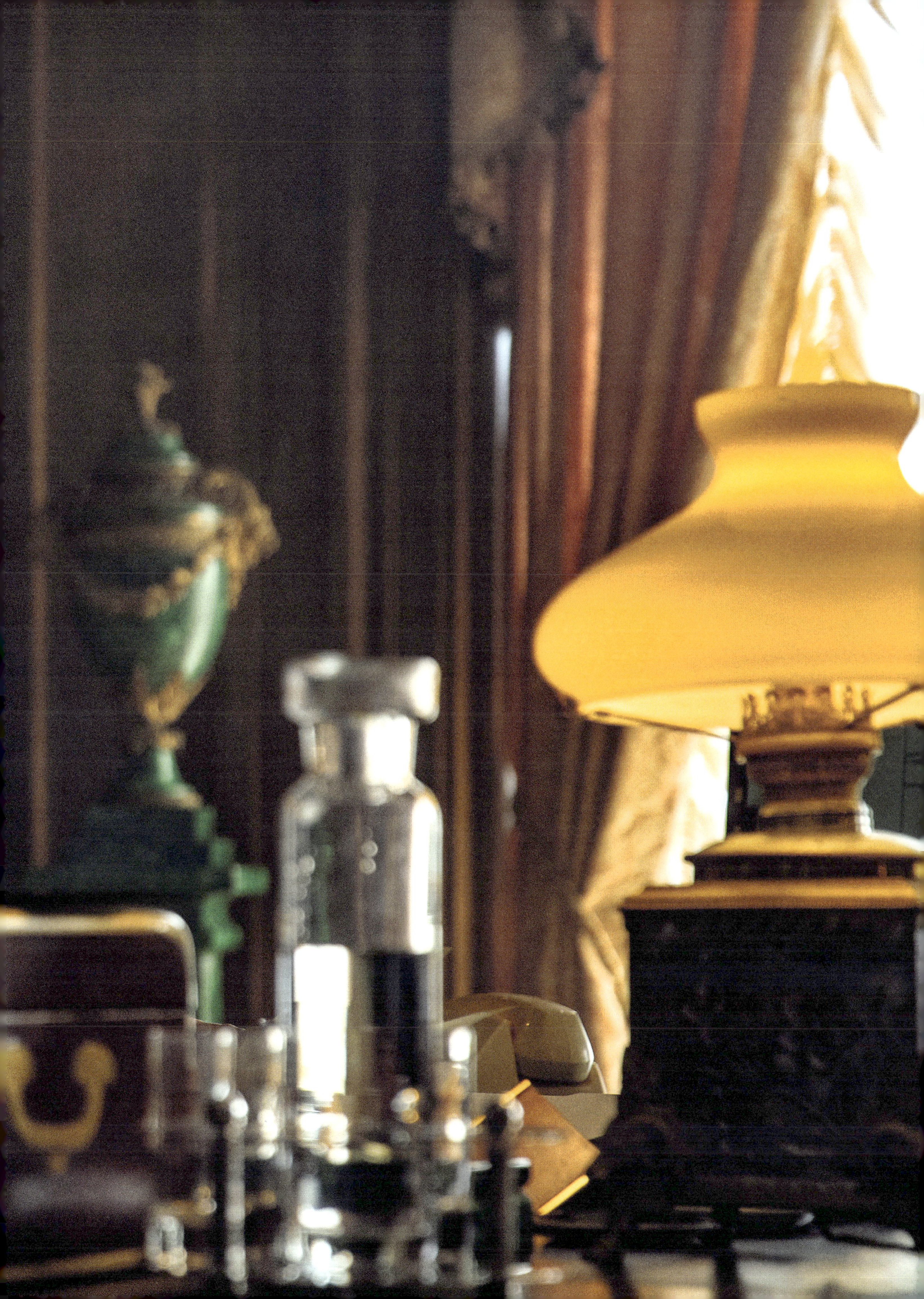

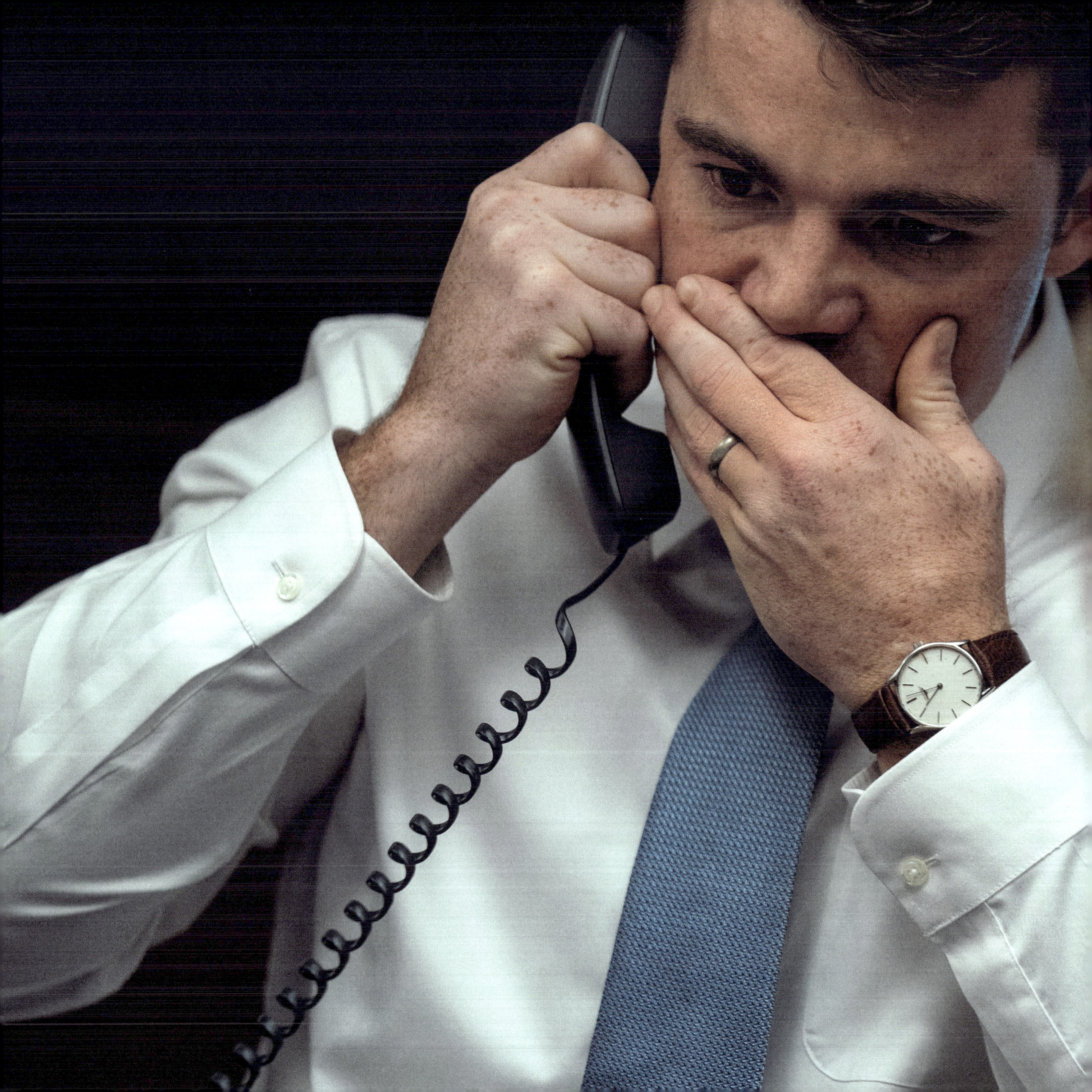

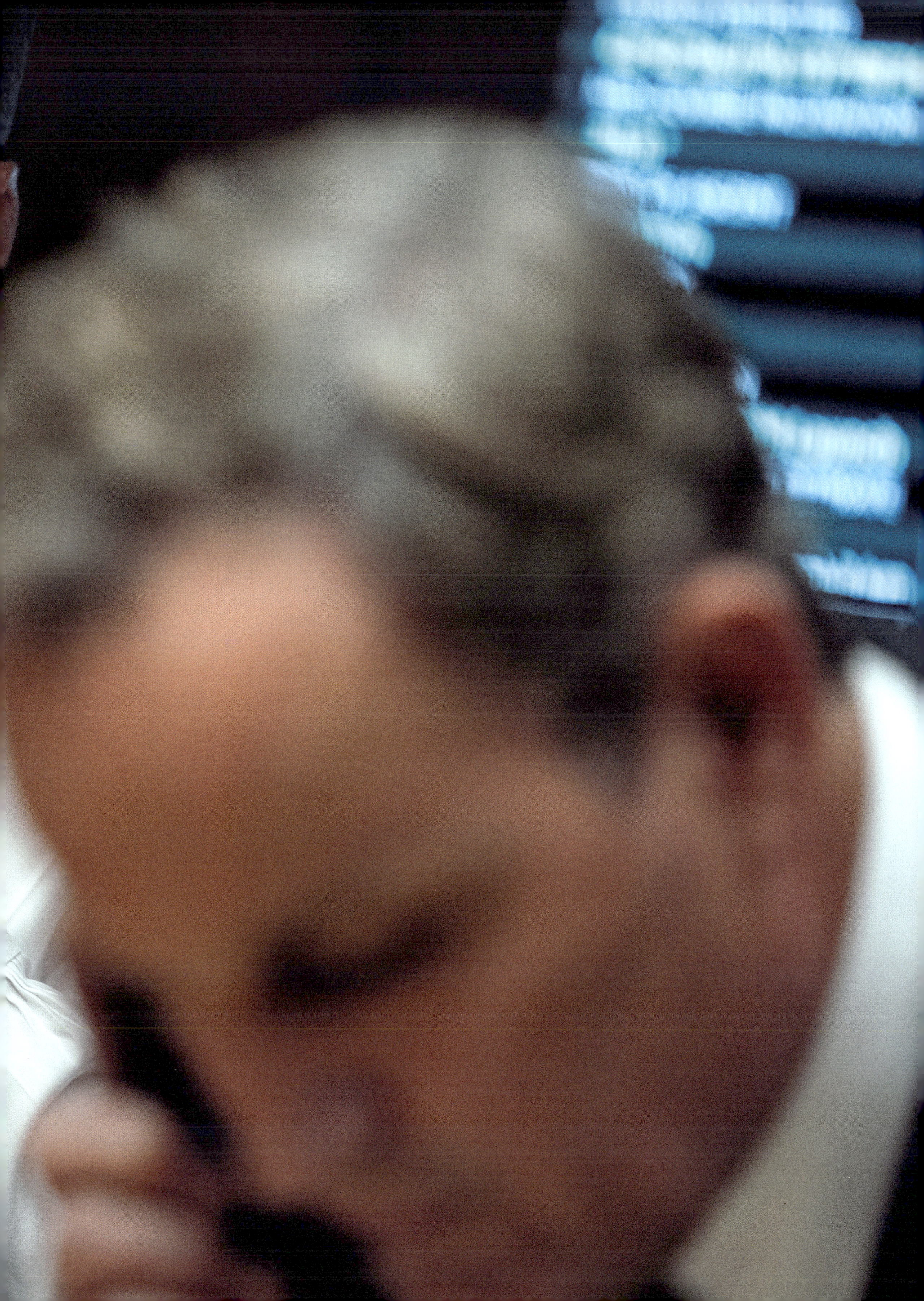

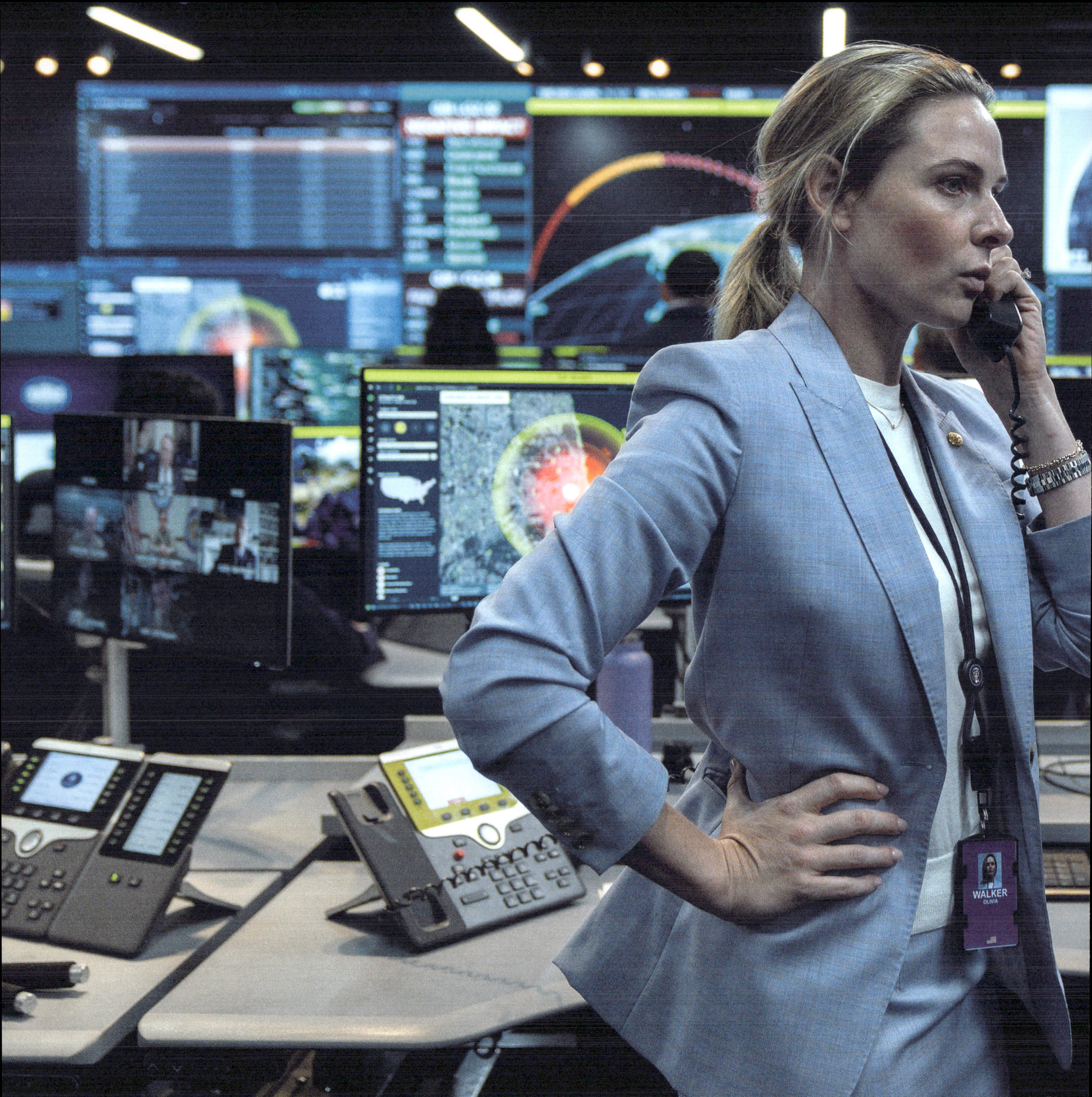
WALKER
OLIVIA

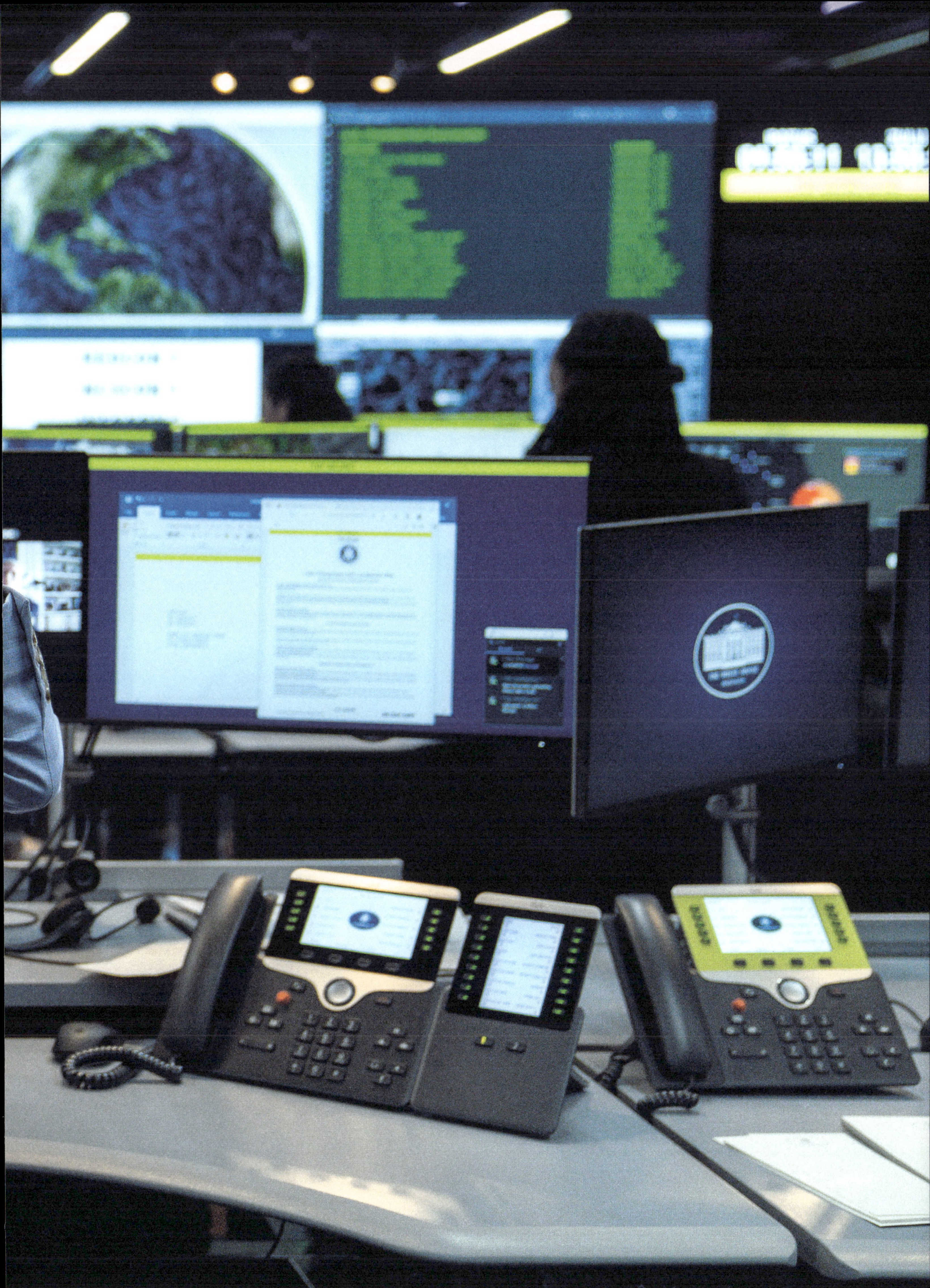

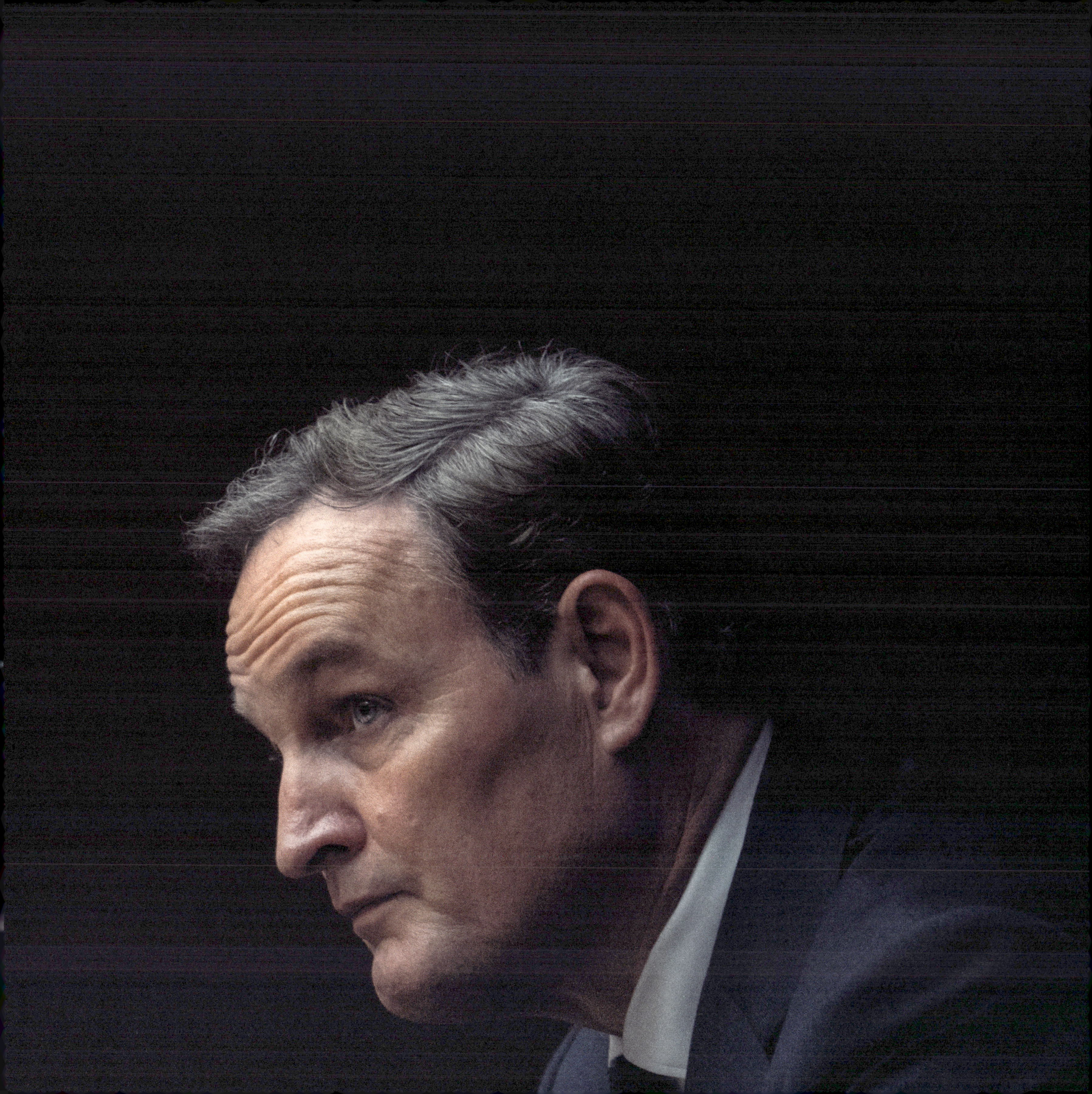

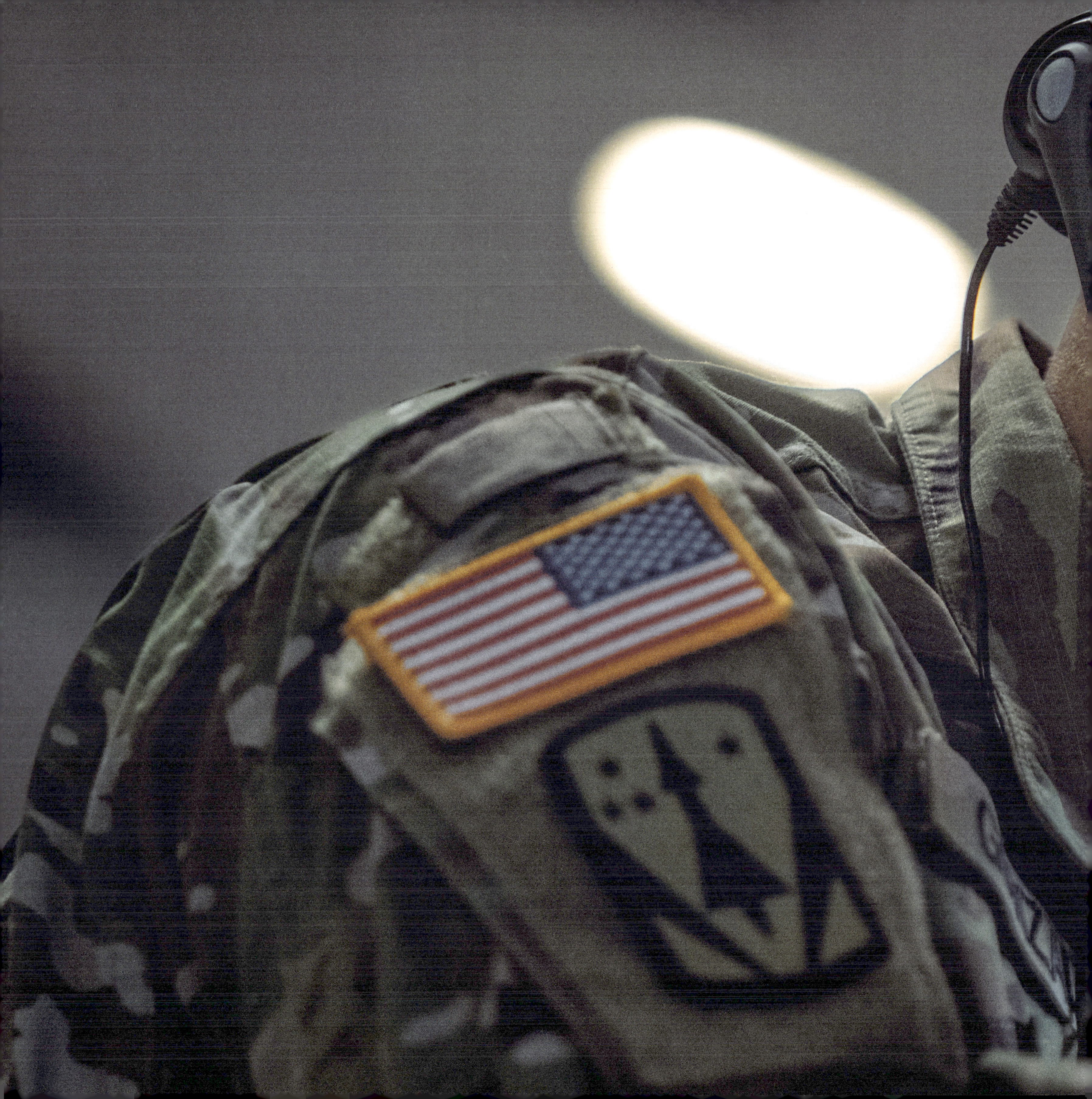

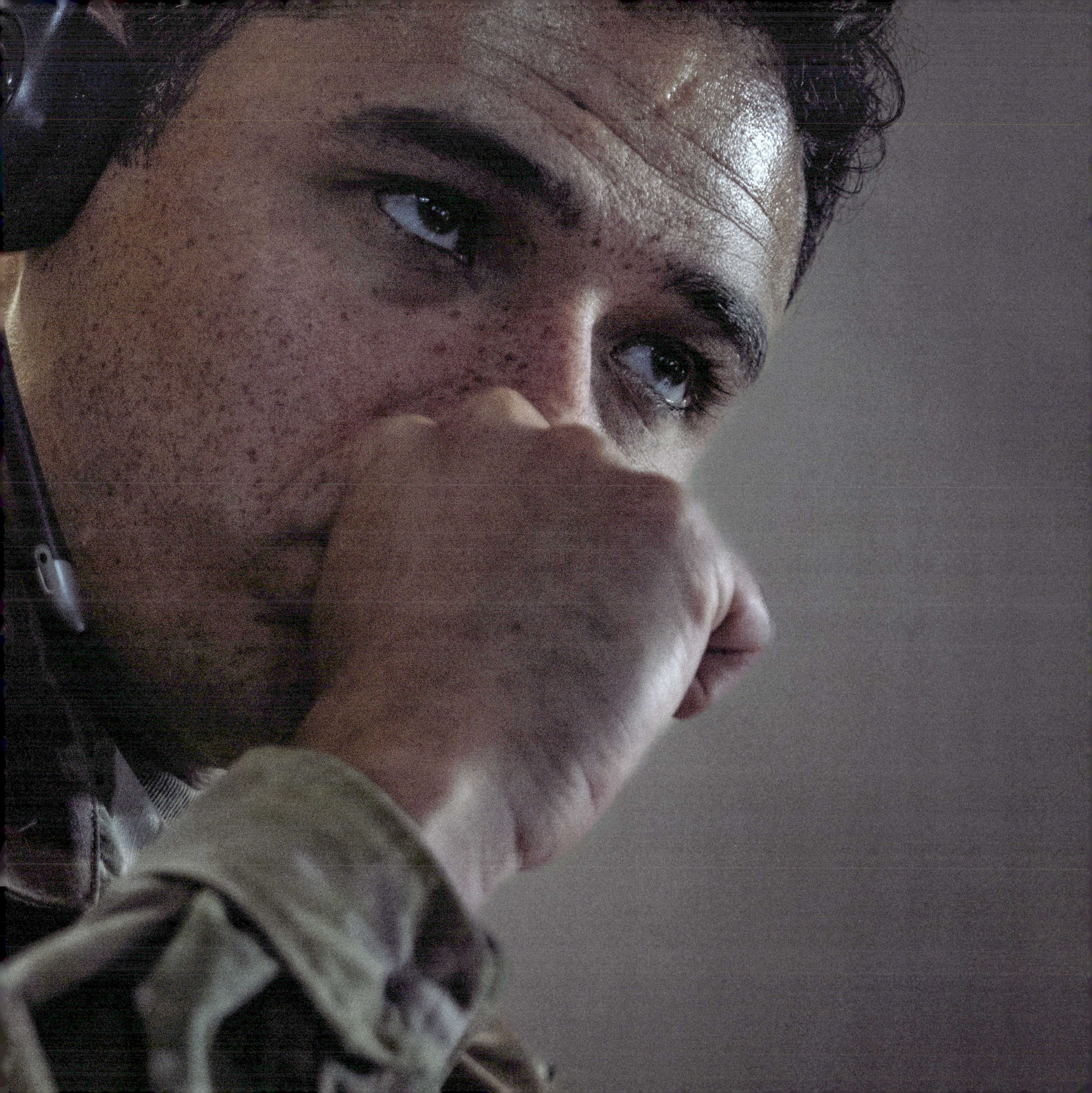

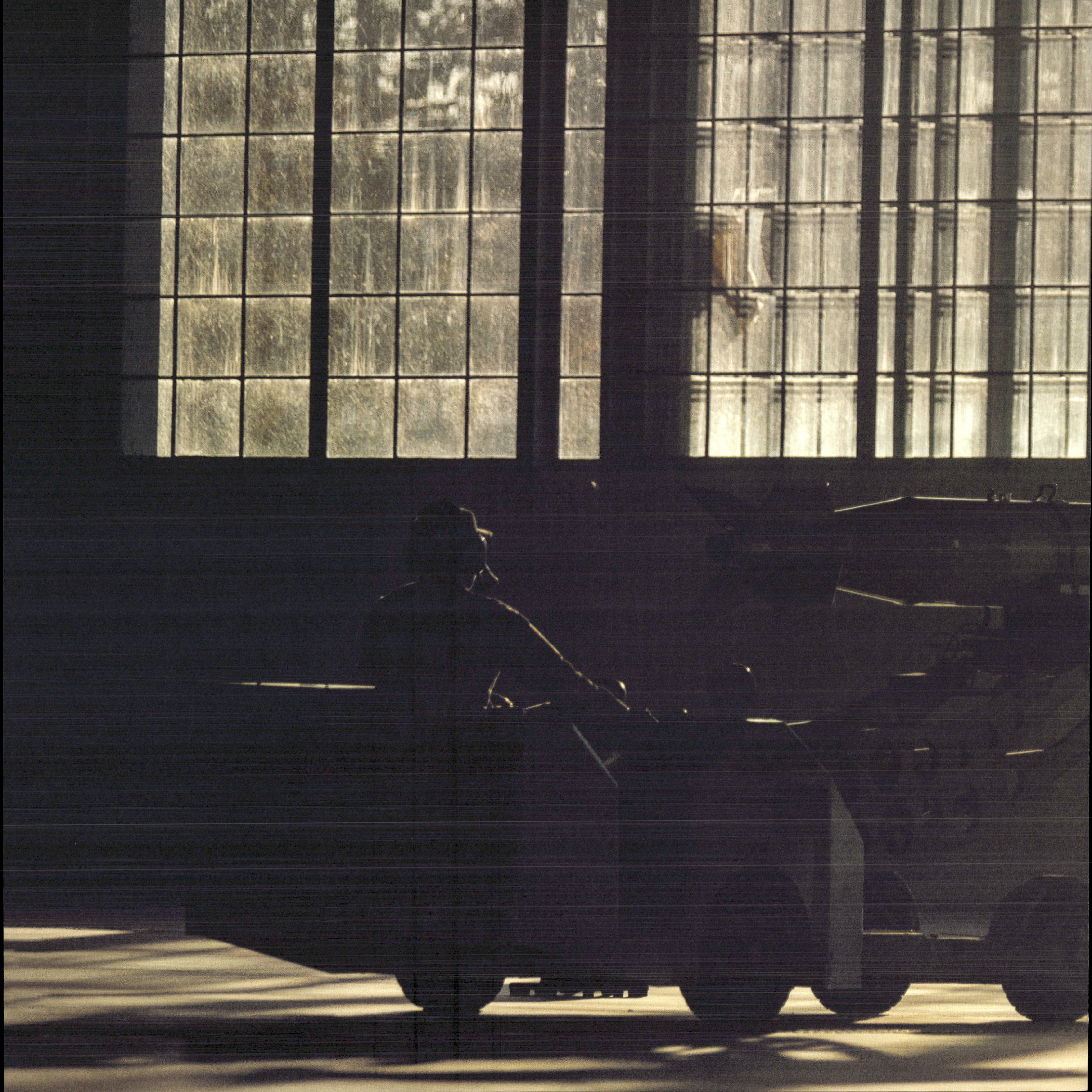

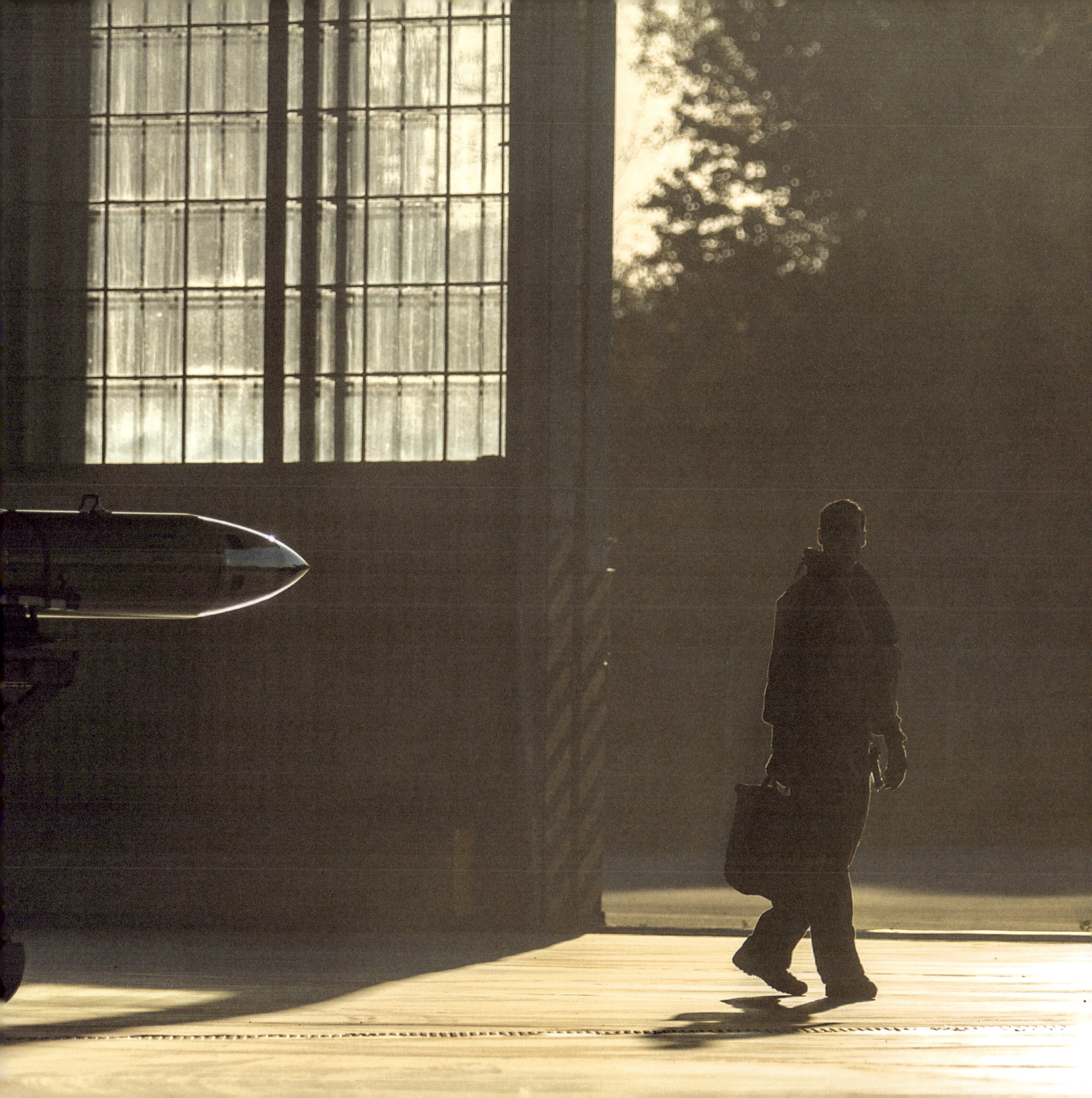

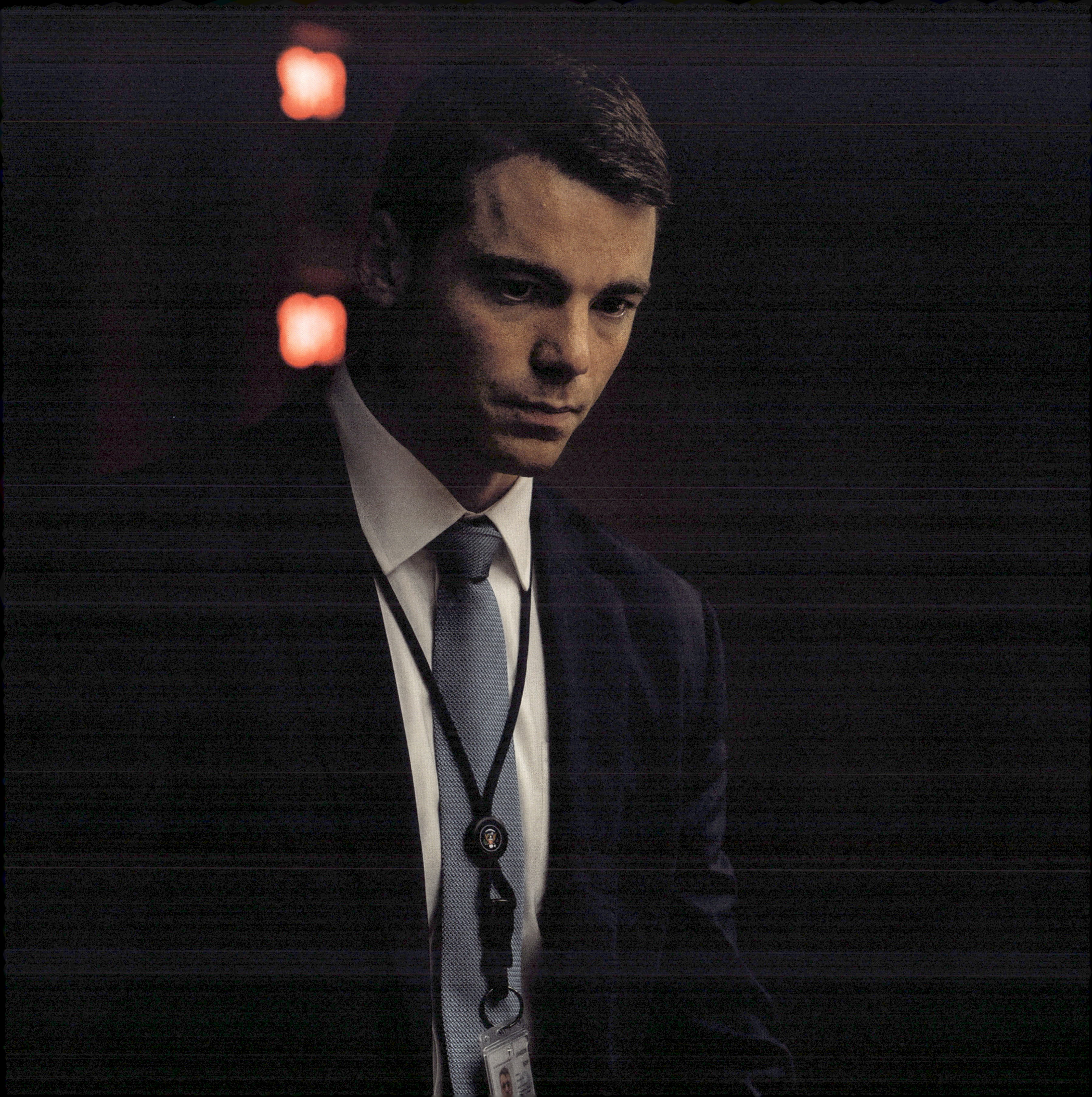

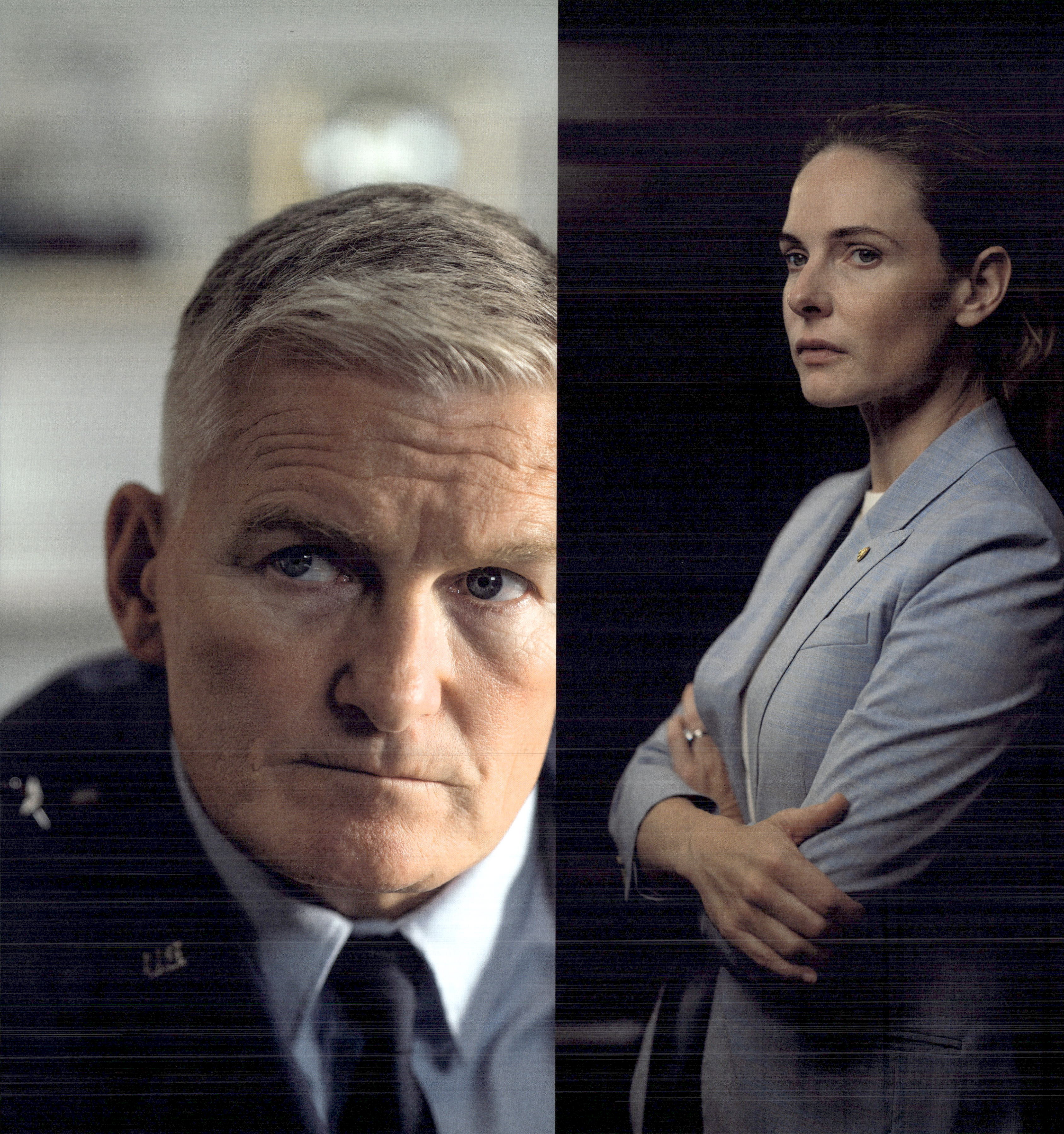

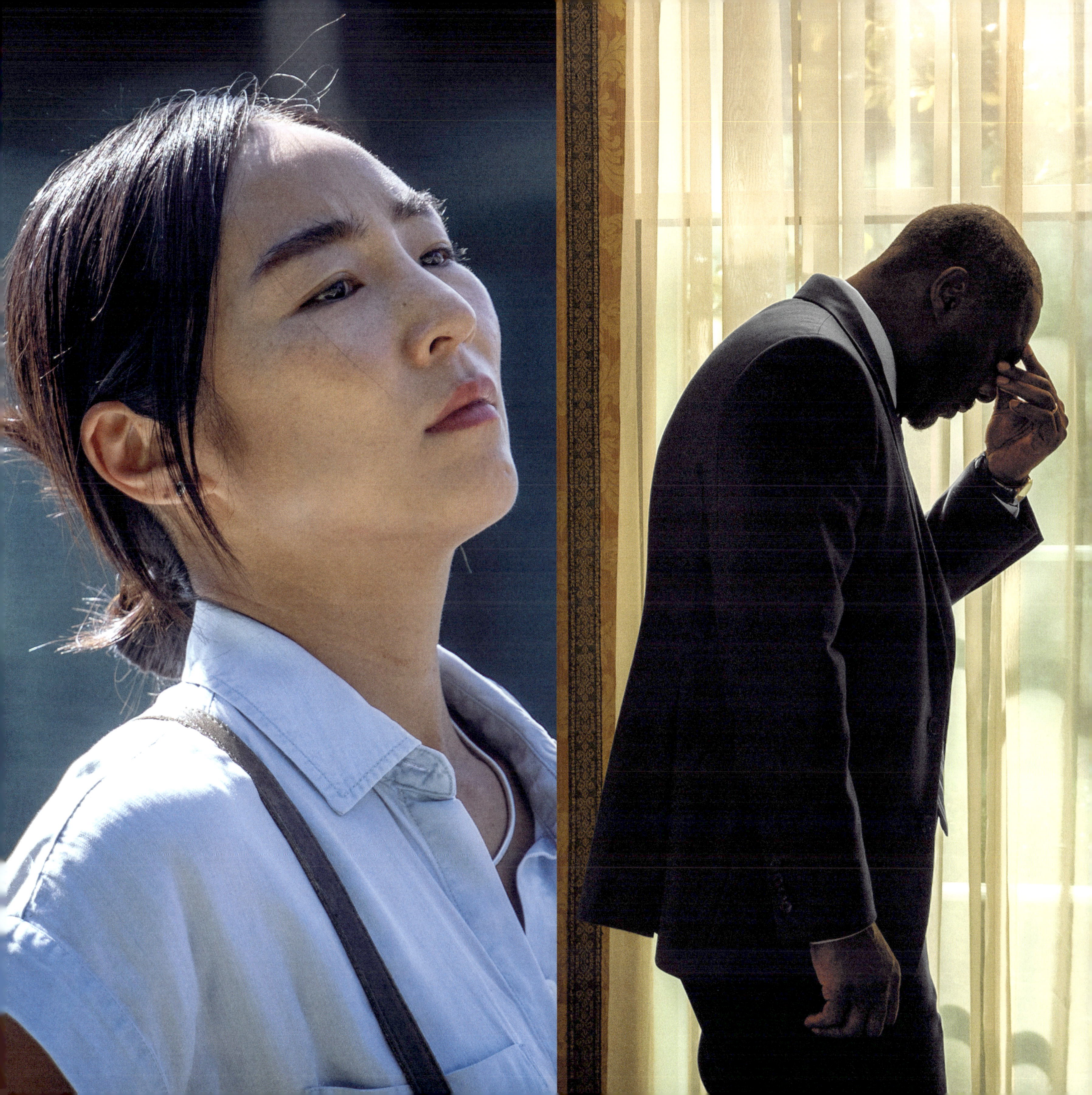

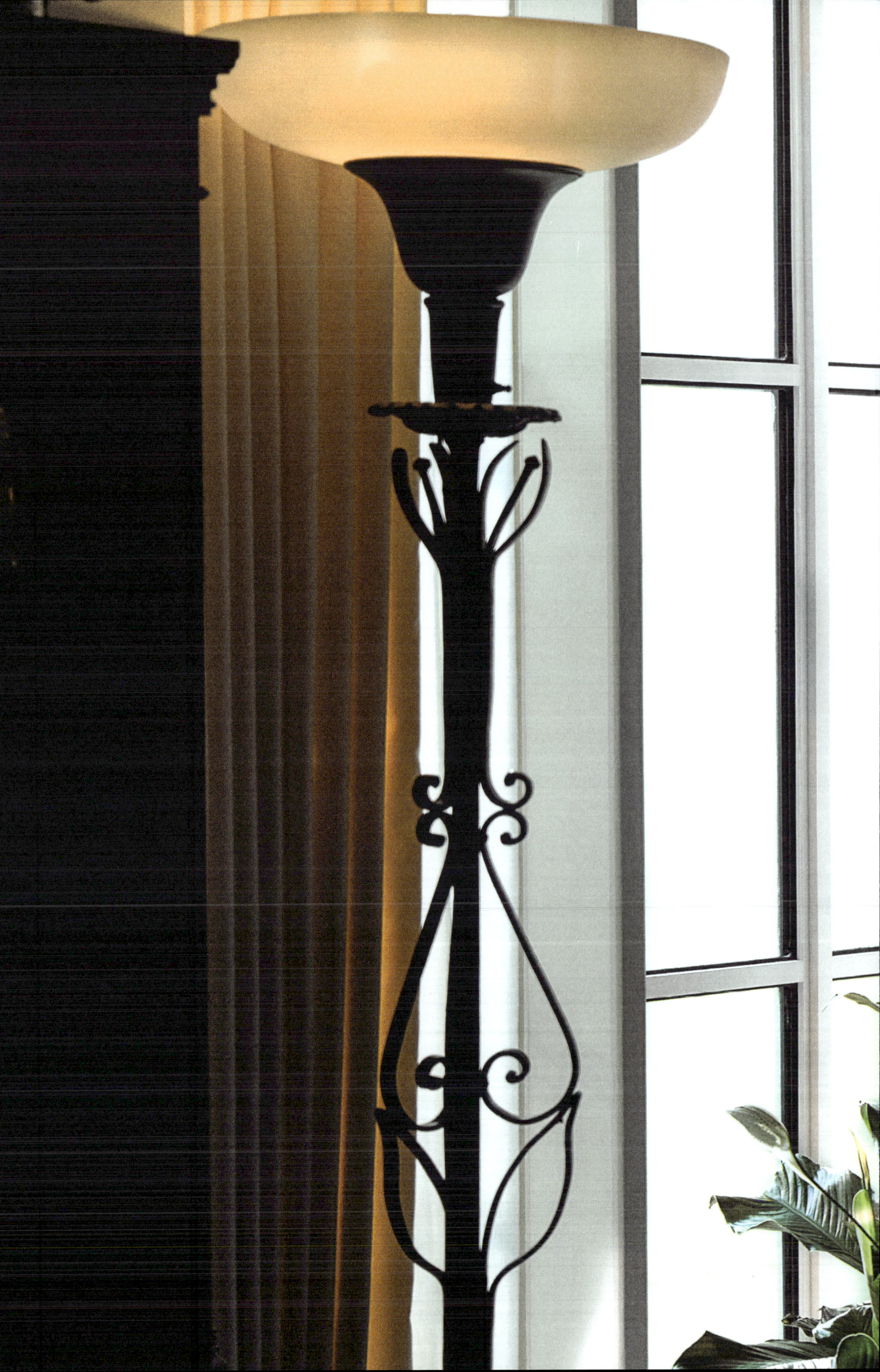

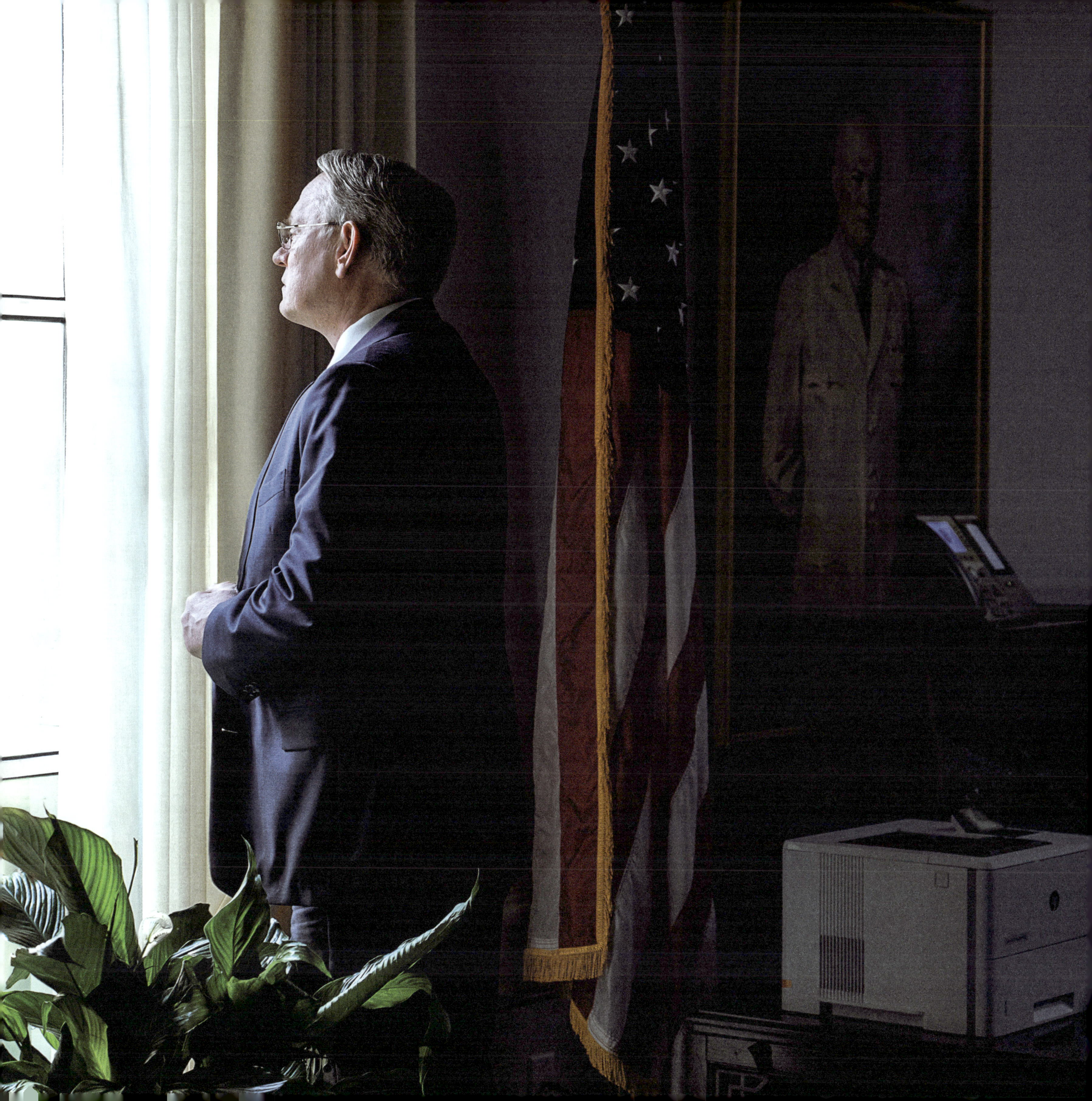

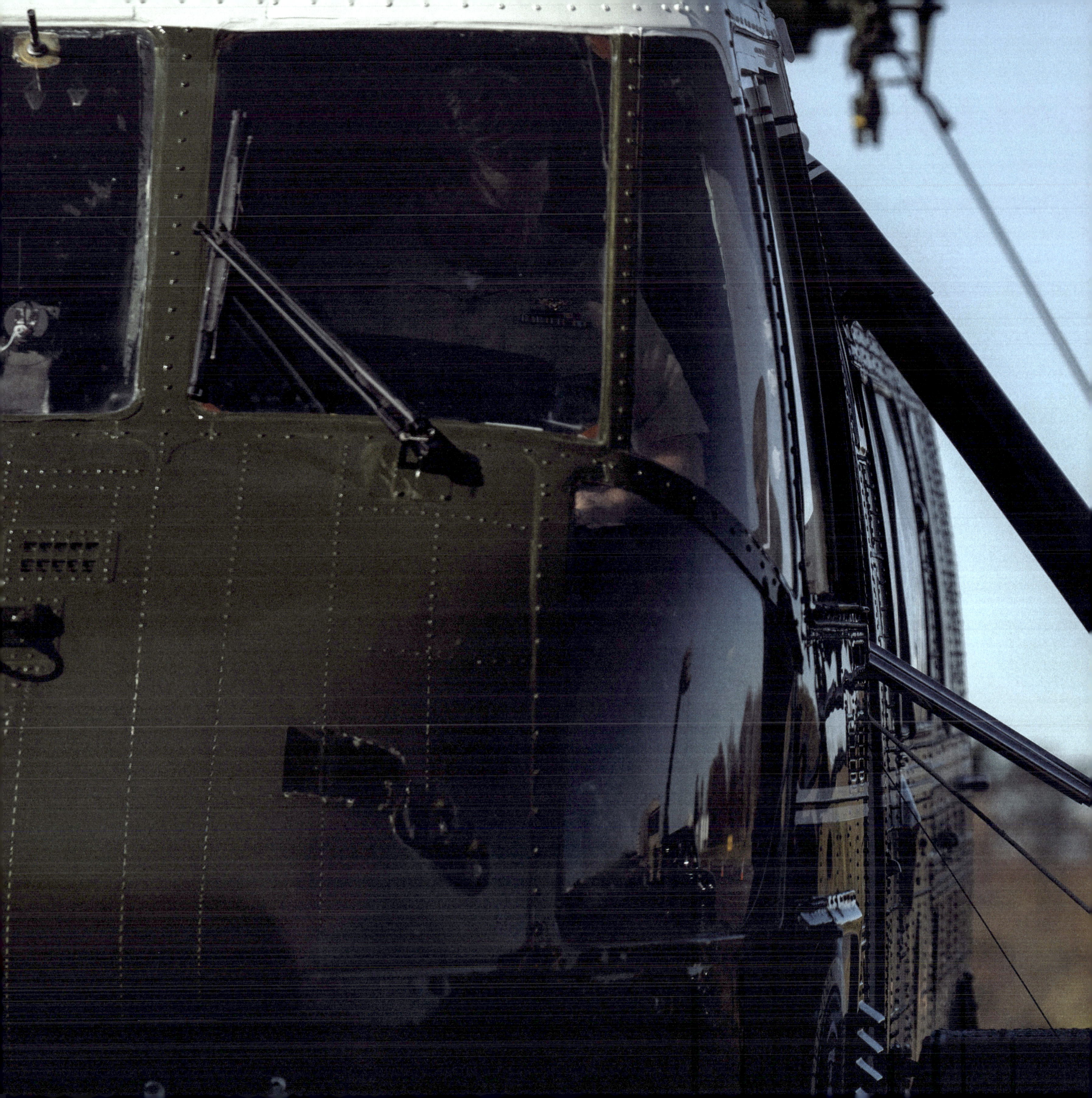

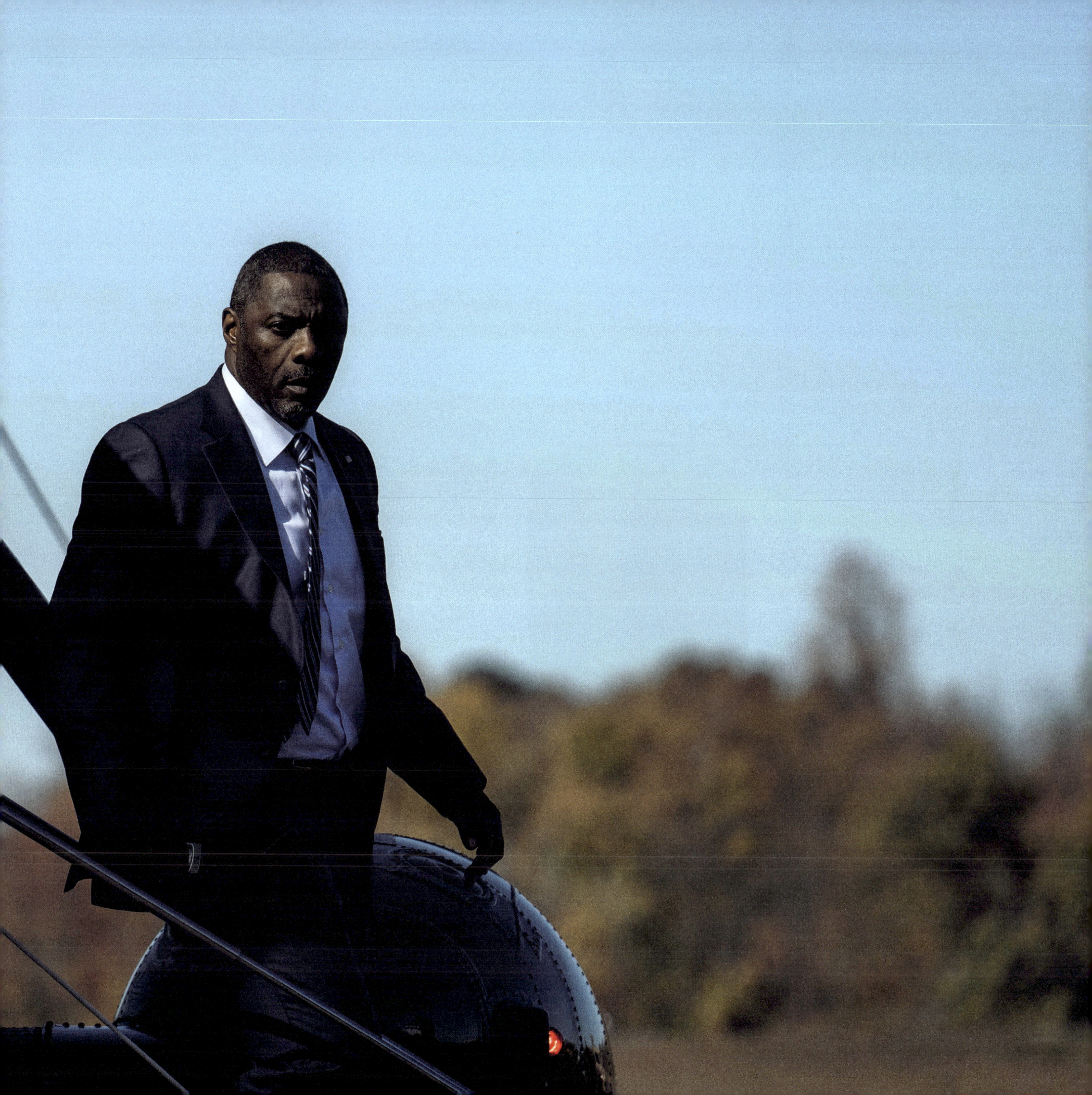

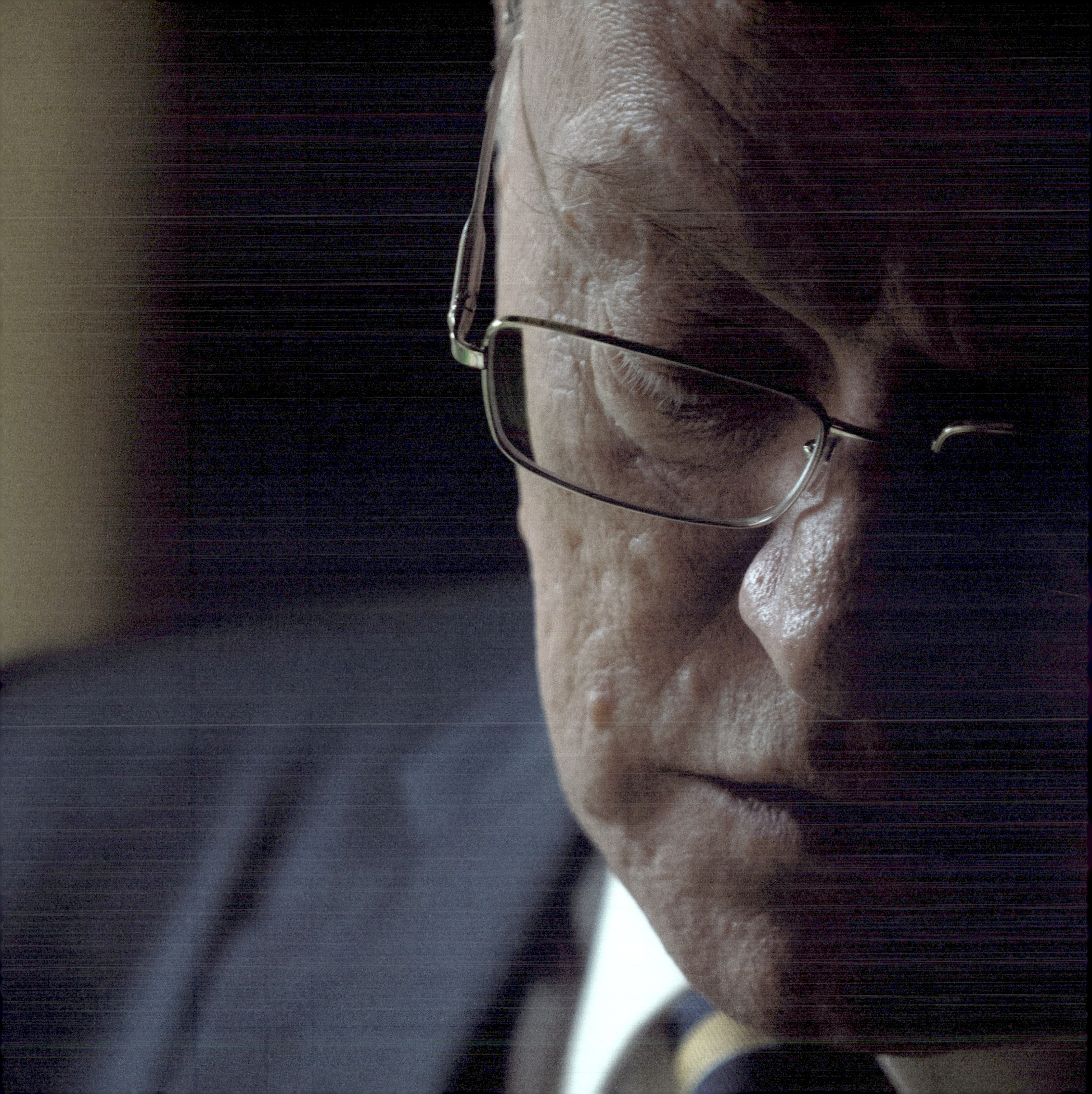

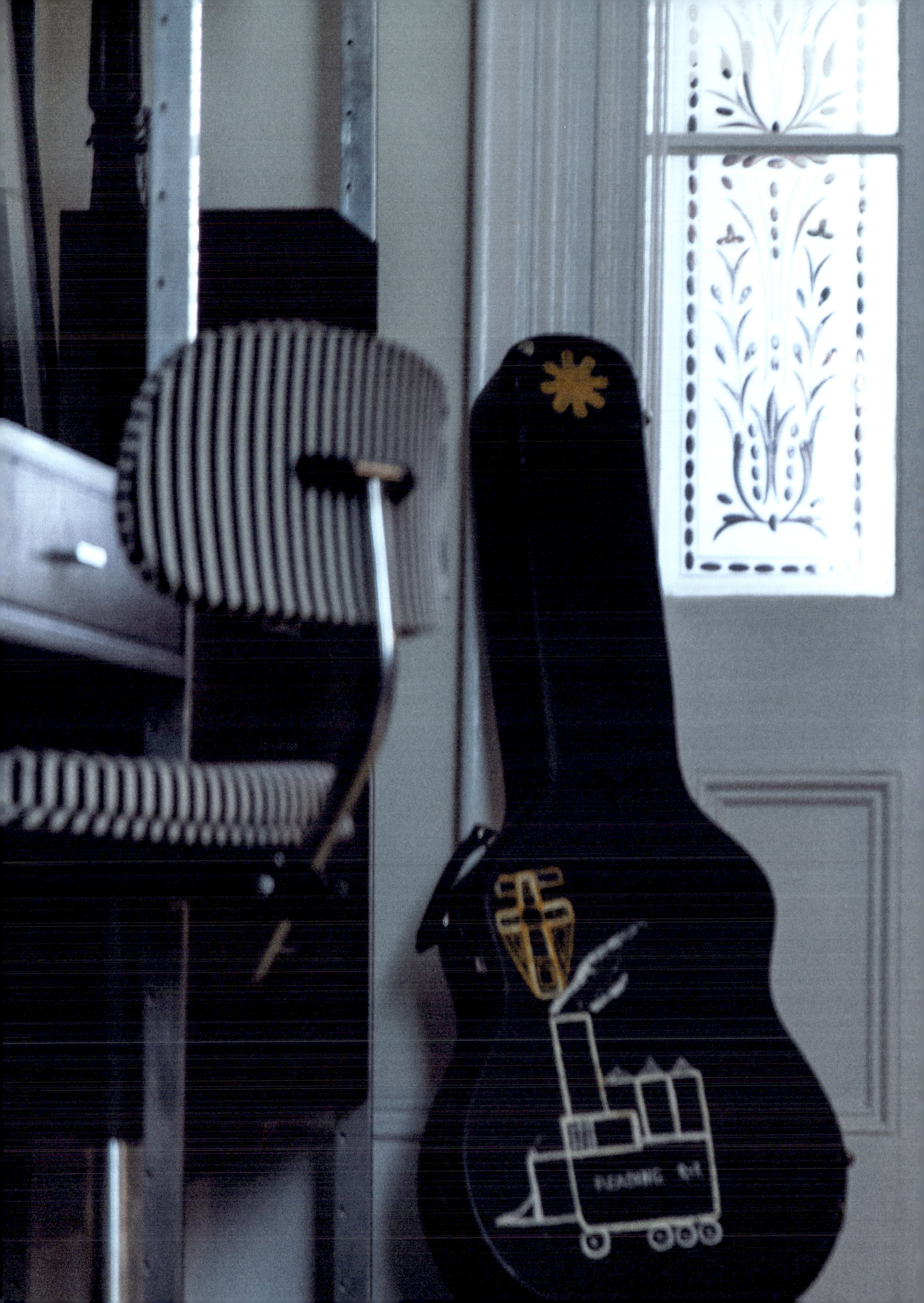

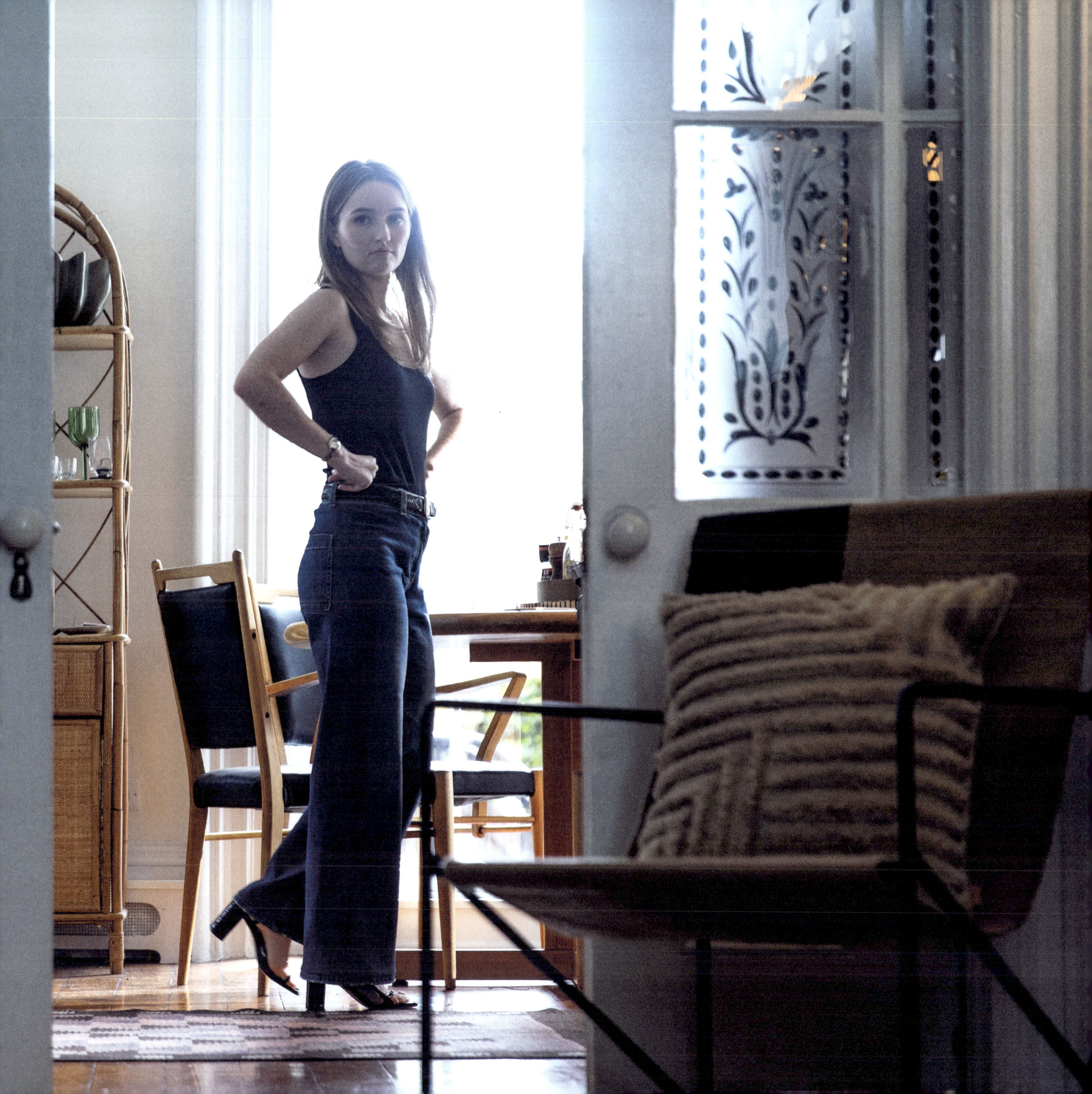

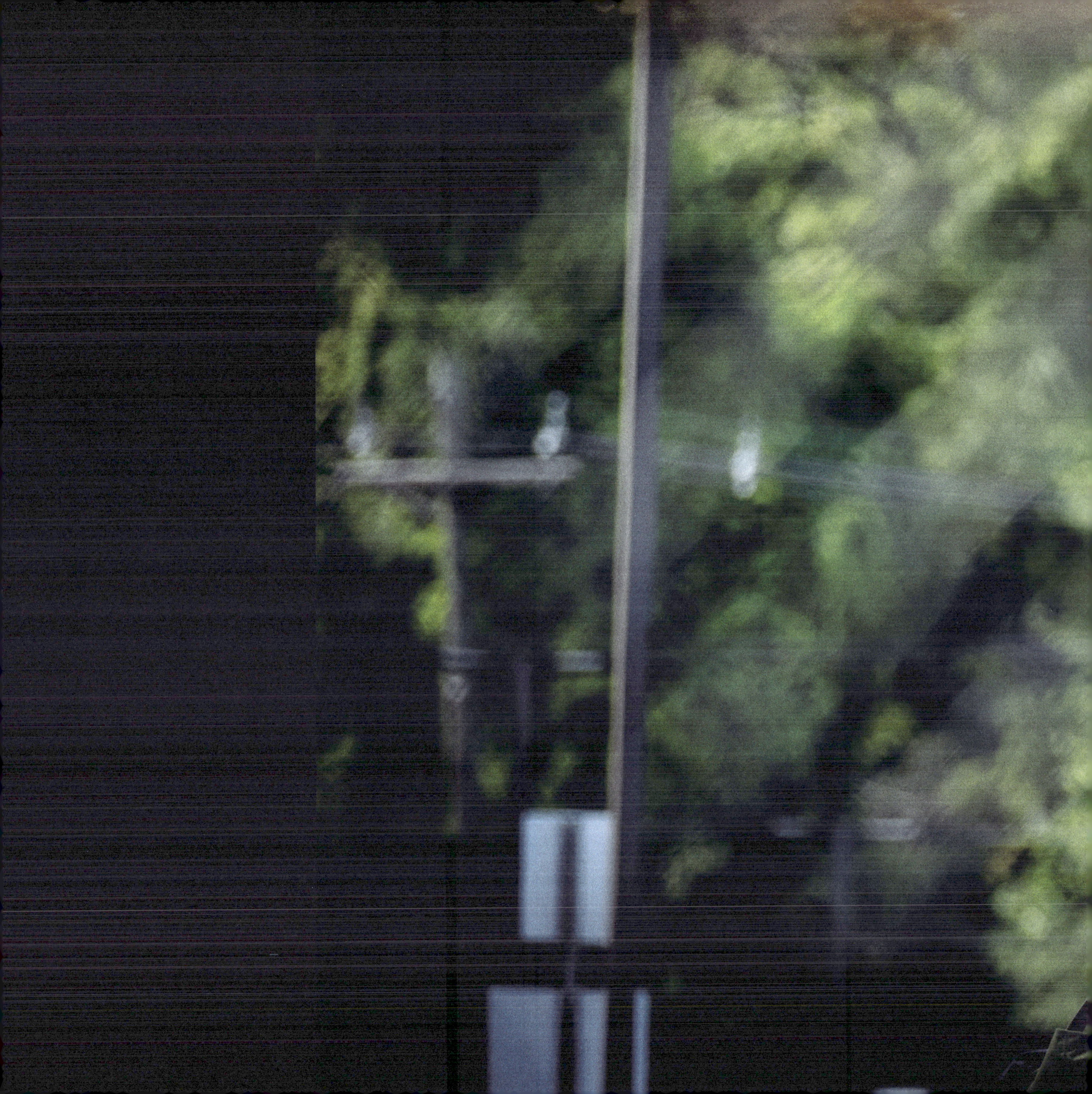

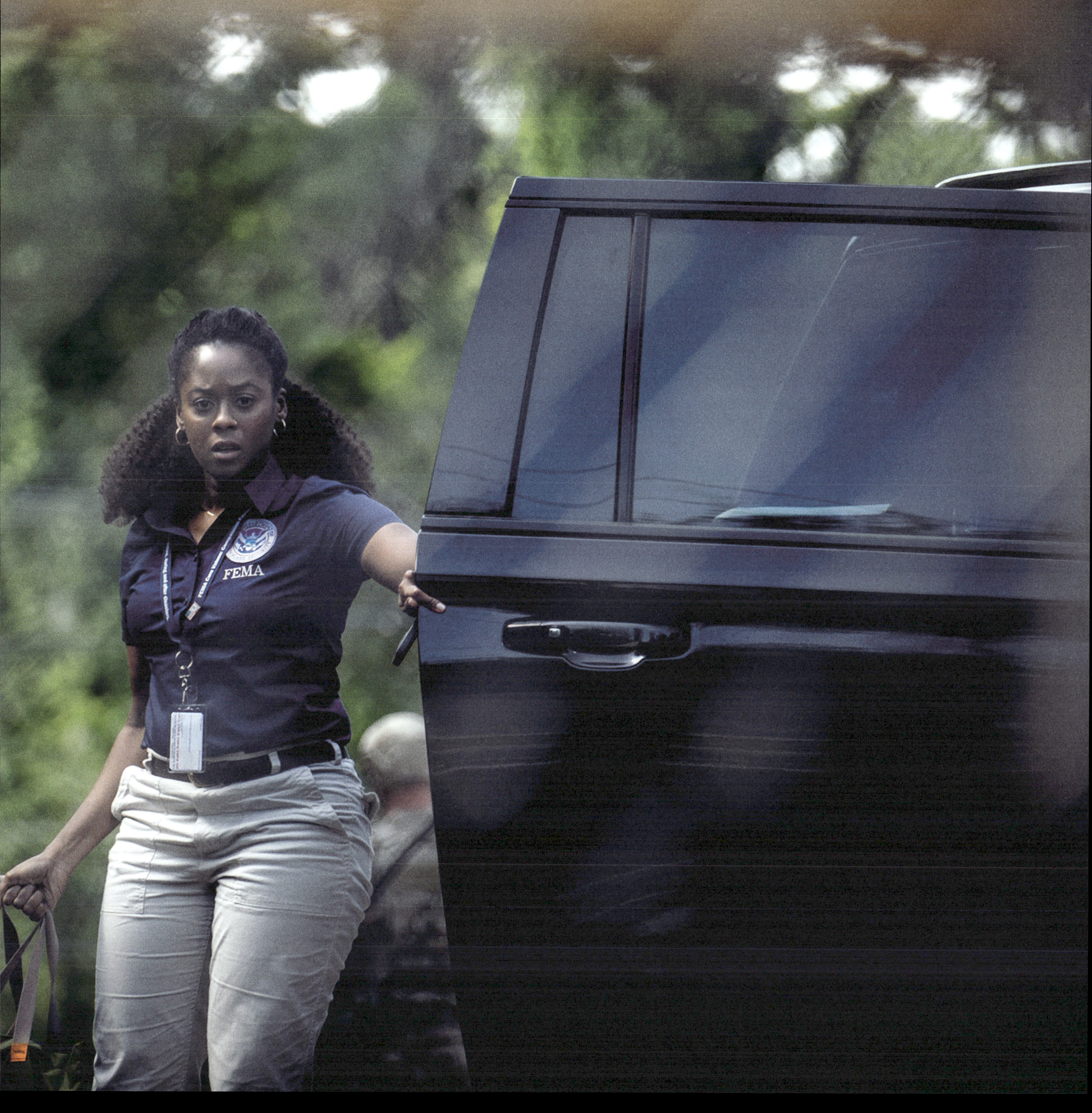
FEMA

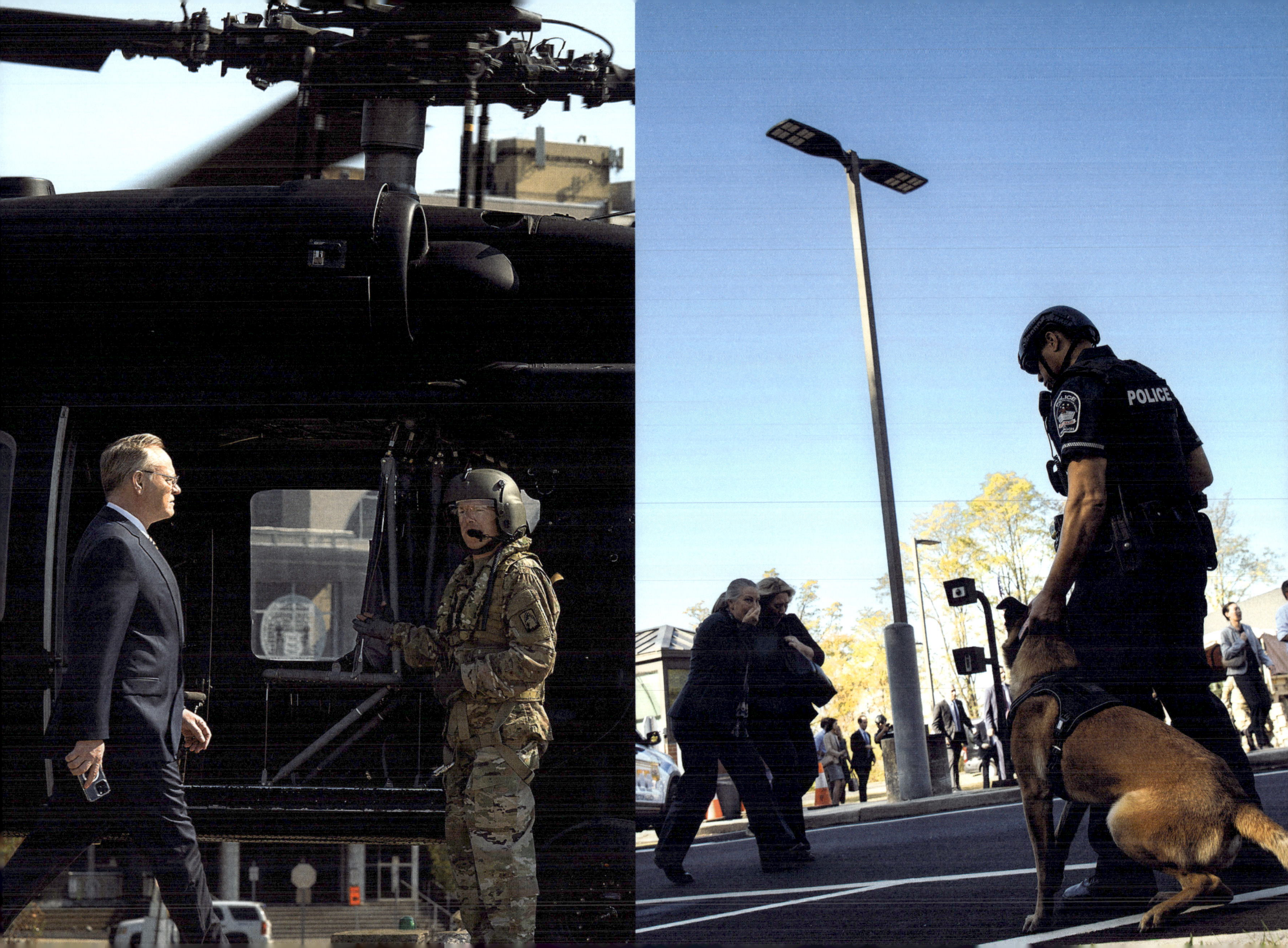
POLICE

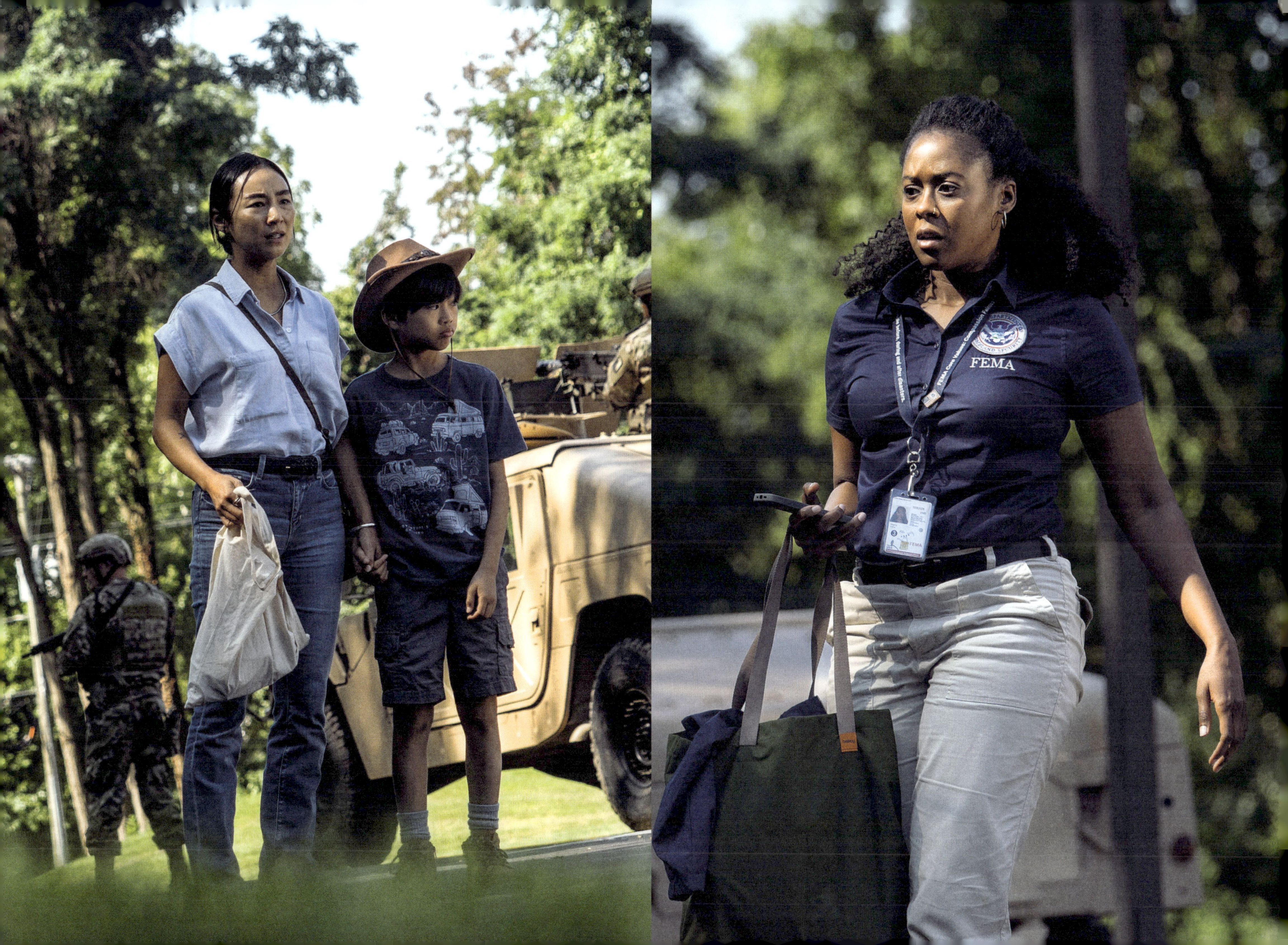
FEMA

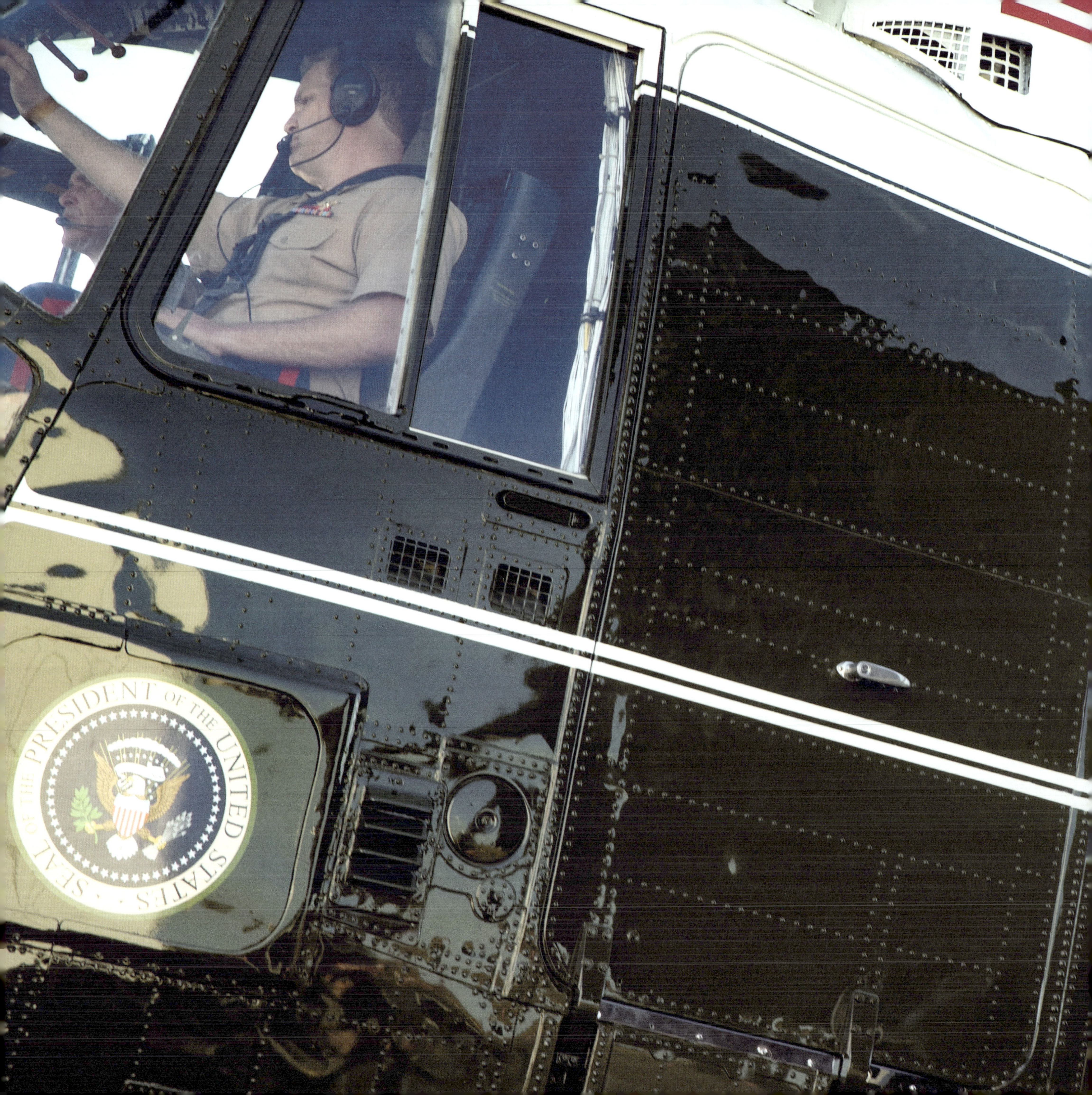
SEAL OF THE PRESIDENT OF THE UNITED STATES

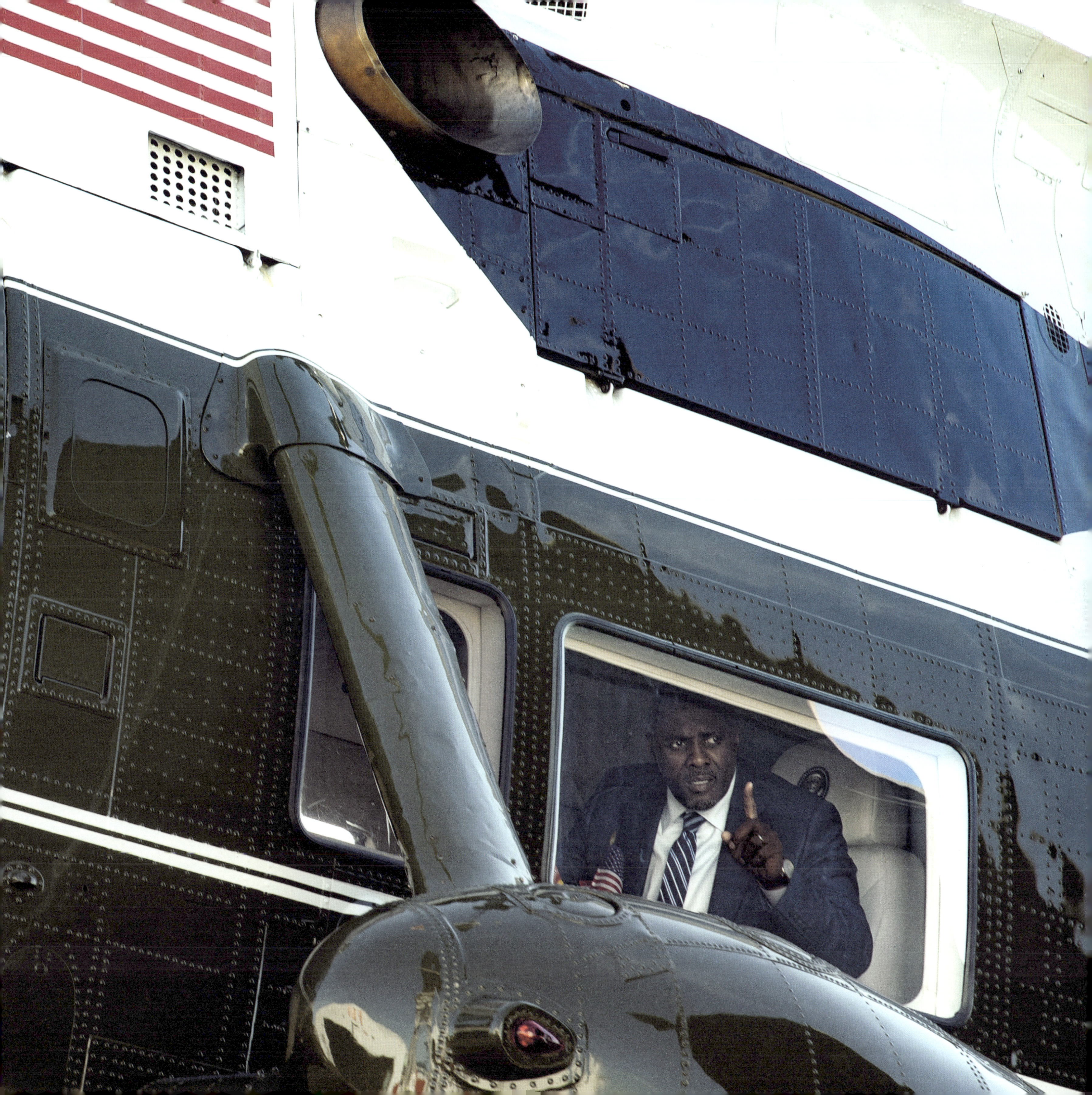

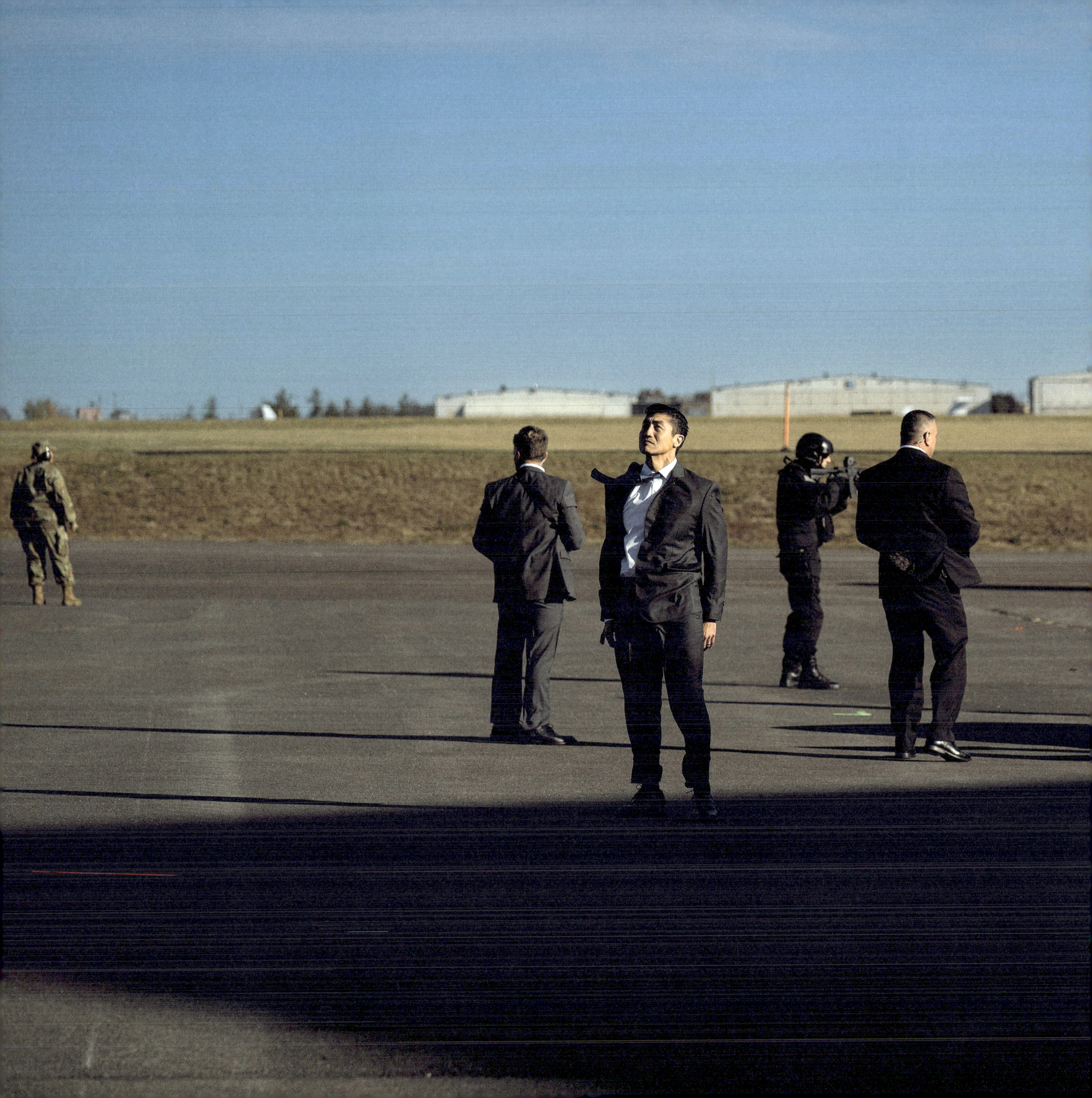

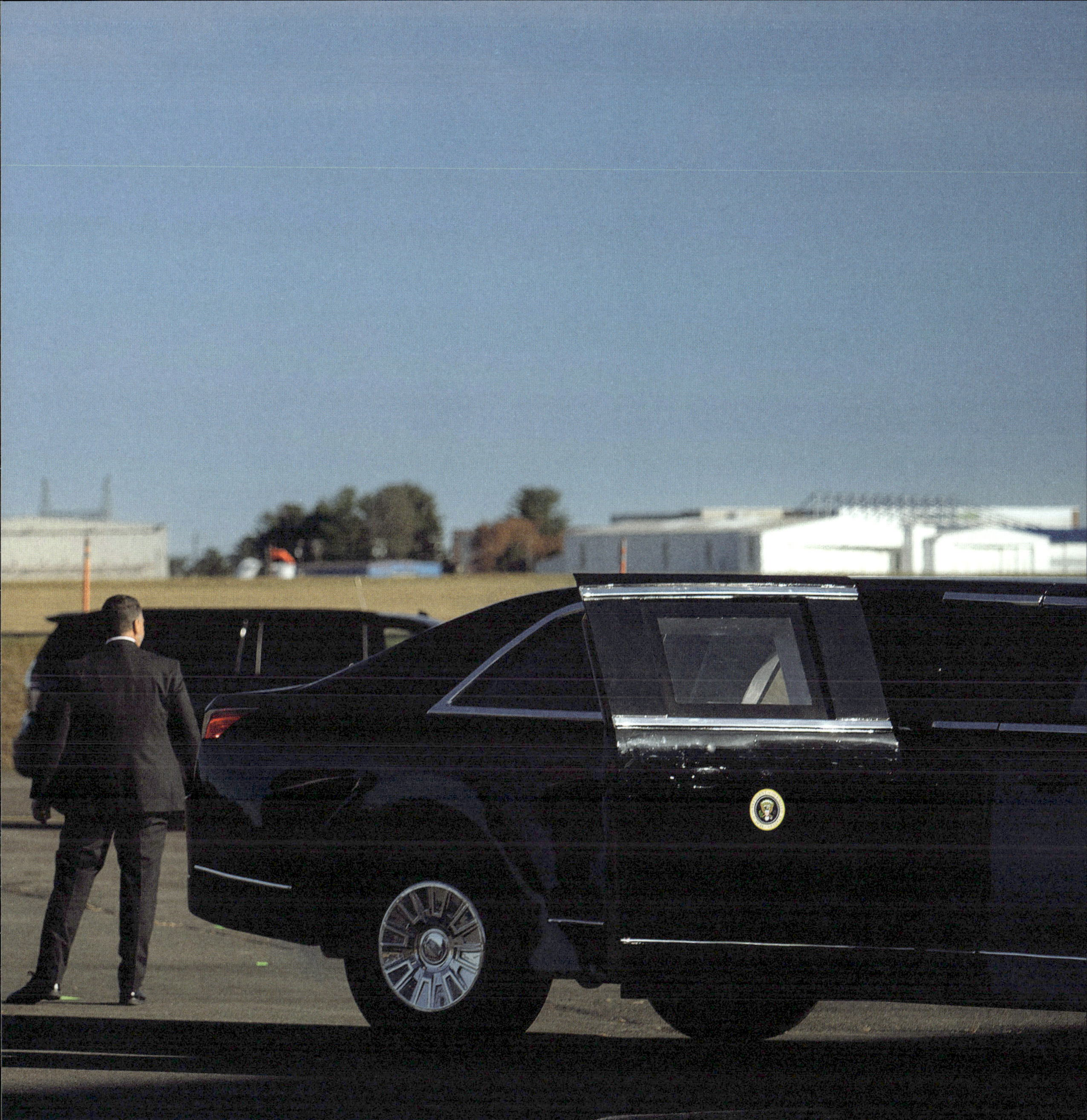

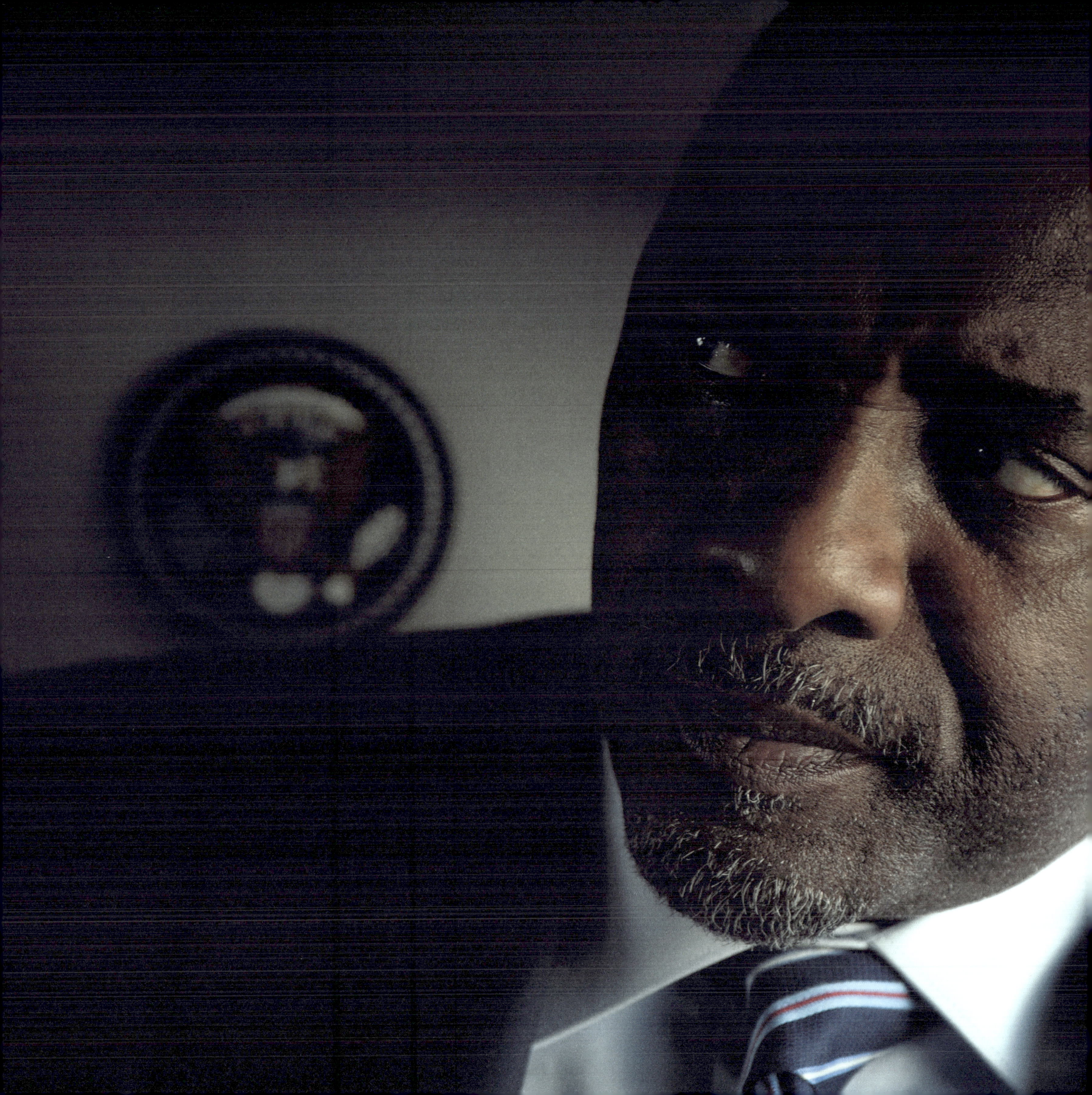

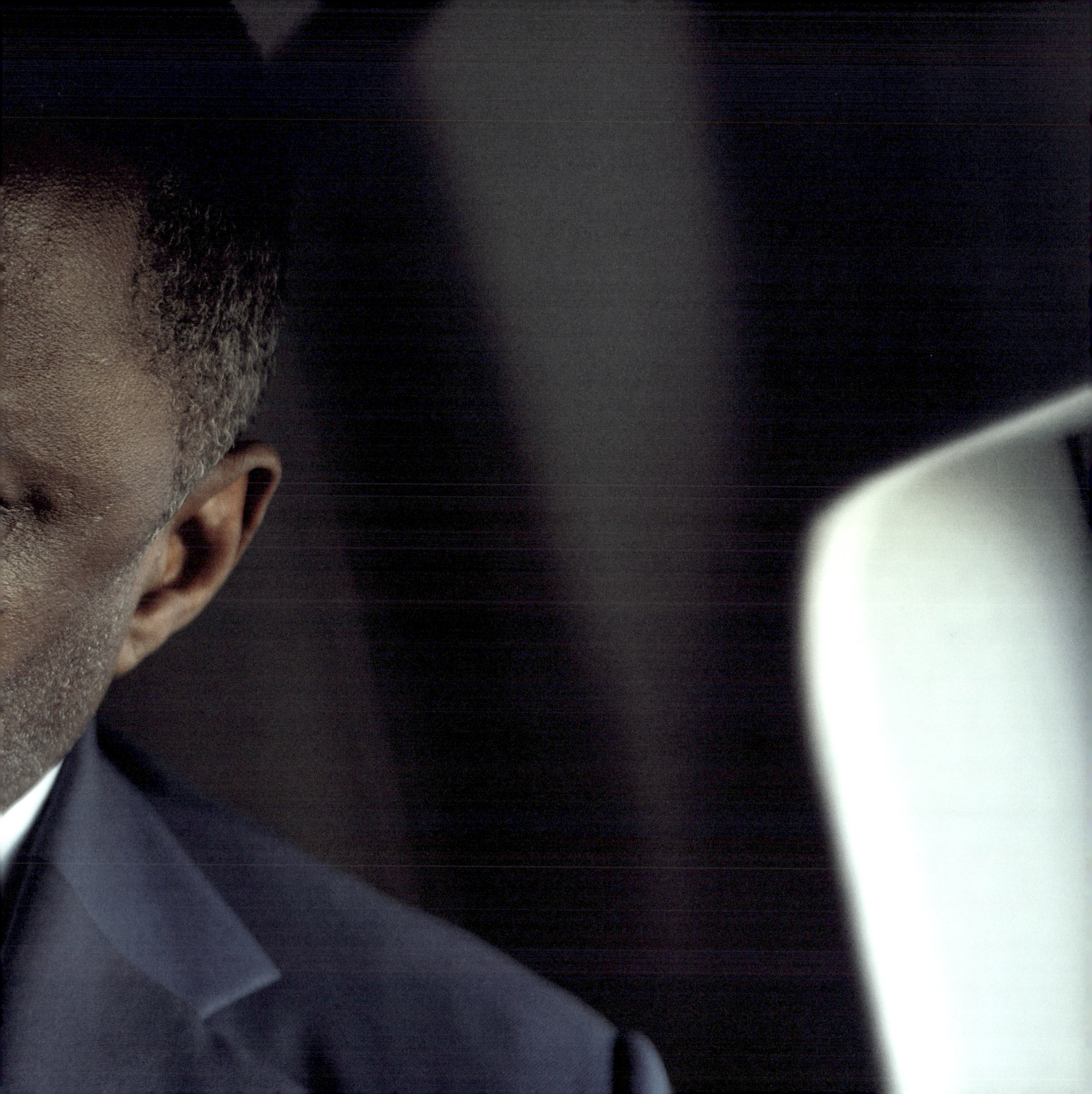

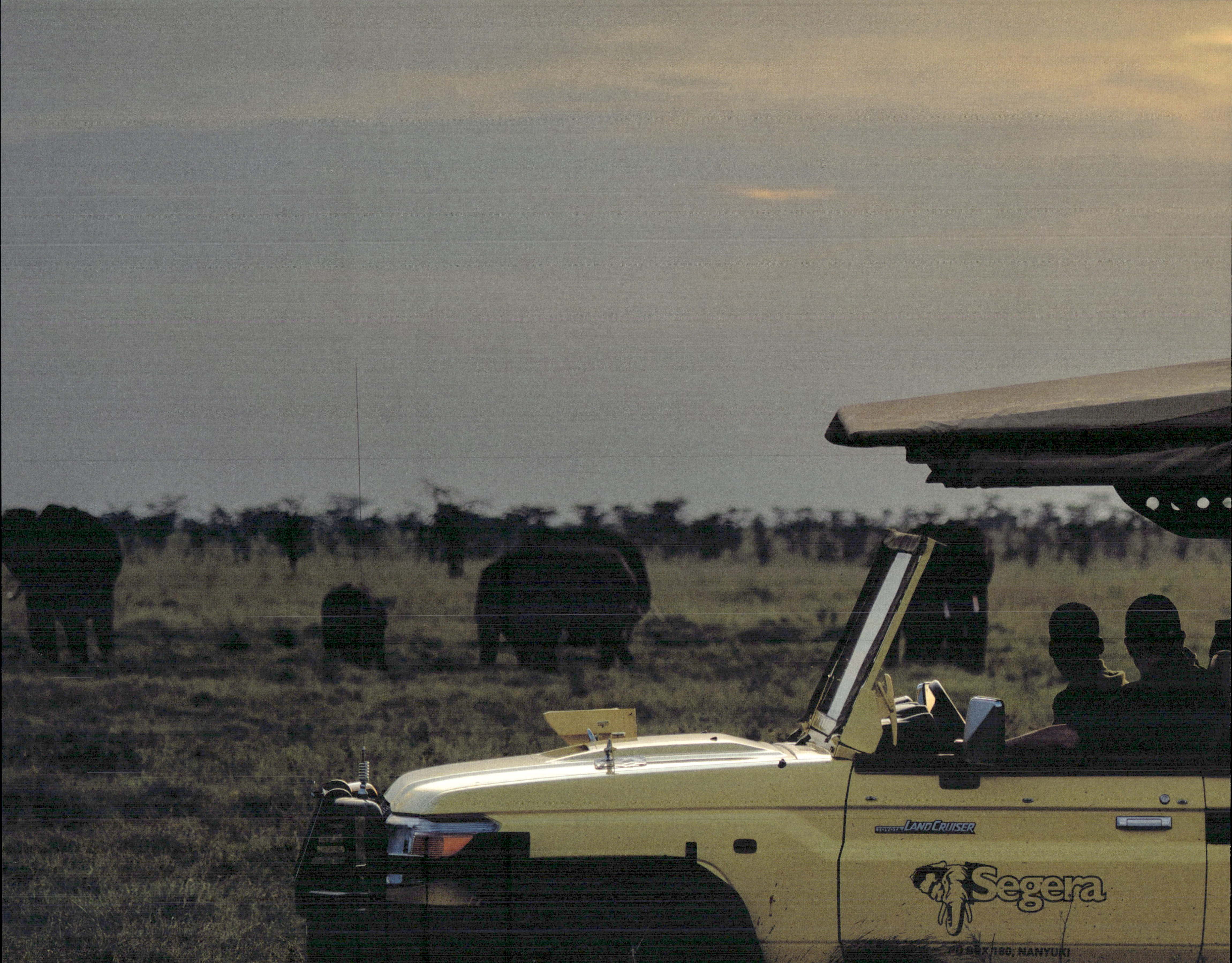
TOYOTA LANDCRUISER
Segera

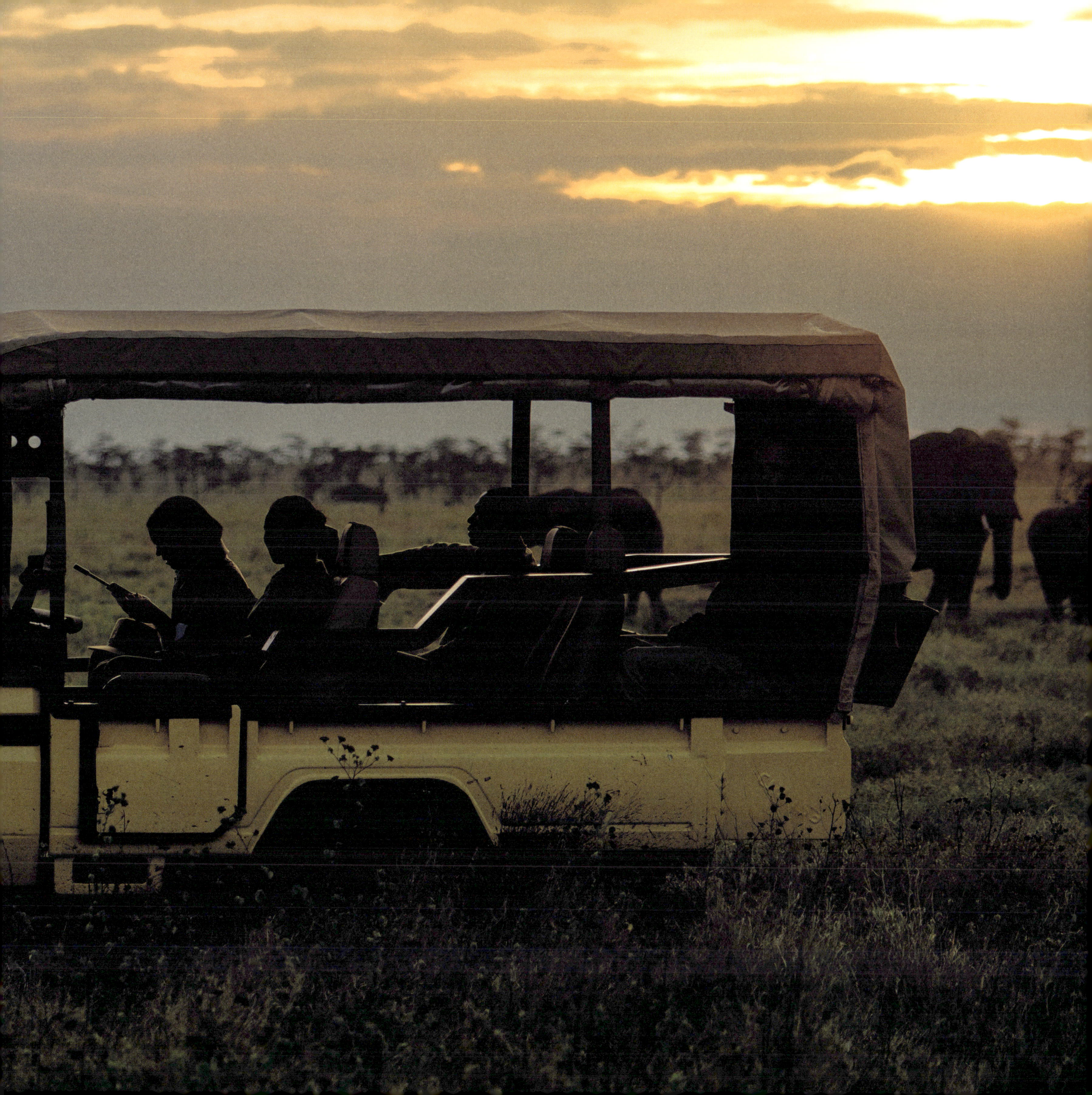

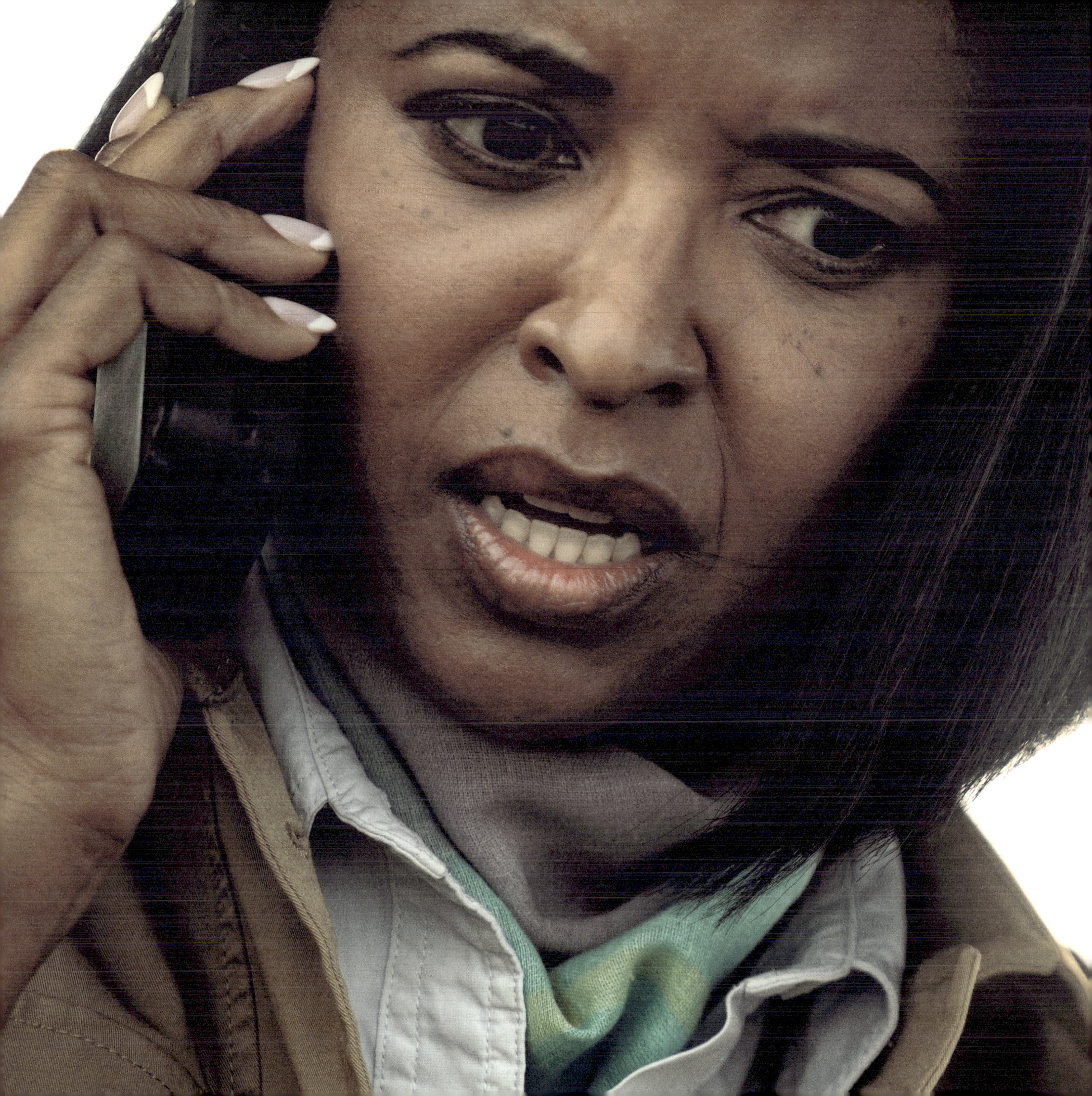

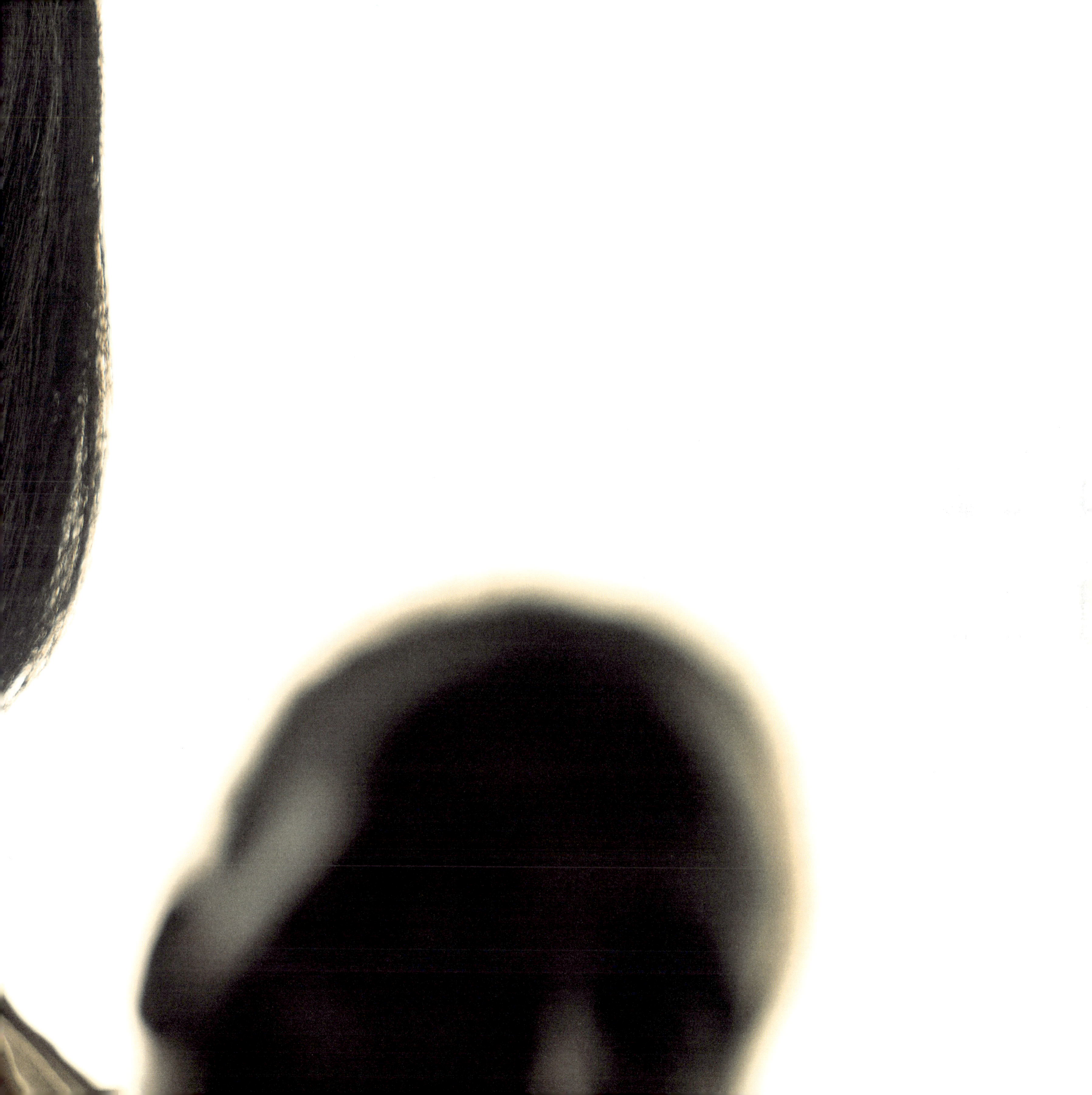

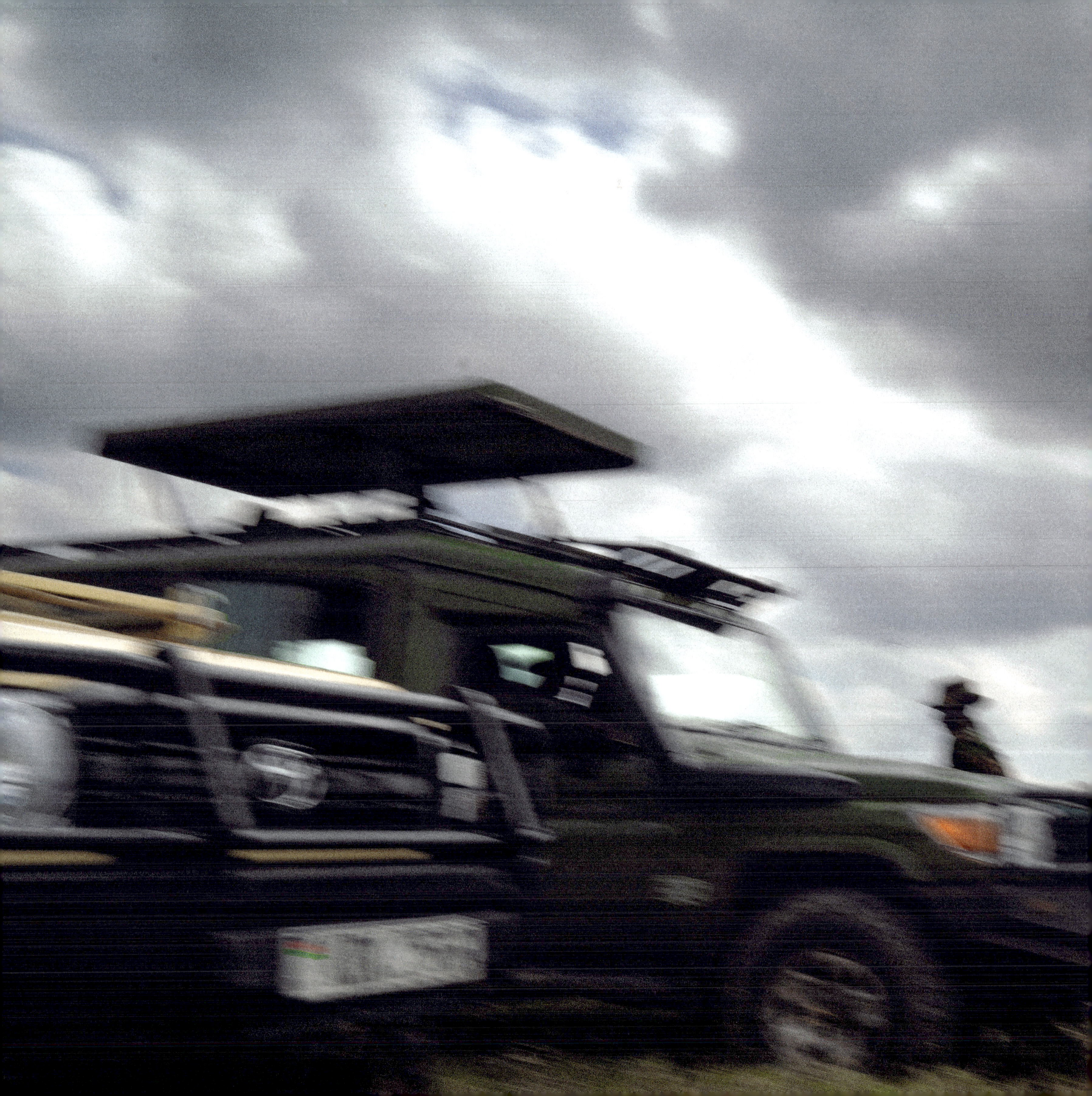

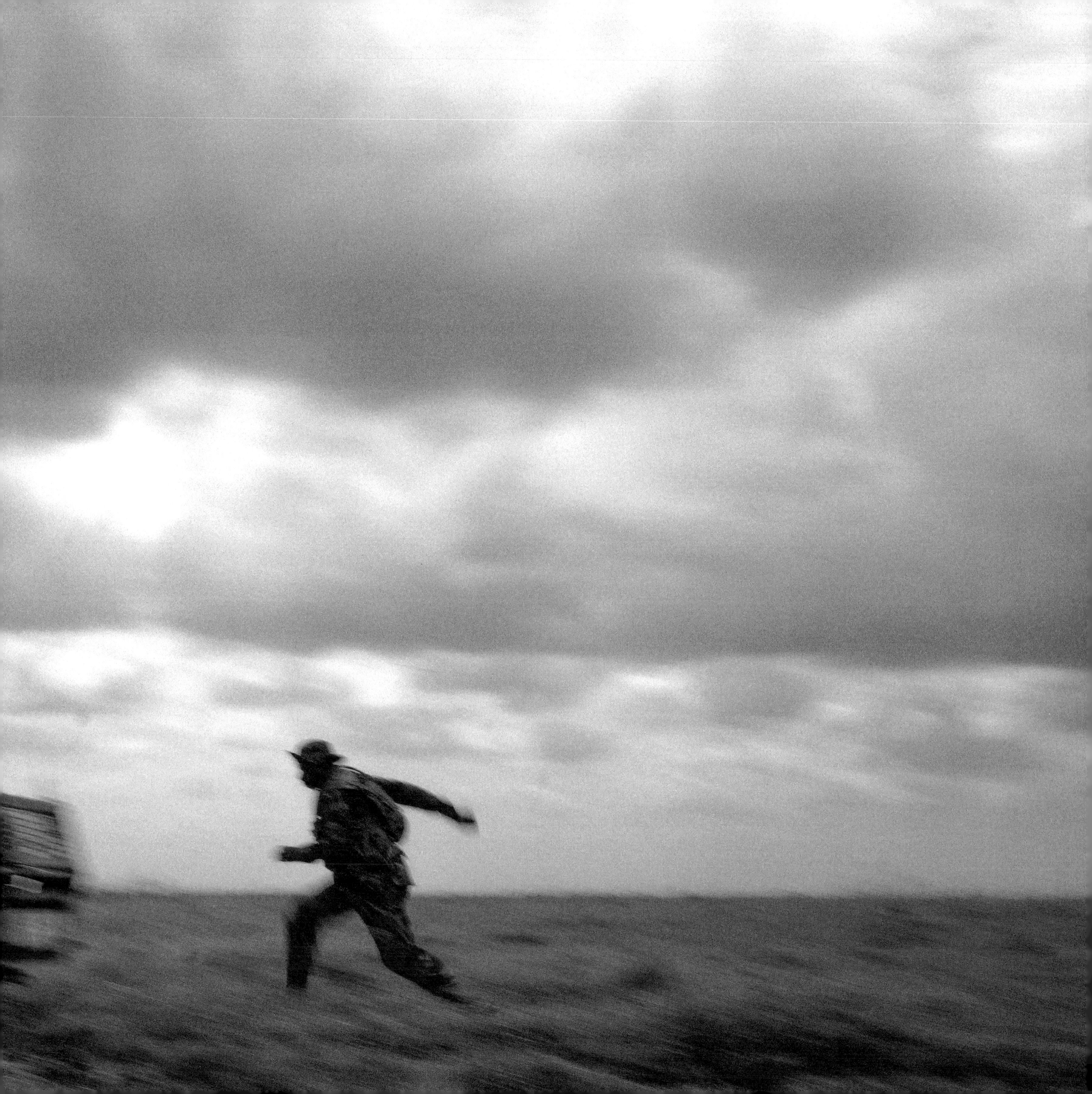

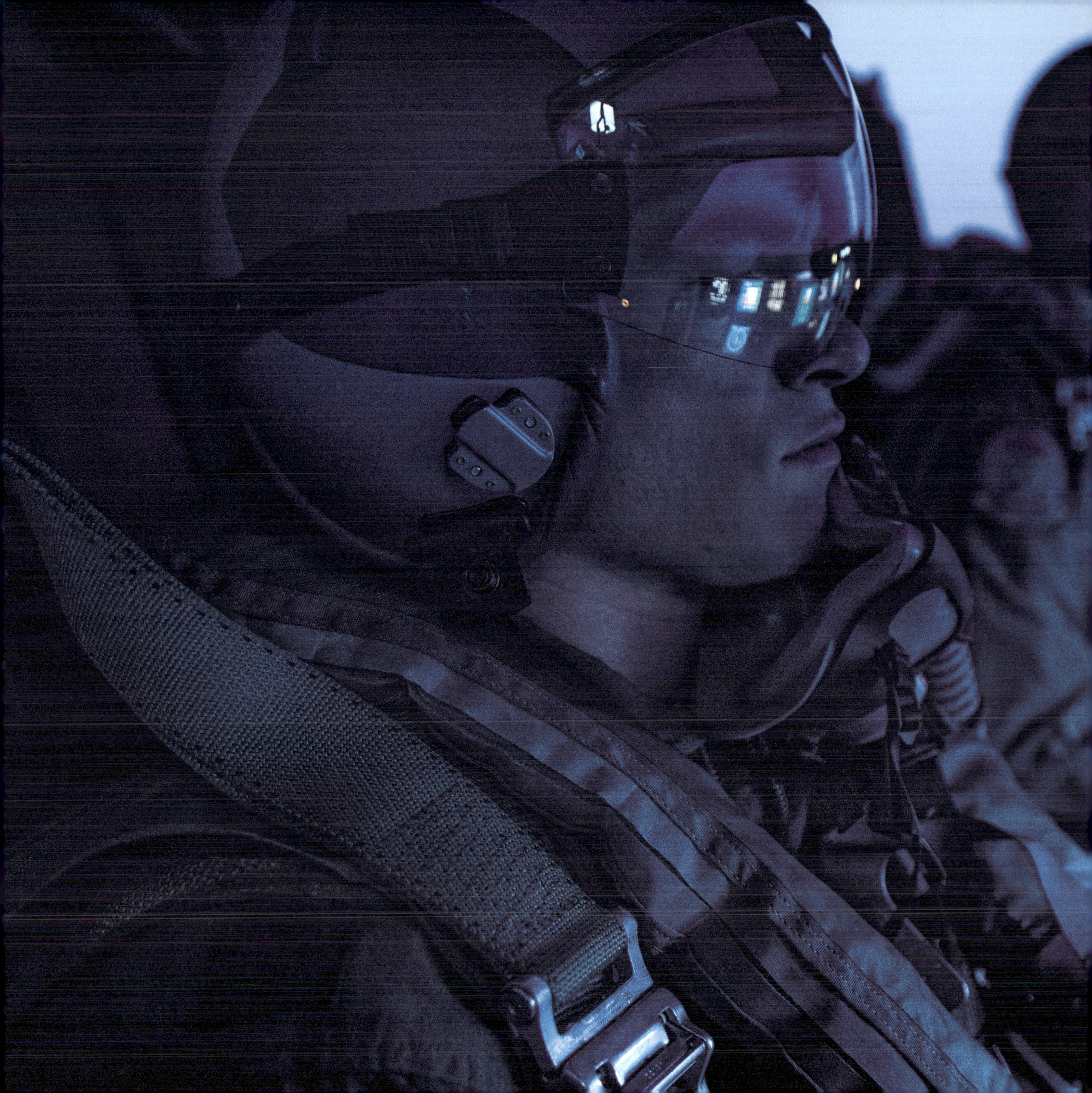

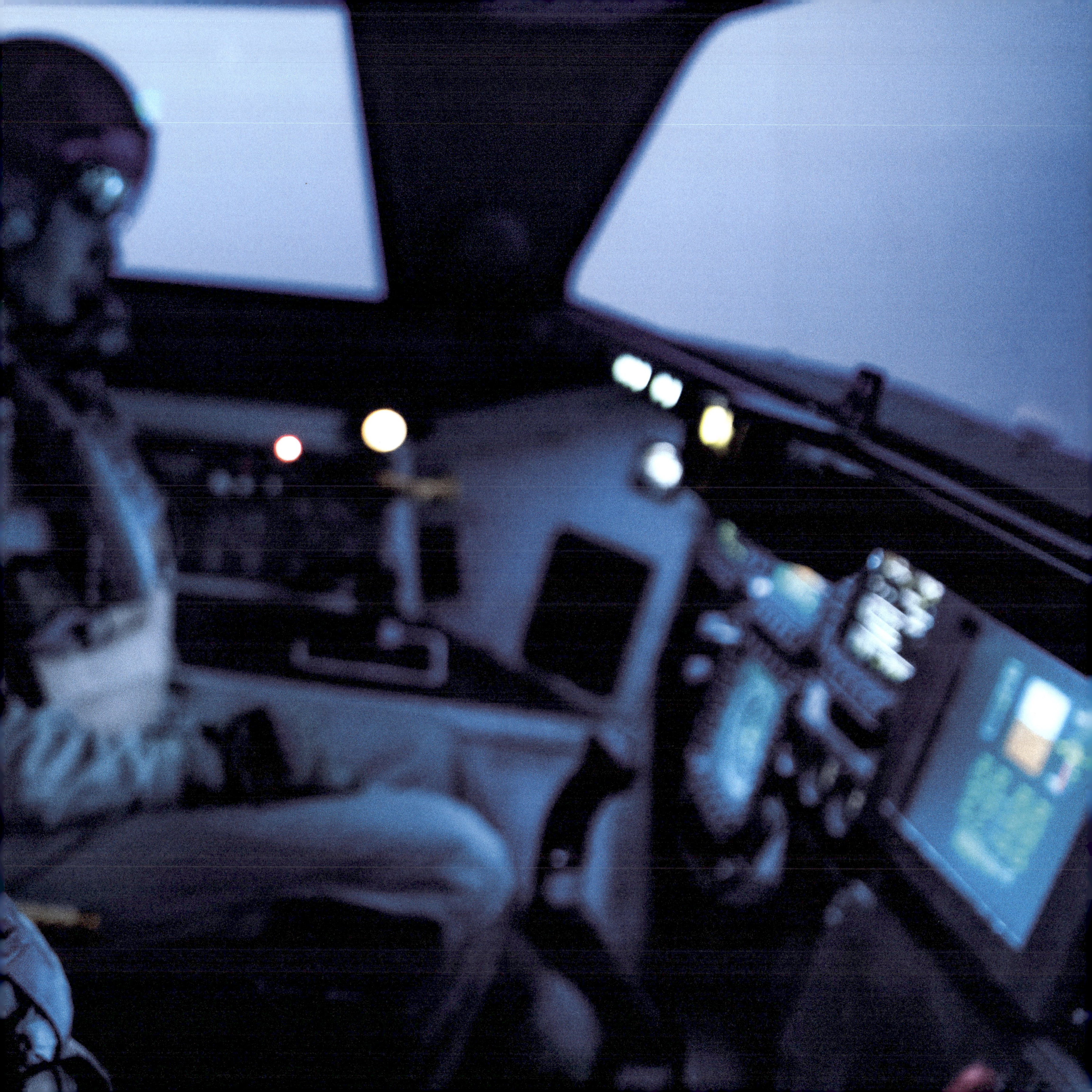

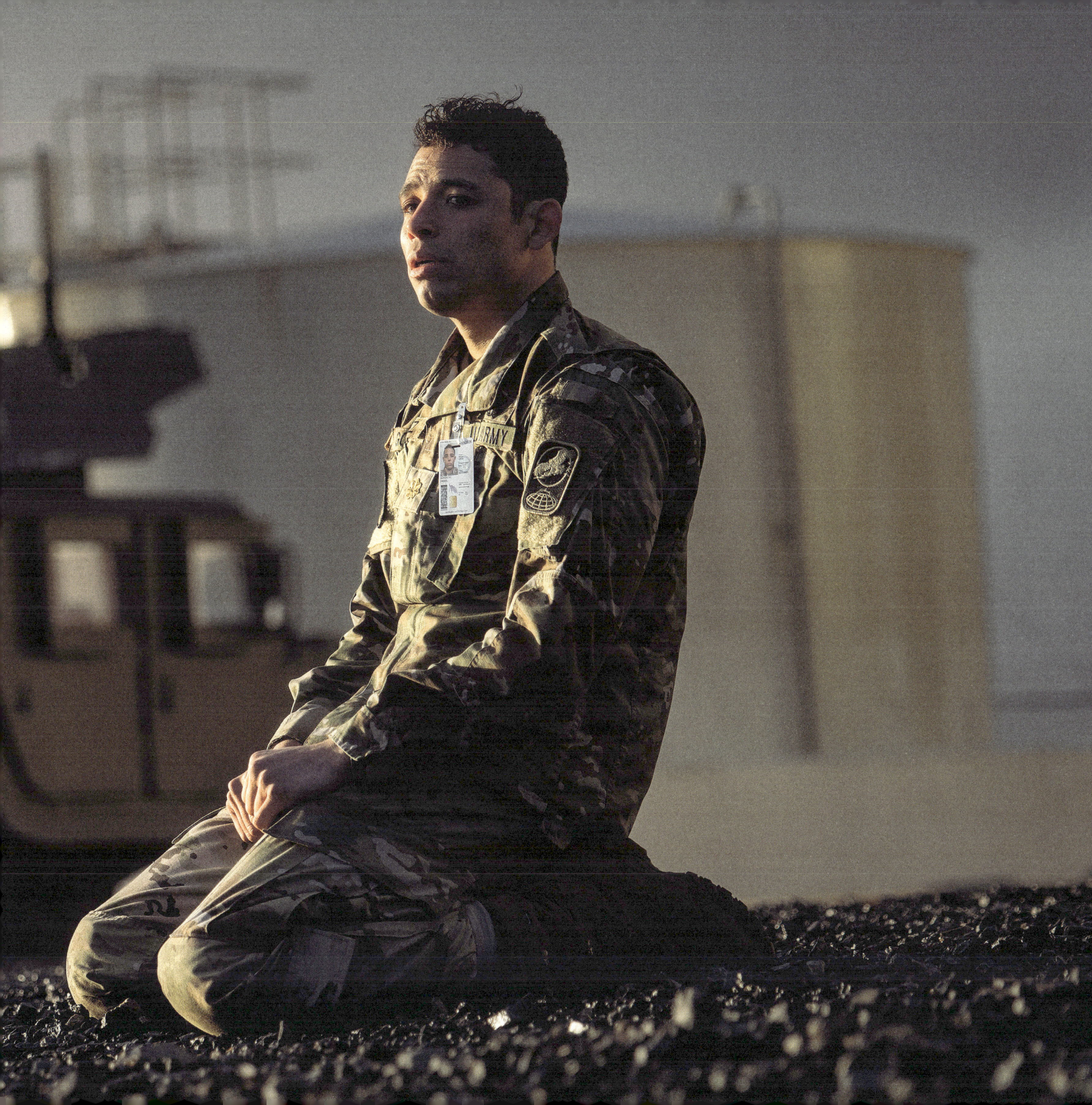
ARMY

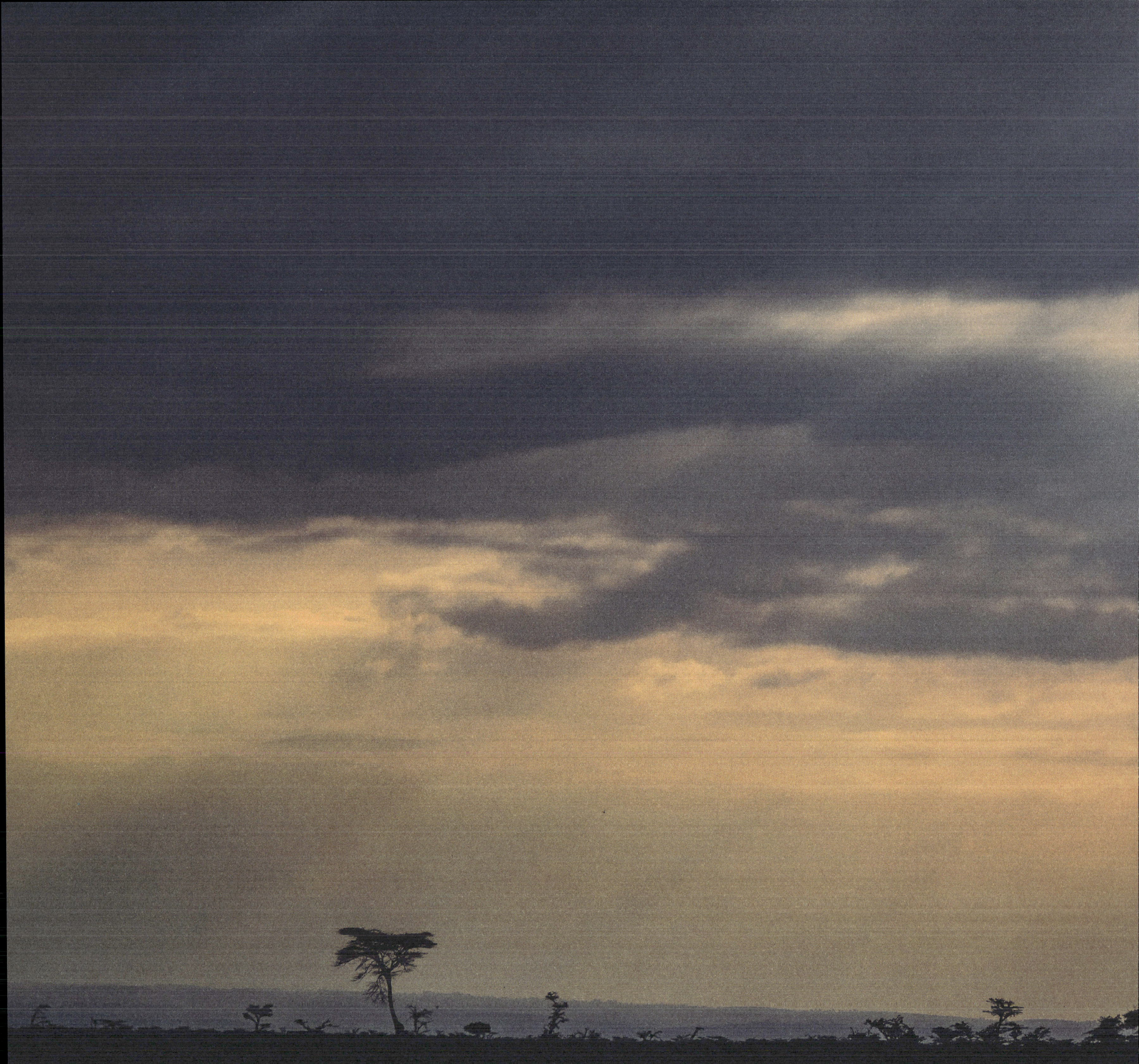

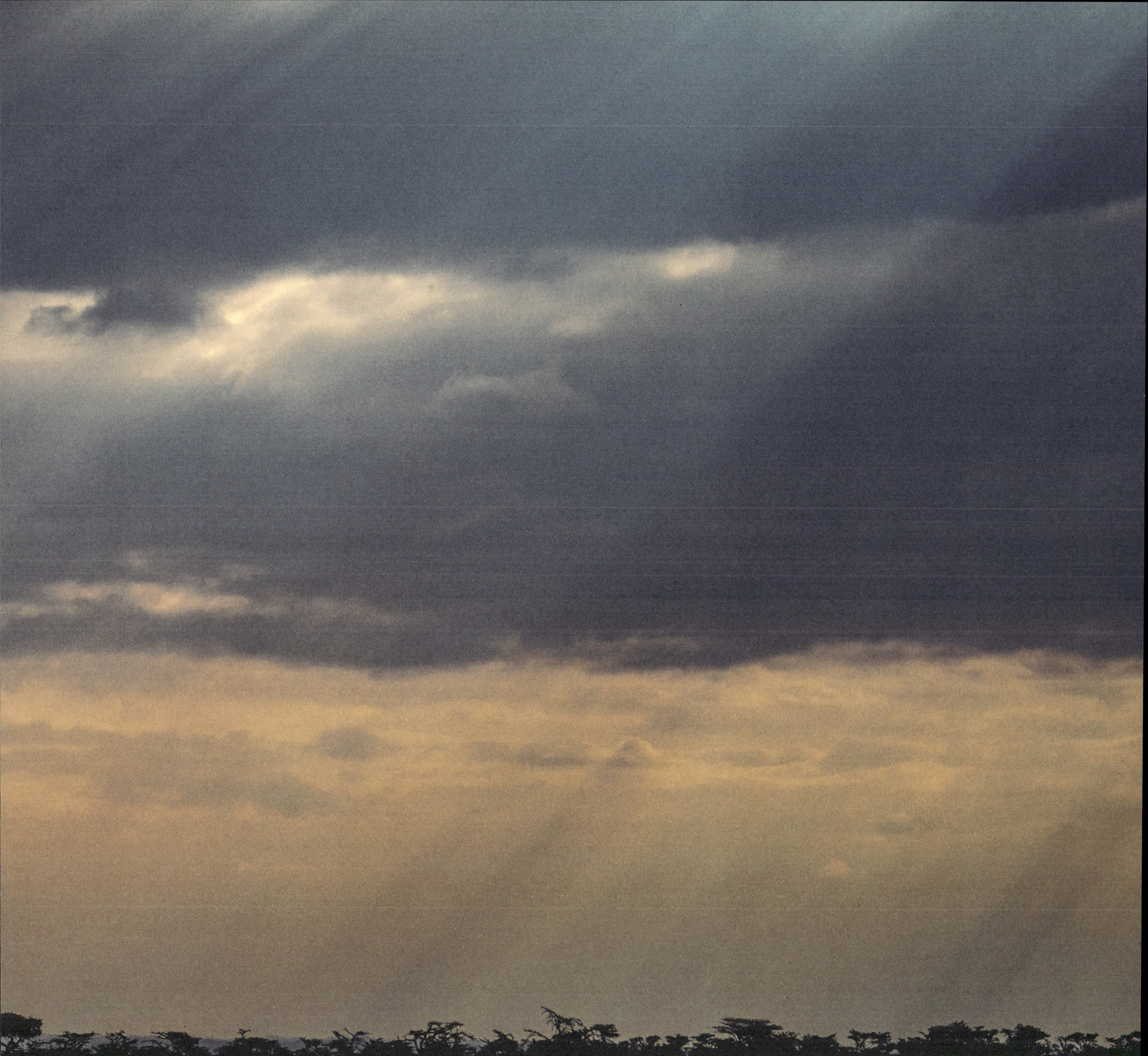

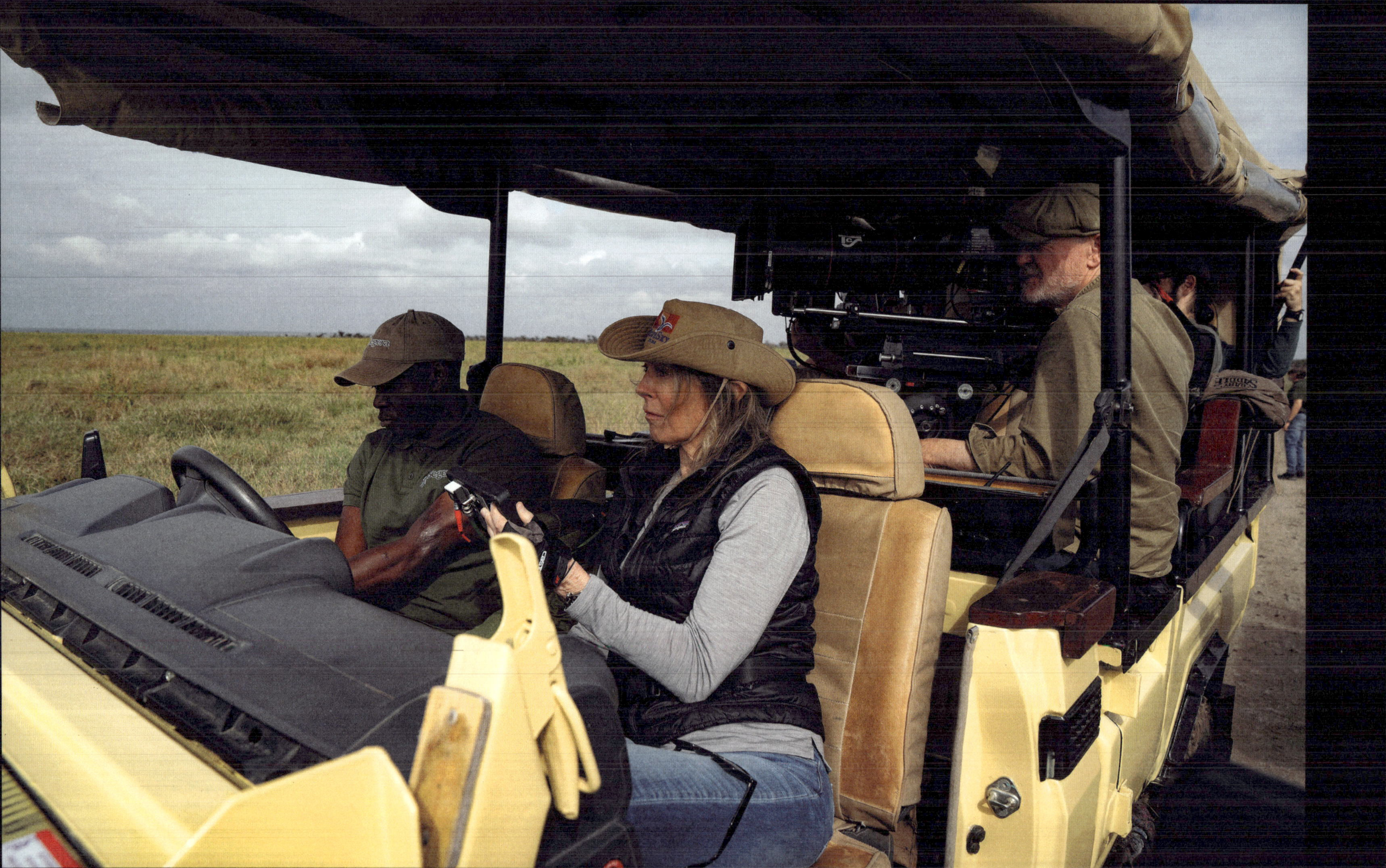

First Published in the
United States of America in 2025
by Rizzoli International Publications, Inc.

49 West 27th Street
New York, NY 10001
www.rizzoliusa.com

Publisher: Charles Miers
Associate Publisher: Anthony Petrillose
Senior Editor: Gisela Aguilar
Editor: Lucie Bisbee
Production Director: Colin Hough Trapp
Managing Editor: Lynn Scrabis
Design Coordinator: Tim Biddick
Book Design: CHIPS

ISBN: 978-0-8478-7673-0
Library Of Congress Control Number: 2025946243
Printed In Italy
2025 2026 2027 2028 2029 / 10 9 8 7 6 5 4 3 2 1

The authorized representative in the EU
for product safety and compliance is
Mondadori Libri S.p.A., via Gian Battista Vico 42,
Milan, Italy, 20123
www.mondadori.it

Visit us online:
Instagram: @RizzoliBooks
Facebook.com/RizzoliNewYork
Youtube.com/user/RizzoliNY

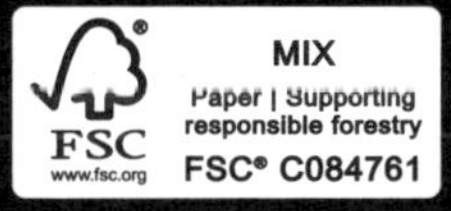

NOT IF. WHEN.